BORROWED TIME

Stories from Swan Valley and Beyond

STEVE LAMAR

BORROWED TIME
Stories from Swan Valley and Beyond

© 2025 by Steve Lamar

All rights reserved. This book is protected under the copyright laws of the United States of America. No part of the book may be reproduced in any form or by any electronic or mechanical means including information storage and retrieval systems without permission in writing from the author, except by a reviewer who may quote brief passages in the review.

COVER PHOTO
Sunset Crags by Steve Lamar

ISBN: 978-09815546-2-4
Library Control Number: 2025903992

PRINTED IN THE UNITED STATES OF AMERICA

PUBLISHED BY
RUMBLE PEAK GEODATA
Condon, Montana 59826

For Sharon
Annie and John
Luke and Sara

ACKNOWLEDGMENTS

I owe a debt of gratitude to the many people who helped make this book a reality. First and foremost, thanks to my wife Sharon who poked, prodded, and urged me to write about my experiences. My daughter Annie, son Luke, John Fraley, Anne Dahl, Suzanne Vernon, and others encouraged me to keep writing.

Many people accompanied me on my journey. I am fortunate that my wife, Sharon, and children Annie and Luke hiked, skied, camped, and climbed mountains with me in the backcountry. Later, son-in-law John Kilgour and daughter-in-law Sara Halm Lamar joined the ventures.

I have fond memories of my childhood escapades with Bugsy and Ronnie Joiner, James Holbrook, David and Gary Cowsert, cousins Jimmy Bayne, Paul Lamar, and Robert Watson.

Special thanks go to Rod Haynes who accompanied me on many memorable trips in the Mission Mountains and Swan Range throughout the years.

Many other friends and co-workers joined in the ventures including Anne Dahl, Kari Gunderson, Tom and Rosie O'Neil, Camille Haynes, Henry and Alice Meyer, Dan and Sheri Burden, Pete and Rachel Feigley, Dan and Sue Stone, John and Nancy Brekke, Barb and Joe Raible, Dave Stenhouse, Kathy Koors, Tom Parker, Melanie Parker, Andrea Stephens, Adam Lieberg, Bill Ferrell, John Cvetich, Ned Banning, Joe Flood, Rusty Wells, Russ Owen, and Barney Jette. Many of them also helped me build our cabin and log home along with Carl and Pat Lamar, Toy Lynn and Don Cross, Jo Barbercheck, Reuben and Nathan Kauffman, Ted Graf, Andy Anderson, and John Gatchell.

Sincere thanks to those I worked with at the US Forest Service, Wilderness Treatment Center, and Northwest Connections.

Of the 148 photos included in the book, most are ones that I took. I'm indebted to Payne Midyett, Russ Owen, Rod Haynes, John Fraley, Melanie Parker, Tom Parker, Sara Lamar, and my son, Luke for providing additional photos.

Special thanks go to the longtime residents who were a great influence on me here in the Swan Valley including Bud Moore, Rod & June Ash, Neil & Dixie Meyer, Leita Anderson, Edna Kesterson, Sue & Bob Cushman, Boyd Kessler, Leonard Moore, and Evelyn Jette.

Please forgive me if I have forgotten anyone due to my lapse of memory.

Thanks for the photos, encouragement, and most of all for playing a part in the outdoor adventures that led to these stories.

CONTENTS

Preface v
Borrowed Time 1
Explorers 5
Turning Point 18
Built on Dreams 21
Electrifying 30
The Eclipse Trip of '79 34
Saved by the Hot Buttered Rum 37
Up in Smoke 39
A Snowy and Cold Time in the Mountains 41
A Memorable Elk Hunt 45
Cat and Mouse 49
Doing the Same Thing With Different Results 51
A Frigid Time in the Backcountry 52
The Silvertip Mountain Caves 62
Belly River Observations 66
Sharing September Snow 74
Cat Fight 77
Asbestos Forest 78
A Ski through the Heart of the Bob Marshall Wilderness 81
The Inspiration Point Grizzly 93
A Snow Survey in the Bob Marshall Wilderness 95
Bear Dreams 104
Windy Times on the Too Much Fun Trip 106
Field Notes 110
Rings of Time: A Historical Journey Through the Bob Marshall Wilderness 114
A Trip to the North Wall 117
Connections 122
Bear DNA 139
A Trip to Lamar Mountain 149
Bear Fight 154
All Miles Are Not Created Equal 156
Decades of Aprils 171
McDonald Peak 174
Five Bears Times Two 182
The Real Panoramic Peak 185
A Climb Up Mount Shoemaker 189
An Unsettling Experience 195
Along the Swan Range 197
Lake of the Clouds 207
Red Mountain 219
Winter Observations 222
References 225

PREFACE

My near-death experience while running for my life during a forest fire blowup in 1977 prompted me to reassess my very existence. From that day forward, I pledged that I wouldn't take my time on earth for granted.

Since that life-altering event nearly 48 years ago, so much has happened. My wife, Sharon, and I put down roots in the beautiful Swan Valley where both our children were born. Nestled between two wilderness areas, much of the Swan Valley has retained its wild and remote character.

Within a month of first visiting the Swan Valley in 1976, we purchased land without giving a thought to employment opportunities. Like many residents of the area, I pieced together a variety of jobs over the years to make ends meet.

During the 17 seasons I was employed by the U. S. Forest Service in the Shawnee National Forest of Illinois and the Flathead National Forest of northwest Montana, I fought fires, planted trees, conducted wildlife surveys, inventoried stands of trees, completed trail work, and worked as a backcountry ranger. As an outdoor instructor, I hiked, skied, and camped in the backcountry guiding groups of young adults, often on 21-day expeditions. I worked as a field assistant for Northwest Connections on the Northern Divide Grizzly Bear DNA Project and the whitebark pine research project. As I hiked the trails, bushwacked through the head-high yew brush, climbed mountains, skied through the wilderness, hunted for elk in the backcountry, and helicoptered into forest fires, I became well-acquainted with the land.

Through these experiences, along with unforgettable adventures with family and friends exploring the forests, lakes, and mountains of northwest Montana and beyond, I have spent countless hours outdoors in all kinds of weather. From sweltering forest fires to frigid subzero campouts, I experienced a wide spectrum of weather moods. And I wouldn't have wanted it any other way.

As a youngster growing up near the Ohio River in southern Illinois, I dreamed of becoming an explorer. While my friends read mysteries or sports stories, I read books about explorers from Magellan to the river pirates. I always wondered what was around the next bend in the trail and over the next hill. One of my teachers tried to dampen my dreams by explaining that everything had already been explored. I didn't buy that line of reasoning mainly because I hadn't explored the unknown myself.

I realized early on that the great explorers kept journals of their adventures. When I was a teenager, I began keeping a journal of my escapades and outdoor adventures. With my journal entries as a reference, I have written over 100 stories of my explorations and observations over the years.

This book contains 41 stories that chronicle my outdoor experiences throughout my lifetime. For the most part, my explorations take place in the forests and wilderness areas of northwest Montana. Ever fascinated with the natural, cultural, and historical aspects of the region, I include information about interesting events, discoveries, place names, geology, geography, and natural history throughout my stories.

I hope these stories spark your interest in exploring the natural world. The mountains rarely disappoint, often opening your eyes and heart to all that nature has to offer. It certainly did for me.

The rugged Mission Mountains. —Luke Lamar photo

BORROWED TIME
1977

◆

Concern turned to fear as the wall of flames pushed us hard from behind while spot fires burned all around us. The situation quickly became desperate. We thirteen firefighters were trapped when the sudden winds fanned the forest fire into a raging inferno, blocking our escape route. We were now in a race for our lives. The odds of escape were quickly diminishing as the whole world around us seemed to be on fire. Fear turned to resignation as the hope of escape diminished. At this rate, we would succumb within minutes. What a horrible way to die.

As a kid, I spent much of my youth exploring the Shawnee National Forest in southern Illinois. I grew up thinking that working for the US Forest Service was about as good a job as I could ever hope to get. When I was in high school, a local youth program hired teenagers for the summer. I hoped against all odds that I could get one of the positions. Unfortunately, my parents' annual income was just a bit too high for me to qualify. I was dejected, but one of my friends got hired. He regaled me with stories of what he had seen and the variety of jobs he undertook during that fateful summer. Even though I did not get hired that summer, the thought still burned within me.

After graduating from high school in 1970 and heading off to college, I got the break I had been hoping for. I was hired by the Forest Service to work weekends in the fall and spring as an emergency firefighter in the Shawnee National Forest. I was thrilled to get part-time work. I received some very basic fire training from a few of the old-timers at the local ranger district. I participated in numerous forest fire suppression efforts over the next three years. Fighting fire in the midwest forests was usually no more than an exercise of raking the leaves away from the forest floor to form a fire break around the slow-burning fire. As the fire burned toward the bare ground, it usually went out for the lack of anything to burn.

After college, I worked as a forestry technician in the Shawnee National Forest and spent my first season doing a variety of jobs that included tree planting, trail work, timberwork, and fire-fighting. In late August 1976, my wife Sharon and I headed west.

I decided I wanted to further my education in the field of forestry and applied to several colleges in Moscow, Idaho, and Missoula Montana. Sharon sent letters of introduction to school districts in those cities. Just as we loaded the last suitcase in our pickup truck, Sharon received a call from the clerk at Missoula County High School District to schedule a job interview. Long story short, we drove straightaway to Missoula, and Sharon was hired to teach at Hellgate High School.

The following spring I landed a job at the Tally Lake Ranger District on the Flathead National Forest. I primarily did forest inventory work but was expected to report for forest fire duty when the time came.

It was two o'clock in the morning of August 1977 when I received my first call to action on a western forest fire. I was dispatched with nineteen other firefighters to Idaho on the Cotter Bar II Forest Fire in the Nez Perce National Forest.

After a bumpy ride in a vintage DC 3 airplane, we arrived in Idaho and were immediately whisked off in a school bus driven by a gruff elderly white-haired man. After a long and tortuous route over miles of gravel road, we arrived at our destination. The driver parked our bus in a huge flat area several hundred yards wide that had been cleared by bulldozers. This cleared area was to be our safety zone. Four or five other twenty-person crews were already there, waiting to be assigned to various areas of the fire.

During a quick briefing, we learned that approximately ten years ago an earlier forest fire burned a large portion of the landscape before us. The previously burned area had been salvaged-logged and now contained head-high brush and small trees. Only an occasional mature, live tree had survived both the previous fire and salvage operation in this steep and rolling terrain. It was hot with temps in the high 90s and little humidity in the air.

Minutes after getting out of the vehicle we grabbed our firefighting tools and hiked along a nearby ridge. Earlier in the day, a bulldozer had cut a trail along this portion of the narrow ridge. Our assignment was to spread out along the top of the spine to prevent the approaching fire below from burning up the steep slope and jumping the fire line. Once we were situated along the ridge top, we took up our positions to wait as the slow-moving fire burned in the grass, and shrubs, and scattered five-feet-tall tree seedlings on its way up to us. Nothing at that point seemed out of the ordinary.

Within seconds the situation dramatically changed. A whirlwind swept up the hillside picking up burning embers, scattering them in all directions. Many of the burning embers fell behind us and we quickly went to work throwing shovelfuls of dirt onto the smoking bits of hot coals. Then, someone yelled, "Look out!" Simultaneously, another voice screamed, "Run!"

A sudden strong wind came roaring at us, pushing a wall of flames toward us. We quickly retreated down the backside of the ridge to a secondary bulldozer line. This was to be our second line of defense. Thirteen of us were now cut off from the original safety zone. We turned momentarily to size up the situation but with the wall of flames bearing down on us we realized that we needed to run.

As we started up the next hill, the fire did not falter as it jumped across the second bulldozer line. We were running hard. The flames were right behind us. We could not seem to gain any distance from the fire. As we were topping the next hill, I glanced back becoming even more frightened. The wall of flames was closing the gap as it was outdistancing us. I knew the situation could be deadly. We kept running and started down the hill. The flames stayed right behind us. As we reached the bottom of the hill my legs felt like lead. My lungs were aching from the effort. I began to pray to God, "Please do not let me die this way!"

Alternately, I kept wishing that I was wearing my tennis shoes instead of the heavy work boots. As we ran through a flat area before heading up the next hill, we passed three tall Douglas fir trees that had survived the previous fire and salvage operation. All thirteen of us ran together as a unit. I was near the front and briefly turned to see if we were gaining on the flames only to see crew member Randy Wiggins bringing up the rear. The Douglas fir trees exploded into flames as he ran past them. At that moment, I thought that we were close to death. I prayed hard, thinking how awful it would be to die by fire.

As we ran up yet the next hill the burning embers landed ahead of us, igniting the parched vegetation. Now we had to weave our way through the burning brush as the wall of flames pushed us from behind. I could feel my adrenaline and energy giving out as I willed my legs to keep moving. I felt the end was near, that there was no way out. I attempted to make bargains with God. The situation was unbelievably dire, as there was almost nowhere left to run. The fire had us trapped. The heat was intense and rising. We were doomed. Surrounded by fire, I resigned myself to the inevitability of death.

Miraculously, the unbelievable happened. The wind stopped completely. A slight opening appeared between the burning landscape. Shielding our faces from the intense heat, we broke free from the grasp of the flames. I could hardly believe it!

I was shaken, but elated. I was so thankful that we were alive. Fear ruled my thinking. I realized I had been carrying my shovel the whole time we had been running. Everyone else had dropped their fire tools at the start.

Realizing that we were still in harm's way if the wind should return, we hustled down an old partially overgrown logging road trying to put some distance between the fire and us. To our astonishment, as we rounded a bend in the road, we spotted an elderly couple in a vintage station wagon driving toward us. The gray-haired couple stopped their vehicle next to us, explaining that they drove from a nearby town to see the forest fire. Little did they know that they were driving into the front of the approaching fire. If the wind had not stopped, they would have driven to their deaths.

The fire division boss quickly commandeered the vehicle. After getting the vehicle turned around, we crammed people inside while the rest of us rode outside. Some rode on top of the station wagon. I stood on the back bumper along with another firefighter. We looked like the boat people with 15 of us crammed inside and others clinging to the station wagon as we drove out of harm's way and back to safety.

Back in the safety zone, we sat in stunned silence. Gradually, some small talk commenced. There was never any mention of what we had just experienced. After a while, it seemed as though most of the crew had forgotten it. I hadn't. I sat there staring out into the smoky haze questioning whether I was cut out to be a firefighter.

As it turned out, I continued to work as a firefighter off and on over the next twenty years. No matter how large or small the forest fire, I never forgot my brush with death. That terrifying experience was forever seared in my mind and would always guide me to put safety first while fighting a wildfire. It was a lesson that served me well throughout the years.

Since that fateful day in 1977, I knew that I was given a second chance at life. Everything since then has been borrowed time. For that, I am eternally grateful.

Flathead National Forest.

EXPLORERS

While growing up in the hills near the Ohio River and the Shawnee National Forest of southern Illinois, I was fascinated with the outdoors. Everything about being outside was a grand adventure from learning about edible plants to exploring the cliffs and caves of the area. I was even more intrigued by the combination of rich local history and the equally remarkable natural history of the region. The area was steeped in Native American history as well as historical accounts of river pirates and outlaw road agents. The legends and lore of the area were often blurred as to what was fact and what was fiction, but to me, that just spiced up the richness of the tale.

Southern Illinois comprised seven overlapping eco-regions, lending to an abundance and diversity of plants and wildlife. The northern hardwoods' southern boundary dipped into this area while the southern hardwoods' northern boundary also intersected with the region. Five other eco-regions blanketed this area to produce an array of species on the landscape.

Even though I stolidly went through the motions of being an attentive student in school, my real passion for learning was in the outdoors. When other students read mysteries and sports books for their assigned book reports, I read about the great explorers of the world. Yearning to see what was around the next bend or over the next ridge bonded me to those bygone adventurers and explorers.

When I was in the second grade my Grandma Watson showed me how to make a quill pen from a chicken or hawk feather. We then collected a bowl of poke berries, otherwise known as inkberries. We mashed them up, then drained the dark purple liquid into a small bowl. I used my newly made pen and ink to write a letter. Writing with a quill pen was at times a bit messy and always slow, but I thought it was great fun.

Grandpa and Grandma Watson, who lived nearby, had a small pond out behind their barn where I would often go fishing. It was full of perch and sunfish as well as a few catfish. When I was around ten years old, James Holbrook, David and Gary Cowsert, and I decided to camp for several days by the pond. James propped his fishing pole on a forked stick. We had barely started fishing when something yanked James's rod and reel which was quickly pulled out into the middle of the pond and disappeared beneath the surface. We could not believe it!

We had never caught a fish over eight or ten inches long, with most of the fish even smaller. James thought there must be a monster fish in there. He was annoyed and determined to not only somehow get his rod and reel back, but also catch the monster fish. We continued to fish with cane poles for a couple of days, but only caught small perch and sunfish. I grew bored on the third day and went home. James and David stayed. Later I heard them hollering in the distance as they approached my house. I ran to see that they had a huge catfish in a dip net. James had somehow retrieved his rod and reel with the huge fish still attached. He had quite a time reeling it to the shore. The two of them could hardly hold the fish up. Later, the fish was measured at 15 pounds and was three to four feet long. I could not believe such a small pond could hold such a large fish.

———•———

One summer day when I was 10 years old the family clan decided to go swimming. The day started innocently enough as Mom, Aunt Marilyn, cousins Sharon and Robbie, my sisters Toy Lynn and Jo, and I rendezvoused with other family and friends at the popular swimming hole on Hog Thief Creek near the Old Furnace.

The Old Furnace, built in the 1800s as part of a thriving pig iron industry, was now relegated to a curious relic of history as a point of interest at the Old Furnace Recreation Area managed by the Forest Service. The stream adjacent to the picnic area was named for someone who I suppose was overly fond of pork.

Tired of the hot, sultry weather, I for one was happy to get into the creek to play and cool off. Most of the swimming hole was shallow, which is where we younger kids splashed about. But upstream was a deep hole that was well over all of our heads. Someone had built a diving board over this deep hole by hammering an old board to a couple of downed trees that lay along the shore. Only one teenager was swimming in the deep water after diving off of the springboard. While he had the deep water to himself, the shallow end was very crowded with kids jumping, splashing, and screaming as general bedlam characterized the scene. In a festive mood, the parents were sitting on the bank resting on blankets while busily talking, eating, and laughing.

With a newly purchased scuba mask, I practiced swimming underwater. I could not swim otherwise. I positioned the mask on my face to form an airtight seal, then tested it by sticking my head underwater. I frequently had to readjust it to keep the water from leaking in. When all seemed just right, I waded out to the waist-deep water, took in a deep breath, slipped under the surface, and attempted to swim. I rarely made it very far. Still, I enjoyed the new-found world of exploring underwater.

When I came up for a breath of fresh air, I found myself standing on the edge of the deep hole. I lifted my mask to catch my breath. The water level was up to my chin. I looked around and saw that almost everyone else was engaged in a game of water tag. I was about to walk to more shallow water when my cousin Sharon bumped into me as she was trying to avoid Toy Lynn's tag. As I was already on the lip of the loose gravel bottom, I slowly slid under the surface of the stream and shortly came to rest at the bottom of the deep hole. My eyes were open and I could look around me in the emerald-green water. I pushed off the bottom, trying to reach the surface. My arms broke the surface but my face did not. I tried to take a breath but only took in water. Half choking, I sank to the bottom of the hole again. I tried to crab-walk back up the steep gravel bottom but just slid back into the bottom of the hole as I could not get any traction in the loose gravel. I was starting to panic as I was out of air, my lungs screaming. I attempted to push off and go for the surface one more time. I did not make it. I was going down for the third time, not able to hold my breath any longer. I tried to breathe but only took in water. I thrashed about in total panic. I thought that I was going to die.

Suddenly, I felt hands grab me, pulling me to the surface. As we broke the surface, I coughed, gasping for air. I looked into the face of my rescuer. It was Jimmy Carraker, the lone teenager who earlier had been swimming in the deep water. Unbeknownst to me, Jimmy saw me go under. He had been resting on the diving board above the fray. When he saw me in trouble he dove in and rescued me. No one else noticed I was in trouble. In fact, no one even noticed that Jimmy had saved me. Everyone was still playing, eating, laughing, and talking. Jimmy asked me, "Are you okay?"

I squeaked out, "Yeah, I think so." Confident that I was okay, Jimmy then went back to his resting spot on the diving board. Shaken, I went over to sit on the bank near the shallow end until I recovered. Later, I rejoined everyone in the shallow water, staying well clear of the deep hole.

Jimmy Carraker, who was three years older than me, lived a few miles up the road from the Old Furnace. A true man of action and deed, he later served in the war in Vietnam, earning the Silver Star and Bronze Star for bravery. I know that he will always be a hero in my heart. He certainly saved my life that day.

———•———

My parent's house stood on an old Indian site. I often found arrowheads and other artifacts in the plowed fields of both our land and surrounding farmland. Friends, cousins, and even my younger sisters would often join me in walking the fields after a fresh rain exposed the flint pieces of the old Indian camps.

Often while walking along the sandy soil of the low ridgelines, I would contemplate the lives of the Native Americans. I was impressed with the skill the flint makers possessed in shaping their tools and the variability in styles and craftsmanship. As the successive layers of soil were exposed from the farming practices, I wondered if I was finding some extremely old pieces mixed in with the younger pieces. I always questioned the age of the artifacts as well as how long these sites had been used. I was also fascinated with the large number of sites that were scattered throughout the region but there was scant information available locally at that time.

Less than a mile down the road was my Uncle Bennie and Aunt Ruth Lamar's farm. Surrounding their house were some incredibly large old maple trees. These trees were much larger than any that I had ever seen. Paul, my cousin, had found some Indian artifacts in their garden that were some of the most artistically and finely crafted artifacts that I have ever seen anywhere. I often wondered if those particular items were used for spiritual purposes rather than for everyday use. I thought that the huge old maple trees and those artifacts were tied together somehow into a religious site used by the Native Americans.

———•———

Once as a teenager I decided to go deer hunting in the section of cliffs between my Grandpa Lamar's lower farm and the rural community of Shetlerville. I awoke several hours before dawn to get to the area I wanted to hunt by daylight. I parked Dad's old truck near the train trestle and hiked down the railroad tracks until I got to the rocky cliffs. I walked to the area by starlight and planned to climb up through a steep, rocky section to get to the top where I could watch a wide area of terrain for any deer movement. As I neared the top of the cliff, I heard something very close to me. I stopped and stared into the darkness, but could not see anything. Slowly, I took my flashlight out of my jacket pocket and turned it on. Standing on a rock several feet away was a bobcat. We were looking at each other at eye level. I was both fascinated and a bit scared. I had never seen a bobcat until then and was not sure what to do. Slowly I backed down the way I had just come. When I got down to the railroad tracks, I breathed a sigh of relief. It was still dark so I decided that I would continue to walk along the train tracks until I came to the end of the cliff section and then enter the forest. As I walked below the rock cliff, I could hear the bobcat following along on top. I got a little nervous, as I did not know its intentions. I loaded my shotgun just be to on the safe side. I wondered if the bobcat was just curious about the human wandering around in the predawn darkness.

———•———

My friends and neighbors, Bugsy and Ronnie Joiner, and I would often go camping together. Except for Ronnie's pocketknife with only one broken-off blade, we had no camping gear. Usually, we each had one blanket to wrap up in as we lay around the campfire. We carried our drinking water in fruit jars, our food in paper or burlap bags, and matches in our pants pockets. If it rained, we got wet. We banked our comfort in our ability to build and maintain a good campfire. Often, we built brush lean-to shelters, but those shelters seldom were anything more than fun structures to build as they rarely kept us dry when the weather turned rainy.

I wanted to get a sleeping bag but did not have any money. I noticed that on the back of my comic books, there were prizes that could be earned by selling greeting cards and one of the prizes was a sleeping bag. There was a family reunion coming up and I thought I could sell enough boxes of cards to earn a sleeping bag. Luckily, almost every aunt, uncle, and cousin bought a box.

Soon my new, rectangular, cotton-filled sleeping bag complete with duck print arrived in the mail. I could not wait to try it out. I called Bugsy and Ronnie to tell them about it. We decided to go camping in the forest out behind their parent's property. We gathered firewood and built a campfire. For our supper, we wrapped some potatoes with a thick one-inch layer of mud and tossed them onto the coals to bake.

Later that night, I crawled into the warmth of my new sleeping bag while Bugsy and Ronnie took their places on each side of the campfire wrapped up in their blankets, burrito style. It was a cold, humid night with heavy dew coating everything. I awoke to hear Ronnie muttering how he was freezing. The campfire had burned down and he was attempting to get it built up again. I had to relieve myself so I crawled out of my warm sleeping bag. I asked Ronnie if he would like to switch places for a while. I volunteered to sit by the campfire while he warmed up in my sleeping bag. He wasted no time as he jumped at the opportunity to warm up.

After relieving myself I tried to find some more firewood as we were about out. Dew was on everything and the wood was too wet to burn. The fire just kind of sizzled and smoldered along not burning very hot. I wrapped up in Ronnie's thin blanket and leaned into the fire trying to absorb any available heat. I looked up and noticed Bugsy was not on the other side of the fire any longer. He had crawled into my sleeping bag too!

Both were snoring away. I grabbed Bugsy's blanket and added it around me, but it did not seem to help. Before long, my teeth were chattering. I kept trying to find wood that would burn hot, but everything was too damp. We did not have a flashlight so I stumbled and tripped around in the darkness in my seemingly futile attempt to find firewood. Finally, when I thought I could not take the cold any longer I tried to wake Ronnie and Bugsy, but they snuggled down deeper into the sleeping bag. There was no way they were going to give up their warm, comfortable world for the dismal campfire, thin blankets, and the cold, damp predawn morning.

———•———

In our youthful exuberance, Bugsy, Ronnie, and I decided to form our own Explorer's Club. We discovered an old map of Hardin County that featured all the cave locations, various historical sites, and points of interest. We pored over the map and planned countless explorations and campouts. At one point, we encouraged my younger cousins, Paul Lamar and Robert Watson to join our club. But first, they had to pass a series of initiation tests. In one of the tests, each candidate had to cross a small stream via a rope that was anchored to trees on each side of the stream. Ronnie demonstrated the technique. When he got about halfway across, the rope broke and he landed in the shallow stream. Because the weather was a bit chilly that day, he immediately hustled home to change clothes. Paul solemnly watched all of this happen, turned to me, and said, "I don't think I want to be a part of your club."

•

On a bitterly cold winter day, Bugsy, Ronnie, and I decided to walk down to the Ohio River to duck hunt. The bare ground was frozen hard and a sharp breeze came from the north. Our cotton clothing was totally inadequate for the conditions we were confronting that day, but as usual, we did not let a little cold weather stop us from getting outside for a little fun.

Before we could go hunting, we needed to buy some ammo. As usual, money was in short supply, practically nonexistent. Luckily, we could buy individual shotgun shells at the local Western Auto Hardware store, a four-mile round-trip hike for three teenagers too young to have driver's licenses. We pooled our money and bought three shotgun shells. With only three shotgun shells and two shotguns among us, we would need to trade off using the shotguns. We would have to make our single shot count. There would be no second chances.

By the time we got down to the river, my toes were numb inside my flimsy leather boots. My face and my hands were just as cold as my toes. I noticed that my breath was visible as we moved along.

The water level had risen and flooded above the riverbank, spilling onto the forest floor that lined the edge of the river. A half an inch of ice had formed on the surface of the river extending out about 70 feet to the open water.

We chatted as we walked along, not really in serious hunting mode. Suddenly, a mallard duck flew up just beyond the ice. Ronnie instinctively pulled up his gun and shot the duck. It fell to the water a few feet beyond the ice shelf. We congratulated Ronnie on his fine marksmanship. We had two dogs with us, but couldn't get either dog to go into the cold water even after we broke up the ice near the shore. We looked upriver hoping a barge would come by to break up the ice, allowing the duck to float to shore. The river barge never materialized.

Finally, after waiting quite a while, Bugsy impatiently looked over at his older brother and challenged him, "You shot it, you go get it!" Ronnie looked a little hesitant. Bugsy exclaimed, "Hey, you can't let the meat go to waste. Steve and I will build a campfire so you can warm up when you get back." Bugsy and I got busy and built a large bonfire from the driftwood that was in abundant supply.

Sighing loudly, Ronnie peeled off his clothes, went to the river's edge, and gingerly waded in. He had to break the ice as he went farther out. The water was deep and Ronnie found himself swimming while at the same time breaking the ice in front of him. He was making good progress and was within 10 feet of the duck when he turned around and started swimming back. He was all bug-eyed and his face had a pale blue color to it.

Bugsy could not believe that Ronnie was giving up. He hollered, "Turn around and get the duck!" He picked up a chunk of driftwood and threw it at Ronnie while yelling at him to turn around. The wood missed Ronnie by inches but splashed him good. Resolutely, Ronnie headed to the shore. Nothing seemed to deter him. When he reached land, he half ran, half stumbled to the fire. He was shaking uncontrollably and his lower lip was blue and trembling. Bugsy gave him hell for not getting the duck after being so close. Bugsy demanded, "Get your pearly white butt back over to the river and get that duck!"

Ronnie could barely respond his teeth were chattering so much but he definitely let it be known that he would not be going swimming for a second time that day.

I couldn't help but laugh at the scene before me, but I was amazed that Ronnie had even attempted the icy swim. I was none too warm even though I was fully clothed, dry, and standing next to the bonfire the whole time.

After Ronnie fumbled around getting his clothes back on, we stood by the bonfire for a long time. We had never heard of the term *hypothermia* but Ronnie got a pretty good idea that day what froze to death meant.

Later, without the duck in hand, we walked home.

———•———

When I was a teenager, I lived about a half-mile from the Ohio River where I spent a lot of my spare time exploring, hiking, hunting, and just goofing off. One of my favorite places along this waterway was a large sandbar on the inner bend of the river. Across the mile-wide Ohio River on the Kentucky side rose the high cliff face known locally as Lover's Leap. Both from my home and along the river I often looked at that high sentinel of rock and wondered what the view would look like from its top.

One hot summer day while walking along the sandbar with my friends Bugsy and Ronnie, we came across an abandoned rowboat. Bugsy yelled, "Salvage rights!"

Being young, enthusiastic, and somewhat overly optimistic we decided that this boat could indeed be salvaged with a little hard work, sweat, and ingenuity. We labored long and hard to remove the sand out of the half-submerged boat. We dragged the waterlogged vessel across the long sandbar, through the dense undergrowth of grapevines and stinging nettles, and across the adjoining pasture where we somehow wrestled the unwieldy contraption into my Dad's old Chevy pickup truck. We then drove across the rolling pasture to my house, where we deposited our newfound treasure in Dad's garage.

When Dad got off work later that day, he took one look at our find, shook his head, and walked away. He knew that no fatherly advice would help in this situation. He figured that after a short stint of sweating and tinkering over this piece of junk, ultimately disillusionment would set in and we would abandon the project. Then, he would haul the remnants off to the junkyard. And it almost happened that way.

After days of working on the boat, Ronnie said, "Aw the heck with working anymore, let's see if this boat will float." Again, we struggled with hauling and lugging the boat back to the river. With a fresh coat of paint hiding the dry rot and the somewhat noticeable gaps in the bottom floor, we proceeded to launch the *U.S.S. Explorer* into the slow-moving, mile-wide Ohio River. Our destination was the opposite shore of Kentucky where we planned to explore the cliffs of Lover's Leap before returning to the Illinois side of the river - modest goals we surmised, or so we thought.

We shoved off and started straining at the homemade oars that were nothing more than modified 2 x 8 boards. We quickly determined that if two of us bailed water as fast as possible while the third furiously rowed, we just might make it to the other side of the river before the boat sank and we drowned. About halfway to the other side of the river, our will to survive took over, as we knew that the boat contained no life jackets and that none of us could swim any farther than we could spit. This scary perception came to us, as the riverbank in either direction looked a long way off.

On the brink of exhaustion and several blisters later we finally beached the leaky craft on the Kentucky shore. The stress factor decreased somewhat. We stood there alternately looking up at the looming cliff face and back at the wide river. Bugsy wisely announced, "Well hell, we'll probably drown on the way back across the river, so we might as well have some fun and see what the view looks like on top." We laughed and agreed, so up we went.

The steep, rocky cliff face seemed several hundred feet tall although, in reality, it was probably much less. The rock outcropping was very smooth, sharply angled, and much too technical for our abilities. We could have coined the expression *being between a rock and a hard place* as we clung shakily to the few nubbins of hand and footholds available. It only took a few minutes to realize that we were again in a precarious position and that surely, we were going to fall to our deaths. Once again, the pucker factor almost shot off the scale!

Lady Luck intervened again that day as we were able to ever so slowly edge our way over to the side of the cliff where we could get off the rock face to safety. We then scrambled up a steep, faint trail running parallel to the edge of the rocky cliff and eventually gained the top of Lover's Leap.

The view from the top was fantastic and awe-inspiring. We could see for miles around the area. Our homes, off in the distance, looked like tiny miniature models. We picked out other landmarks that we knew. We were elated, soaking up the scenery for quite some time. As explorers, we felt we had cut another notch in our belt.

Later, we slowly worked our way back down to the boat. The three of us stood silently on the Kentucky shoreline while the water lapped at our feet. We stared off at the distant Illinois shoreline. Finally, Bugsy broke the silence when he exclaimed, "Well dammit, let's get it over with."

As Ronnie grabbed a makeshift oar, he blurted, "I'll row if you two bail."

We pushed off, took up our positions, and began our long ordeal. We fought furiously. We changed positions. We cussed. We prayed. We began to think that we would never make it. When we figured things could not get any worse, we heard a loud warning blast from the whistle of a river tug barge. We looked up to see a huge river barge, heavy with coal quickly bearing down on us. The pucker factor now amped up ten-fold as we became madmen flailing urgently trying to get out of the way of the fast-approaching vessel. We barely avoided the crushing blow of the bow only to get nearly swamped with the large wave from the barge. I am sure the barge workers and pilot looked at our situation with both concern and possibly humor. We were too busy bailing water to notice.

We continued our battle, slowly eating away at the remaining distance. The boat was over half full of water and filling quickly. After what seemed an eternity, sweating from exhaustion, our muscles screaming for relief, we finally made it to the Illinois shoreline. We stumbled out of the boat and lay on the sandy shore, exhausted but happy to be alive. The scene reminded me of three shipwrecked survivors lying face down in the sand, gasping for breath. The boat gunnels were the only thing left protruding out of the water. After a long rest, we finally got to our feet and walked home. We abandoned the boat for the next round of foolhardy explorers.

———•———

In June 1969, three teenage friends, my 10-year-old cousin, and I spent a week camping on the small island just southeast of the larger Hurricane Island located in the Ohio River. These two islands harbored a bit of the local legend and lore of the area. The spring on the larger island was known as the Ebb and Flow Spring. This spring would alternately flow then ebb and disappear for a short time before flowing again.

In the early 1800's this spring served as a freshwater source for people traveling down the Ohio River on flatboats. The spring was often recommended to travelers for its cool, sweet taste. River pirates operated a tavern a few miles upstream from the spring in the famous Cave-in-Rock where many of the flatboat travelers were persuaded to pull over for refreshments and supplies. The pirates would size up the wealth of the travelers, and if deemed worthy, would be robbed there or later at the Ebb and Flow Spring. Pirates would hide near the spring, waiting for the unsuspecting travelers. Many visitors were murdered when they kneeled to get a drink of water. The pirates would then steal anything of value and sink the flatboat out in the deeper water. As the story goes, so many travelers were killed one day that the spring flowed red with blood. Legend has it that on moonlit nights you can hear the mournful cries of the murdered victims whose spirits wandered around the island.

Ronnie, Bugsy, Danny Spivey, my cousin Paul, and I made up the gang of friends of this expedition. We intrepid explorers held weekly meetings, planning everything in detail. Then, the following week at our next meeting, we would change everything. At first, we planned to take just a few survival items and live off the land for the week. As the actual time of the trip drew closer, we started adding a bit more gear and some basic food items to supplement our survival experience. We even made a rule that each of us had to bring a can of food to add to our growing supply of goods for the trip at our weekly meeting. By the time we were out of school for the summer, we had collected a sizable amount of food and gear to bring with us.

Danny convinced his dad to take us over to the island in his motorboat and drop us off with instructions to come back in seven days. We had so much gear and food that it took two trips to get all our gear and all the explorers over to the island. The motorboat broke down after the first trip, stranding Paul and Bugsy on the island. They stayed busy gathering firewood while the boat was being repaired. Eventually, after the boat was fixed, the rest of the crew and supplies were deposited on the island.

It was a hot evening as we unloaded the boat and carried the gear and supplies up a short, but steep sandy riverbank to a flat area in the forest. We proceeded to clear the weeds and debris away from our campsite. Paul and Bugsy had piled a large stack of driftwood near the fire pit. We built a rough brush lean-to shelter before darkness. For supper, we roasted hot dogs on our long slim sticks over the campfire. It was a grand adventure in our young minds. Could life be any better?

A couple hours later we found out as it clouded up and started to rain. Most of us had been lying around the campfire when the rain started. We grabbed our blankets and hustled to our shelter. While huddled together we discovered that our shelter was not very waterproof. The wind picked up bringing even more rain into our shelter from the front and sides. We quickly became soaked and cold. It rained for hours. Later, when the rain finally subsided, the mosquitoes attacked relentlessly. We were miserable.

Finally, with sleep impossible we piled out of the shelter and built a fire to warm up. While one side of our bodies enjoyed the warmth of the campfire, the mosquitoes were dining on our other side. The hours until daybreak went by ever so slowly. It was a long night with little sleep.

The next day, after hanging our wet gear to dry, we put the campsite in order and fortified our shelter. We found a couple of boards in the driftwood debris and used them to make a comfortable seat for our latrine. A kitchen table was made from sticks and rope lashed together. Another wide board was used for a camp seat. More firewood was gathered. After the morning of busy activity, the campsite had a comfortable feel to it.

In the afternoon we proceeded to explore the small island. The water level in the river had dropped a foot or so exposing a small sandbar on the upper end of the island. We discovered quite a few mussel shells in this wet, sandy area. As part of our goal to live off the land, we boiled some mussels in a pot of water, pried off the shells, and attempted to eat a couple. It was like chewing rubber! My teeth literally bounced off the meat while trying to chew. We spit out the rubbery meat of the mussel and decided that we would try fishing instead.

We found a patch of cane growing on the island and cut a few cane whips to use for fishing poles. We found some worms and grubs under fallen trees lying on the ground. We tied our fishing line and hooks to the poles, baited the hooks, tossed the line into the water, and waited. The minutes turned into hours without so much as a nibble from the fish. Finally, hunger took over and we cut up some potatoes to fry in a skillet over the campfire. With a pleasant, warm breeze that second night, we slept like babies.

The next morning, we debated whether to swim over to the larger island. It was less than a hundred feet in distance to the other island. Danny, a strong swimmer, went over first and found the water shallow on the other side. There was a strong current flowing between the islands though. Paul and I decided to wear life jackets as neither of us were strong swimmers. As I started to swim, I found that fighting the current was difficult, and became tired quickly. I was afraid that the strong current would take me away from the islands and out into the middle of the river. I was lucky that the distance was not greater as I was exhausted when I finally made it to the shallows of the other side.

We decided to search for the Ebb and Flow Spring but were not sure where to look. This island was several miles long and was so large that it did not even seem like an island. We discovered that much of the interior of the island was cleared farmland. We saw a farmer on a tractor working in that area. We had erroneously thought that these islands were still as wild as the former days when the river pirates operated on the island. We were afraid that we would be accused of trespassing on someone's private property so decided to return to the small island. The return swim was not as bad as the current worked in our favor.

One lazy day blended into the next. The time on the island had a Huckleberry Finn flavor to it. We fished. We threw sticks out into the river. We built another table out of sticks and rope. We napped. We watched the clouds float by. We waved to passing boats. We played ballgames with old balls found in the driftwood debris. We explored. We sat around the campfire telling stories.

One moonlit night I was awakened by a chilling "o- o- o – o – uh" sound. I bolted up wondering if I had been dreaming. I sat looking around at the silvery moonlit areas and the dark shadows. Then I heard it again. It sounded like a ghost calling!

I immediately thought of the ghosts of the Ebb and Flow Spring legend. I attempted to wake everyone else up. Bugsy sat up, looked at me with a strange far away look, and mumbled, "The cheese is in the refrigerator." He then rolled over and went back to sleep.

The rest of us sat up listening. Then we heard it again. We agreed that it was a ghost calling. We sat there in awe at what we were hearing. The hair on the back of my neck was standing on end. Then we heard it again, but it sounded a little different. We could now distinguish the soft ghostly sound as a baying coon dog. What a relief! We laughed at how our imaginations had run wild.

One night we could hear voices over on the Kentucky side of the river. They sounded loud and unruly. Bugsy started hollering back at them. Ronnie told him to knock it off; that whoever it was might be drunk. Then, we heard a motorboat start up. We were apprehensive as the boat approached. We did not want any visitors. Out of the boat came several rough-looking men, obviously drunk. They looked through our supplies and wanted us to cook them some food, but we told them that we had only enough food for our stay on the island. We kept hoping that they would just leave. We were scared, staying huddled up for mutual protection. They staggered around, repeating that we should cook them some food. Finally, after what seemed a lifetime, they got back into their motorboat and left. We breathed a sigh of relief. Later, Ronnie gave Bugsy hell for enticing the drunks over in the first place.

One evening Danny and Ronnie were sitting on the sandy bank near our campsite looking through the binoculars. They had spotted a woman sunbathing on the far shore of the river. She was wearing a bikini. Bugsy wanted to see, but neither Danny nor Ronnie would give up the binoculars. Then, Danny informed us that the woman had taken off her bikini top. Again, Bugsy tried to wrestle the binoculars away from them with no success. After several minutes of staring through the binoculars and playing keep-away with Bugsy, Ronnie announced that we had missed the show as the woman had put her top back on and left the shore.

The last night we ate like kings when we realized that we had enough food to last another week. It was a fun time around the campfire that night as we ate, told stories, and relived what we had done for the past week.

At the appointed time the next morning, Danny's dad arrived with the motorboat and picked us up. We were proud of our expedition and could not wait to tell everyone about our trip. Even though our original goal of living off the land had not been tested, it had been a grand adventure nonetheless.

Shawnee National Forest in Southern Ilinois.

TURNING POINT
1972

◆

Our group of two outdoor instructors and six students traversed several snowfields and glaciers to reach the final route to the summit of Fremont Peak. For safety, we roped up while traveling across the Upper Fremont Glacier. The route to the summit was a steep ascent on the snow with a climb around a yawning bergschrund, a deep and broad crevasse near the head of the glacier where the mass of moving ice pulled away from the stagnant ice. On our final climb to the summit, we used a variety of fixed lines and roped belays on both snow and rock to reach the top. The view from the summit was spectacular with a sea of mountains in all directions. The backside of the mountain was a sheer drop with lots of exposure. I had to lie on my stomach to look down the other side. Our reverie was cut short as a thunderstorm began to brew off to the southwest and was headed our way.

To descend the mountain as quickly as possible, the instructors decided that our group needed to rappel off the rock section and over the bergschrund. We promptly set up the ropes and one by one took turns rappelling downward toward the cavernous crevasse.

When it was my turn to rappel, I tried to stay calm as I looked down into the dizzying depths of the bergschrund. I jumped out and away while letting rope run through my brake hand, while at the same time swinging on the climbing rope into the yawning crevasse before swinging out, letting more rope out, and landing on the bottom lip of the bergschrund. Without delay, I unhooked the rope, glissaded down the steep snow to the runout zone of the glacier, and came to a stop.

Climbing to the top of Fremont Peak was both exhilarating and terrifying. My fear of heights was put to the test. Fremont Peak, at 13,751 feet, the third tallest peak in Wyoming, was the second peak I had climbed on my 38-day trip in the Wind River Range of Wyoming.

Once our group got off the summit in what seemed like record time, we roped back up, crossed the Upper Fremont Glacier to the rocky moraine at the toe of the glacier where we planned to bivouac without sleeping bags, and spent the night. This exercise was planned to show us that it was possible to survive the night if caught out away from camp. At the toe of a glacier at 13,000 feet in elevation, it was a cold night with what seemed like a million stars in the clear sky. Sleep was scant that night. The challenging climb and bivouac experience was something I would never forget.

As a 19-year-old college student, I considered myself a capable outdoorsman but craved more challenging outdoor experiences. I had heard stories about a survival school but knew no details. I was about to finish my second year of Junior College in Southern Illinois before transferring to Murray State University in Kentucky in the fall. I asked my college advisor if he knew anything about survival schools. He came up with information about two organizations, Outward Bound and the National Outdoor Leadership School (NOLS). I read the information and decided that I liked what NOLS had to offer.

Founded by mountaineer Paul Petzoldt, NOLS provided courses that taught environmental ethics, technical outdoor skills, wilderness medicine, risk management, and leadership skills on extended wilderness expeditions.

I signed up for a 38-day wilderness expedition course in the Wind River Range in Wyoming. In late July 1972, I traveled to the NOLS headquarters in Lander, Wyoming where our group was outfitted with the proper gear and food we would need for the trip. We would be re-supplied by pack stock mid-way through the trip.

Over the course of the 38-day trip, our group was given instruction and training that included plenty of backpacking, mountaineering, rock climbing, rappelling, and route-finding skills as we were rarely on any trails. We learned about No-Trace backcountry techniques, map and compass, fly fishing, flora, fauna, edible plants, first aid, and so much more.

The mountaineering instruction included lots of rock climbing, rappelling, rope work, protection placement, and more route-finding. There was also plenty of snow climbing training including how to properly use an ice axe, self-arrest techniques, snow anchors, and rope work.

Wind River Range, 1972. —Payne Midyett photo

We also learned the basics of cooking in the backcountry. There were no freeze-dried meals, only basic ingredients and spices. We cooked everything from fish chowder to German chocolate cakes. We used lightweight camp stoves and also small campfires to cook and bake our meals.

My greatest challenge on the trip was the technical climbing and mountaineering exercises. Since I was a small child, I have always been afraid of heights. I was terrified at times. But it also made me examine myself at a deeper level.

Near the end of the trip, I decided that to overcome my fear of heights I would set a goal to climb 100 mountains in my lifetime. I had the first two under my belt from this trip. I had climbed Stroud Peak and Fremont Peak. I only had 98 to go! I eventually met that goal and although it helped dilute my fear, I was never able to completely overcome my fear of heights.

The trip ended with a five-day survival trip. We were divided into groups of four and had use of all of our gear but no food. We were told to subsist on fish that we caught and edible plants that we foraged. We were about 45 miles from the spot where we would be picked up at the end of the exercise. With few established trails in the backcountry, we were challenged to test our route-finding skills by bushwacking through tough terrain. At one point, putting our skills to use, we had to rappel down a cliff face to continue on our route. I thoroughly enjoyed the challenge of the survival portion of the trip.

We fished at every body of water we came to and did better than most of the groups. We collected a few edible plants, berries, and roots along the way including mountain sorrel and American bistort. Although most of our meals consisted of fish soup, one morning without catching any fish, our breakfast consisted of grouse whortleberries. We laid on our stomachs and filled our camp cups with BB-sized berries. Once there were enough berries for a mouthful, we'd gulp them down before resuming the task.

It was interesting to see how hunger affected our group. Sometimes, we were lethargic and it took quite a while to get up and moving whether to resume our trek, to fish, or to set up camp. Some people got short-tempered, but we all talked constantly about the food we wanted to eat once we were back home. Dreams were often of food.

Wind River Range. Steve Lamar on the left, 1972.
—Payne Midyett photo

I had grown up spending a lot of time in the outdoors while camping, hiking, hunting, fishing, and exploring in the Shawnee Forest of southern Illinois. I thought that I was knowledgeable and knew a good deal about the outdoors. I went to NOLS feeling confident in my skills but I found out that I didn't know nearly as much as I thought I did. I was amazed at how much I learned during that short time in the mountains. I kept thinking that if more schools were like NOLS, students wouldn't need to spend so many years in school.

I was riding an emotional high after the NOLS trip and it was exactly what I needed at that time in my life. For me, it was a life-altering experience and a turning point in my life.

BUILT ON DREAMS

◆

I always thought that log buildings were special, their rustic appeal fascinated me. Log buildings harkened back to a simpler time when people were more independent and self-sufficient. Our forebears often built their own sturdy log houses. They gardened, foraged, fished, and hunted for a great deal of their food. They sewed most of their clothes, as well as crafted many of their tools and everyday utensils. As my Grandpa Alva Watson once told me, "We either grew it, raised it, gathered it, made it, or went without it."

While growing up I listened to the stories of my elders. I read the history of the settlers, the homesteaders, the trappers, hunters, and explorers. A strong dose of independence, self-reliance, freedom, and pride seemed to be a common theme of my ancestors' life stories. I found that type of lifestyle very impressive, a strong potion that tempered my dreams.

By the time I was 18 years old, I knew that I wanted a lifestyle that included as many of those elements as possible. I wanted to own a piece of land and build a log house. I wanted to grow some of my food, as well as forage, fish, and hunt. I wanted to live in a place where there was plenty of wild country to explore. I set a goal to accomplish those goals within the next ten years.

At that time while living in the midwest, there were few people still around who had any experience in building with logs. What few books I found that addressed the subject, came with poor instructions on building crude, one-room cabins. But I kept up the dream, gleaning a tip here, a skill there. I stockpiled the information for later use.

I was doubly blessed when at the age of 23 I married Sharon, the love of my life. She was just as excited about living the type of lifestyle that I dreamed of. We moved to Missoula shortly after our marriage in August 1976 and wasted little time looking for a piece of land where we could follow our dreams.

We found land in the beautiful Swan Valley of northwest Montana. The area had a rural and rustic flavor, with plenty of forest, water, and mountains. Two wilderness areas bordered the valley to the east and the west. The broad valley consisted of checkerboard ownership, comprised mostly of national forest and corporate timberlands. Private, non-corporate lands made up less than nine percent of the remaining land base, mostly original homesteads, some of which had been broken up into smaller tracts.

We bought 35 acres of mostly logged-over land bordering Rumble Creek to the north with a sensational view of both the Swan and Mission Ranges. The land needed a lot of work, as the logging slash was thick and plentiful upon the land.

We embraced the challenge as we dreamed of working and living on our piece of heaven.

Being financially strapped, we did not have the money to build a log house, but we thought we could build a small log cabin to both gain experience in the construction process, as well as have a place to live until the time came when we could build a larger log house. We talked to many people and read what we could find on the subject of log house construction. We were fortunate that there were many Swan Valley residents with log-building experience. I gained further knowledge and skills by working for The Rustics of Lindbergh Lake, one of several log house construction businesses that dotted the area at that time.

After numerous sketches and plans, we were ready to build our cabin. We fashioned it after the small log cabin that we were renting at the Buckhorn Camp (present-day Mission Mountains Mercantile). We spent that summer and most of the next winter completing the small cabin. It seemed that we spent every available minute after work and on weekends working to get another log peeled and notched. The fact that we were greenhorns, stumbling along, learning as we went, made things even slower. But we loved it. A dream was coming true right before our eyes.

Carl and Steve Lamar working on the cabin, 1978.

We moved into the small log cabin in June 1979. Later in October of that year, with the help of a team of three midwives, our first child, Annie was born in our snug, cheerful cabin.

The small 12 x 16-foot cabin had a half-loft with a mattress for sleeping. We had a small wood stove to heat the cabin and running water from a nearby well. We had to heat water for dishwater and baths on the stove. The cabin contained

Lamar's Cabin, 1979.

a small cook stove, refrigerator, sink, and kitchen cabinets. A table and two chairs along with a bookcase and rocking chair made up the remainder of our furniture. A wood box on the front porch was filled with kindling and firewood. A long, galvanized tub stored on the porch was brought into the cabin for baths. A larger stack of firewood was nearby and farther away was an outhouse.

We enjoyed our year in the cabin. I harvested a nice young 4x4 buck during hunting season to provide meat for the winter. Earlier in the summer, Sharon had picked lots of huckleberries while I was away at work. We had cleared a garden area and fenced it that winter in anticipation of planting a variety of vegetables the coming summer.

With Annie bundled up and in a *Snugli* baby pack, we often cross-country skied through the fresh powder snow in the nearby forest where we saw deer and an occasional elk.

Unfortunately, a dark cloud appeared on the horizon as my job situation worsened the following year. I had been working seasonally for the US Forest Service and liked the work but the budget did not look good for the upcoming spring on the Flathead National Forest.

A forest ranger at the Shawnee National Forest in Illinois where I had worked previously told me about a full-time job opening. He said that I would be the frontrunner for the position if we were willing to move back. Sharon and I talked it over, and on the prospect of full-time employment, we uprooted, sold our land with the small cabin, and moved away.

The full-time position never opened up, but I found seasonal work with the Forest Service and then as a pulpwood logger. Finding life away from Montana and particularly Swan Valley less than satisfying, we returned within a year. We were able to rent the former cabin that we had built while we looked around for a new piece of land to purchase.

After looking at numerous places, we purchased 10 acres near Smith Creek in the spring of 1981. Later in 1985, we bought an additional 10 acres adjacent to the original acreage. Our land bordered Burlington Northern Timberlands (later Plum Creek Timber Company) to the west and north. To the east of our house site was a large pothole filled with water, teeming with birdlife of all varieties. Our view to the east included a great view of the Swan Range, particularly the double waterfalls pouring out of the high basin of Condon Creek. Our view to the west toward the Mission Mountains Range was limited due to the forest cover. Our nearest neighbor was half a mile away.

We designed the house plans ourselves after looking at other people's houses, numerous floor plans, as well as what seemed to be hundreds of sketches that we drew up. Finally, we decided on a plan that we both liked.

With plans in hand, we cleared away the trees and shrubs at the house site. Our neighbor and local mason, Ted Graf, built our basement while we roughed in the plumbing and rounded up building tools. To save time traveling from our cabin to the house site, we decided to move into the basement. The downside of that plan, as we found out later, was that when we worked above, the subfloor leaked to the basement below when it rained. We tried a variety of methods to stop the leaks, but none worked well.

Before we progressed far into the building process, we hired Jeff Wilhelm to drill our water well. Using a forked willow stick, he first witched the area to determine where the water source was located. He said that he did not know how or why it worked, but it seemed to deliver results for him. After determining where to put the well, he set up his machinery and drilled through the glacial till soil. At 62 feet he hit over 50 gallons of water per minute. There was so much water that he thought that he had hit an underground stream.

We discovered that our property had a few house logs, but not enough to complete a house. Our land had been logged in the 1950s, with the best trees taken. I looked around for an alternative source. While walking around one evening just north of our property line, I noticed that there was an area that had large, straight lodgepole pine trees. Many were barely alive with only a few green limbs, while a number of them were already dead.

I approached Burlington Northern Timberland officials about the possibility of buying those trees. At first, they were reluctant to work with me on such a small project, but eventually agreed as long as a logging contractor did the work. We later learned that it was one of the last house log sales offered to individual landowners.

On December 23rd, the logger cut and skidded over 100 house logs to our house site. Also, on his last run, he brought out 12 large, dead lodgepole trees that were for firewood. I thought that he had brought the firewood out for himself and went out to help him saw up and load them. He told me, "No, these are for you. A guy can always use a little more firewood. Merry Christmas."

Our house logs were older lodgepole pine that were newborn seedlings around 1857. Most of those trees were approximately 134 years old, tight-grained, and very straight with few limbs. Sun-loving trees, lodgepole pine trees are usually one of the first species to grow back after a forest fire. After determining the ages of the trees in three different areas on our property, I surmised that forest fires had burned our land around 1857, 1899, and 1919 forming a mosaic upon the landscape.

Before putting the logs up on the basement foundation, I needed to peel the thin bark off of the trees. In my box of tools was a drawknife, used for that purpose. It was a present from a 90-year-old friend of my parents. After my Mom told her elderly friend of my plans to build a log house, her friend listened intently. He later gave her a box that contained a drawknife that had never been used. He told Mom that he had bought that tool when he was a young man with dreams of building a log house, but had never got to pursue his dream. He wanted me to have it, to use in building my dream house. It was a gesture that struck a special chord in my heart, something I'll never forget.

Peeling logs with drawknife, 1978.

Because our house was built into a hillside, it was a challenge to lift the heavy logs onto the foundation and then onto each successive round of notched logs. Andy Anderson, a local craftsman with experience working with various cable systems, agreed to help me set up a workable system to lift the logs into place. Unfortunately, the standing trees near our house site were not large enough for a durable cable system. Andy was able to help me get a cable system that would at least get me started but would need to be replaced with a different system later on.

Later, Nathan Kauffman, another neighbor and lifelong Swan Valley resident, showed up one morning with his small bulldozer to help us out. He showed me

Round 4. Using jammer to lift logs onto the foundation, 1982.

how to build a *jammer*, another type of system for lifting logs. Again, the system worked for several rounds of house logs but was too short to complete the job. I finally rented a boom truck to finish the job.

Nathan and I created some excitement when we tried to lift the jammer into place. It had been raining hard that day with muddy conditions around the house site. As he lifted the jammer into position with his bulldozer, one of the support legs slipped, sending the whole jammer crashing onto the basement roof. The impact punched a five-inch hole through the top. All of the rainwater that had collected above poured into the basement down below. It startled Sharon as she was standing in the basement only a few feet away from where the impact occurred.

She quickly grabbed Annie and ran out of the basement wondering what the heck was going on. It continued to pour rain all day and through most of the following night. We tried to patch the hole, but the water kept draining through. We positioned our galvanized washtub to catch the water. It was a long night as I stayed up reading a book, stopping every so often to empty the tub.

It was a heavy snow year as I struggled to keep our road plowed, as well as keep the snow off the worksite and the deck of logs piled up near the house site. The weather was 15 degrees below zero in early January. A winter storm with wind conditions of 69 mph closed the Swan Highway. On January 21st, the temperature with a wind-chill factor on Marias Pass was 105 degrees below zero. On January 25th it snowed 30 inches, then rained the next day. By the end of January, there were 26 inches of packed snow at our place with new snow practically every day. By February 4th it was 36 degrees below zero. I was beginning to wonder if I would make any progress in building a log house that winter.

Despite the bitter cold and snow, we managed to get the first house log up on February 9th, 1982. Less than a week later, we discovered the exciting news that Sharon was pregnant and that the baby was due in early October. We were thrilled and again planned to have the birth at home. I would have liked to have our log house built and ready for the birth, but that scenario did not seem likely.

There were several styles for notching the logs to form the corners of the walls of a log house. I used the western saddle-notch, a popular method used in Swan Valley. This technique allowed each log to fit tightly over the log below it, with no gaps to chink. This method required more work initially but had a strong, solid appearance that was functional, yet visually appealing.

Rough cut notch, 1978.

Cutting notch, 1978.

In contrast, my Grandpa Watson once told me a story of an old log house that he and Grandma had lived in when they first got married. It had been built by a method that required chinking between the logs. The problem was that most of the chinking had fallen out over time. Chuckling, Grandpa recalled, "When we first moved into that old house, we would lay in our bed in one corner of the house and watch the sun come up through the other corner of the house."

Progress was slow. On a good day, I'd manage to get two logs up on the building, maneuvered into place, scribed, rough-notched, finish-scribed, and finish-notched. Each round of logs consisted of four walls plus a log wall dividing the house in the middle. Thirteen rounds of logs were needed to get the desired height. In addition to the log walls, there were the tie logs, as well as the purlin and ridgepole logs. A total of 81 logs of various lengths were used, as well as several posts. The walls were up by mid-July, with the purlins and ridgepole set by mid-August.

One day early in the process of notching the house logs, I had quite a scare. I was working on top of the log wall while Annie was playing down below. She was draped over a ten-foot-long log rocking back and forth, singing a song, when suddenly the log rolled pinning her headfirst into the snow and mud. I quickly jumped down, moved the log, and wiped away the mud that was stuck in her eyes, nose, and mouth. She screamed bloody murder, but she was unhurt.

By the end of September, the tongue and groove boards had been nailed onto the purlins and ridgepole with felt paper overlaid on top of the boards. The log house, although far from finished, was finally weatherproof, just in time for the birth of our son, Lucas on October 8th.

Little did I realize how long the rest of the work would take to finish the house. It was a slow process of juggling family, jobs, finances, and life in the quest to complete the project. Only partly in jest, I joked when I told people, "We started building in 1981, and 24 years later we are almost finished."

One historic aspect of our house was the maple hardwood living room floor. Previously it was the high school gymnasium floor where my Dad and I both played games when we were each on the Rosiclare High School basketball team. When the school was torn down, my cousin had salvage rights to the building and my Dad rescued some of the old flooring. The date, 1927, was stamped on the

10th round. Note old boom truck for lifting logs, 1982.

Steve putting the cedar roof shakes on. Annie in the foreground, 1983.

back of some of the boards. There was so much varnish and painted lines on the flooring that our neighbor Rueben Kauffman ran everything through his planer to get the bulk of it off. We scraped decades of homecoming and prom glitter from the grooves as we installed the pieces. Even after installing the flooring, it still took several rounds with a floor sander to completely rid the flooring of varnish and painted lines.

Lucas, who was born in our unfinished home, wanted me to put up a basketball goal on the side of the living room wall so that he could say three generations of Lamars had played ball on that floor, but I had to tell him that his mother would never go for his reasoning.

Building our log house is a dream come true. We live in a home that we mostly crafted with our own hands. We have a garden in our backyard that provides us with fresh vegetables and fruits. We hunt each fall for deer and elk to fill our freezer with wild meat. We grill trout caught from high mountain lakes. We have huckleberry jam on our breakfast toast and huckleberry pie on special occasions. We hike, camp, climb, hunt, and fish in the most beautiful landscape found on this earth, much of it accessible literally out our back door. We thrive on a lifestyle built on dreams.

Lamar's log house, 1984.

ELECTRIFYING
1979

◆

My dream of manning a fire lookout finally came true on a hot day in August 1979. Pete and Dana Klein, the longtime Cooney Lookout duo, had scheduled a day off and I volunteered to fill in for them.

Back in 1932, USFS employees Tauno Strom and Dave Halme built the original 20-foot-tall Cooney Lookout at the end of Rumble Creek Road in Swan Valley. The structure, an L-4 model consisting of a 14x14 foot hip-roofed cabin on stilts, was used for more than thirty-five years before being replaced in 1968 with a safer, lightning-protected 30-foot flat-roofed model.

Cooney Lookout, 1956. —USFS photo, USVHS Archives

As Pete began a tour of the lookout, he told the story of how the new fire tower was built right next to the old one. When the Forest Service crew prepared to topple the old tower, they were fearful that it might hit the new one. Pete, along with Butch Harmon, solved the problem one evening by simultaneously sawing down the old tower while at the same time pulling it with Butch's truck with a cable attached to the top of the lookout. When the Forest Service personnel showed up the next day, the old lookout was down, dismantled, piled, and ready to burn.

After climbing the three flights of stairs, Pete showed me around the glassed-in 14x14 foot room perched atop four tall, squared timbers. The room was sparse but efficient. A single bed was built into the northeast corner with a cookstove, bookshelves, and a couple of chairs spaced around the rest of the room. Communications consisted of a telephone and Forest Service radio. A lantern hung from a nail. Water stored in milk cans stood under a shelf along one of the walls. Outside a narrow walkway led around the perimeter of the lookout.

The Osborne Firefinder occupied the center of the room. Forest Service lookouts used this instrument to sight forest fires and pinpoint the direction as well as the probable distance of the smoke from the fire tower. This circular device consisted of a rotating, heavy metal ring that was approximately two feet in diameter. It sat upon a four-foot-tall study table. Inlaid upon this circular device was a stationary topographic map centered on the location of the tower. It had a pair of upright sights located on opposite sides of the ring. By looking through the front and rear sights while rotating the ring until pinpointing the center of the smoke or fire, the lookout could calculate the location of the fire by using the instrument and area landmarks.

Pete pointed out prominent landmarks that might help pinpoint the location of a fire such as Gray Wolf Peak, Lindbergh Lake, and Elk Point. In this area of Swan Valley, most thunderstorms move in from the southwest, often through the Lindbergh Lake country sweeping across the valley toward Cooney Lookout.

After a lightning strike, there might be fire immediately or it might be several days before a smoldering fire becomes active and detectable. Pete demonstrated how he plotted the lightning strikes so that he could continually watch those areas for any telltale signs of smoke.

The color of smoke could vary depending on the type of fuel the fire was burning. Pete cautioned me to make sure what I was seeing was indeed the generally blue-gray smoke of a fire and not the white-gray dust from a logging truck or water dogs that sometimes formed when moisture was in the air.

Thunderstorms were ferocious when they traveled directly over the lookout tower. For protection from lightning, the Forest Service grounded the lookout tower with lightning rods. As an additional safety precaution during a storm, Pete told me to stand on the hot seat, a small stool that had glass insulators attached to each leg. He also advised me to not use the radio or phone.

After the briefing, Pete bid me farewell and left me to my aerie perched on a knoll above the valley floor.

The sky was cloudless as I began my day. I took the binoculars and scanned the area. As a resident of Swan Valley for three years, I knew most of the landmarks. Nevertheless, I studied the maps and the terrain. I could see several prominent peaks along the jagged skyline of the Mission Mountains: Gray Wolf, Mountaineer, Daughter of the Sun, and McDonald. A bit closer I could see Lindy Peak and Elk Point. I practiced with the Osborne Firefinder until I felt comfortable with its use. I enjoyed the vista with the sea of green forest, the rugged mountains, the cool invigorating morning air, and the refreshing silence.

Even though this lookout was located at the end of a road with several residents living within a half-mile, I enjoyed the relative solitude that was interrupted by an hourly radio check-in to the Forest Service office at the Condon Work Center.

I had always wanted to spend a summer as a fire lookout and now I was getting a taste of it. As a lookout, I felt like I had stepped back in time as more and more fire towers were being phased out due to so-called better methods and technological advances in fire detection. Of the twenty-plus lookouts that once dotted the

Cooney Lookout, 2009.

high country of the Swan Lake Ranger District in Swan Valley, only the Cooney and Mission Lookouts were in use in 1979.

By the mid-1970s, the Forest Service had begun to rely more heavily on spotter planes for smoke detection, rather than lookouts. After checking all the old fire records, Pete researched the number of fires that had been spotted by planes and how many had been spotted by the lookouts, especially at Cooney Lookout. He discovered that Cooney beat all the lookouts and the planes combined. Because of Pete's efforts, the Forest Service decided not to destroy Cooney Lookout.

By afternoon the temperature rose to the 90s with thunderhead clouds starting to build off to the southwest. The sunshine penetrated the glass windows of the lookout making the temperature on the inside uncomfortably hot. I moved my small, wooden chair outside to the narrow hemmed-in walkway. The weather broadcast over the Forest Service radio reported a good chance of thunderstorms moving through the area.

The dark towering clouds continued to build. It was not long before I could hear rumbling off in the distance. The dark anvil-shaped clouds began their march across the valley. Lightning lit up the clouds. The rumbling and the wind increased. I could feel the tension in the air as the storm approached. I moved inside close to the Osborne Firefinder. Suddenly, a lightning bolt blasted from the sky and torched a tree. I quickly plotted the burning tree in the Loon Flats area.

Another lightning strike hit in the same general area. In quick succession, there were several more ground strikes. I had a hard time keeping up with all the action. I quickly reported by radio that I had seen several lightning strikes, giving the legal descriptions. As the thunderstorm approached and sheets of rain began to fall, I signed off.

The wind became stronger as nearby trees bent and swayed wildly. The increasing wind buffeted the lookout as the darkness enveloped the fire lookout. The thunder boomed with bright flashes of lightning lighting up the dusk-like darkness. It started to rain large droplets of water. A few drops at first, then a deluge of rainwater fell from the sky.

I moved the small, insulated stool to the center of the room and stood on it just in time as a tremendous blinding flash of blue light shot through the windows. I must have jumped three feet into the air it startled me so. It was as though someone touched off a shotgun blast next to my ear. It felt as though my eardrums had burst. I had never experienced anything like this before. The storm was intense. The frenzy of rain, wind, thunder, and lightning kept up for several minutes before moving on over the Swan Range and into the Bob Marshall Wilderness.

Although the skies had cleared, the excitement of the storm had me charged up. I had to remind myself to calm down and concentrate on the job at hand. I grabbed the binoculars and scanned the areas where I previously observed lightning strikes. I saw a puff or two of smoke. I promptly called the fire into the office at the Condon Work Center and continued to scan the area for more telltale signs. However, the rain had doused any other fires.

Later, in the cool evening temperatures, I sat outside on the walkway of the lookout and enjoyed the play of low light and the effect of the changing colors and shadows across the landscape. The storm had completely dissipated with only a few scattered, red and orange clouds over the Mission Mountains to the west. The air appeared cleansed as the mountains stood out in sharp relief.

As I reflected on my experience as a fire lookout, I smiled at the thought. My first day as a lookout had been the whole gamut from peaceful and idyllic to stormy and electrifying.

THE ECLIPSE TRIP OF '79
1980

◆

On February 28th, 1979, along with four friends, I skied into the Mission Mountains Wilderness for a three-day campout. One of our primary goals was to climb high enough in the mountains to break through the cloud cover and experience the total solar eclipse that would take place over this part of Montana. We also looked forward to camping in the snowy terrain while skiing and exploring the backcountry. We decided to set our sites on the chain of lakes in the upper reaches of the South Fork of Cold Creek.

Our group was made up of young Henry Meyer, the three Johns – Brekke, Brenneman, and Addington, and myself. We all lived in Swan Valley, loved the outdoors, and were excited about getting up into the mountains for an adventure.

After riding with Henry in his old four-wheel-drive pickup toward the South Fork of Cold Creek, we soon came to the end of the plowed portion of the road. The three Johns followed in another pickup truck. We donned our backpacks and started skiing up the drainage. We were sporting new Trak Bushwhacker skis that were wide, short, and very maneuverable in wooded, rugged terrain. We skied over three miles up old logging roads until we came to the wilderness boundary.

Shortly before noon, the total solar eclipse took place as we were crossing the boundary into the Mission Mountains Wilderness. At that point, we were above the majority of the cloud cover that had much of the lower valley socked in. Only a very thin cloud cover was between blue skies and us. We stopped skiing when the eclipse started taking place as it quickly started getting dark as though dusk was melting into the darkness of night. It became so dark that it was hard to see the ski tracks in front of us. Even though we knew not to stare at the total eclipse, as solar radiation could damage our eyes, we nevertheless stole quick glances at it. The sun was a dark disc with a bright glow radiating out from around it. It was a strange sensation as we marveled at the noontime darkness.

In awe, Henry asked, "Wow, I wonder how the wildlife is reacting to this darkness?" Other questions came to mind. Would the birds roost early? Would the elk and deer get up to feed? After a few minutes, the darkness lessened as the total solar eclipse faded. In a few short minutes, the noontime daylight returned. We stood around amazed by the experience, talking excitedly for several minutes about witnessing a total solar eclipse.

Solar eclipses occur when the moon passes more or less in a straight line between the sun and Earth and are witnessed approximately twice a year somewhere on Earth. But total solar eclipses are rarer, being observed somewhat less

UP IN SMOKE
1981

In September 1981, sixteen Forest Service firefighters, including Swan Valley residents Barb Raible, Kathy Koors, and myself, were flown to a helispot on the ridge above the forest fire burning on the steep sidehill in the canyon on the north side of Holland Creek. The fire had been very active the day and night before but was lying down early that morning. There were crews of firefighters already working the lower portions and the sides of the fire when the decision was made to put firefighters above it and aggressively pinch the fire off from all four sides.

As we unloaded from the helicopter, one of the supervisors told us to drop our packs that contained our food, extra clothing, rain gear, and sleeping bags in a pile near the landing area. We were instructed by our crew boss, Jim Greytek, to take only water and tools. While the fire conditions were relatively calm, we were told to hustle down to the upper part of the fire and establish a fire break.

Meanwhile, the district ranger, Bill Pederson, was closely observing the fire from a vantage point in the valley below where he could easily observe the whole fire area.

As we were hiking down toward the fire, we received an urgent radio communication from the ranger. His contact was direct and to the point, "Get the hell out of there! The fire is blowing up below you!"

Luckily, the night before we arrived, a burning ember had landed uphill and burned out a sizeable area, probably several hundred feet in an oblong shape. We quickly moved into the blackened area as the fire moved up the steep ground toward us. It burned up and around us, eventually burning over the helispot area. We later learned the fire burned all of our gear and food that we left near the landing area.

After the fire passed, we waited for the area to cool down and proceeded down through the blackened landscape. We eventually found a place where we could pass safely into unburned terrain along the southeast perimeter of the fire boundary. At that point, we started to dig a fire line. We continued to build a fire line for the next 34 hours.

Boyd Kessler, who was running the support operations at the Condon Work Center, radioed us that he would try to get some hot food prepared by Leita Anderson's kitchen crew to us if there was an available helicopter to drop in supplies. Unfortunately, there were many forest fires in the Swan Valley area at that time, and the longed-for hot food never materialized. After 24 hours, a helicopter flew over and dropped a case of Army Meals-Ready-To-Eat rations down to us. By then, we were famished, and we devoured the prepackaged food.

We worked close to the edge of the fire, putting in hotline as we constructed the firebreak. Following safely behind the chainsaw team that cut the trees and brush from the firebreak's proposed route, the remainder of our crew was spread out digging the fire line.

After 34 hours of digging, I felt like a zombie in a trance, mechanically digging and scraping an eighteen to twenty-four-inch-wide tread as I methodically plodded along until I hooked up my section of fire line with the person ahead of me. I moved up to the next person and said, "Bump." I'd take over where they were working. In turn, that firefighter would move up along the line and bump the next person. As a crew, we methodically constructed the firebreak.

The fire was often active enough that it often provided all the light we needed to see while we worked. Occasionally, a large tree's roots burned out and came crashing down. Rocks and logs bounced down the steep terrain from time to time.

It was hard to stay mentally sharp as the long work shift wore on. After a prolonged 34-hour shift, we took a 45-minute catnap break. We continued to work a couple more hours before being relieved by fresh crews that were brought in.

It felt terrific to get a hot meal at Leita's cookhouse at the Condon Work Center and a few hours of sleep before being sent out to the next forest fire.

The Condon Air Field east of the Condon Work Center during forest fire activity. —USFS photo

A SNOWY AND COLD TIME IN THE MOUNTAINS
1983

◆

When I awoke at dawn, I knew the temperature had plummeted overnight. Breathing the frigid air through the cinched-up opening of my mummy sleeping bag told me that it was extremely cold. It was difficult to breathe in deeply without an involuntary cough escaping my lungs. Ice had formed a thick crust around the opening of my sleeping bag where the moisture from my breath froze to the fabric. My fellow campers and I were about to experience winter on a different level, a much more dangerous level where mistakes can have serious consequences. Mother Nature had thrown us a curveball and we needed to adjust.

In 1983, while working as a wilderness instructor for the Wilderness Treatment Center (WTC), I helped lead a winter trip into the Bunyan Lake area along the eastern foothills of the Mission Mountains. The Wilderness Treatment Center, a drug and alcohol treatment program, utilized an outdoor component as part of the 60-day therapy process. Each patient was required to complete a 16 to 21-day wilderness expedition as part of the therapy regimen in an attempt to come to grips with their addiction. The program was geared for 14 to 24-year-old males. Each patient spent a month at the facility working through the various levels of progression dealing with their addiction before they qualified to move on to the next level of therapy - the backcountry trip. The outdoor trip was a combination of challenge, reflection, and application of lessons learned earlier in their therapy treatment.

It was mid-December with lots of fresh, loose, unconsolidated snow. Luckily, snowmobilers had made a packed trail into the area that allowed for easy skiing. We were equipped with Sorel boots with wool liners and sturdy Bushwacker skis. Our backpacks were heavy, containing enough food, gear, and clothing for a seven-day stay along the perimeter of the backcountry. We would be camping on what was then Plum Creek Timberland property.

The first day was a long ski from the road junction near the homes at Lindbergh Lake to the Bunyan Lake area, a distance of over seven miles. It was a sunny day with temperatures in the low 20-degree range which made for good skiing. Our small group included two instructors and two patients. The day was interspersed with teaching the young men the various skills and techniques of winter camping and travel.

Arriving in the late afternoon at our campsite, we packed down the snow where we would set up our two tents. While waiting for the snow to set up and harden to form a level base for our tents, we dug out a kitchen area and fired up our lightweight camp stoves to begin heating water for hot drinks and cooking supper.

We got our water by skiing over to Bunyan Lake, digging down through the snow, and chopping a hole in the ice. This effort saved time and fuel from having to melt snow to keep hydrated. With what little sunlight was left on the short December day, we cooked our meal, set up tents, and got camp ready for the long winter night. With clear skies, the temperature started to dip as soon as the sun set behind the Mission Mountains. The snow took on a squeaky sound when we walked in our beaten-down trail between our cook area and the tents.

Sometime during the night, it warmed up as clouds moved in and it began to snow steadily. By morning, the snow continued to fall with six inches of fresh snow on the ground. Our itinerary called for moving camp adjacent to the wilderness boundary, less than a mile away. By the time we packed up, it had snowed another six inches and was still coming down heavily.

We shouldered our heavy packs and skied up the ridge to our next camp. The total snowpack was now over waist-deep with no real base to it. It was tough skiing off the snowmobile track as our skis sunk straight down and encountered rocks, stumps, and brush. It was difficult pushing through the deep snow and obstacles while trying to gain elevation up the ridge. One of us pushed through for a while then stepped aside so that the next person in line could break trail. Even rotating at short intervals quickly tired everyone out. The snow continued to fall heavily and stacked up quickly. By noon, the snow was chest-deep and still coming down. Finally, we made it to our campsite. I couldn't believe how much effort it had taken to go such a short distance. It was obvious that at this pace our plans for the next few days would need to be adjusted. During the night it snowed another 12 inches or more.

The next day we decided to take a day ski but quickly found that even without heavy backpacks it was tough going. We couldn't ski downhill on the steeper terrain without having to push forward. I was in good physical shape but these kinds of conditions quickly took the starch out of me. I was amazed at how much energy and effort it took to go only a short distance.

The snow conditions did not improve for the rest of the trip. Each day was a repeat of the next. It was frustrating. I hoped that during our stay in the area we could ski to the top of Lindy Peak but it was obvious that was very unlikely.

Finally, it was time for the solo exercise where each patient camped by himself, alone in a designated area where he built a snow cave to sleep in, and was given his individual therapy homework for three days and two nights. We two instructors did numerous periodic checks to make sure all was going well and to bring the patients hot drinks to supplement their food and water. We stressed taking responsibility for their actions and doing the little things that were important to living safely in a wintertime setting. We reminded them to eat and drink sufficiently and dry out damp clothing inside their sleeping bag using their body heat.

The temps inside of the snow caves stayed a comfortable 32 to 35 degrees while the outside temperatures remained in the high teens and lower 20-degree range. The heavy snow had slacked off but the snow flurries continued.

When I awoke on the bitterly cold morning, I could tell that the skies had cleared off during the night. This did not feel like an average cold winter morning. My eyelashes were frosty and the hairs in my nostrils were tingling.

I woke the other instructor, discussed the turn of events, made hot drinks, and went to check on the patients. The first young man was fine. He had taken care of the little things and was snug inside his snow cave.

The second patient was a different story. When we skied up to his snow cave, we found him standing outside without his wool hat. He complained that he had no feeling in his legs from the knees down. He said he had forgotten to bring his damp boots into the snow cave during the night and the boot liners inside his boots were frozen solid. He wore forbidden cotton socks that he had sneaked into his pack before leaving for the trip. He had forgotten to dry out his damp wool socks and had replaced them with cotton socks.

I immediately helped him get inside his snow cave and put on his hat. I then took off his boots and checked his feet. The big toe on each foot had sure signs of frostbite. The tips of his toes were a pale egg-white color. I knew he needed medical attention and that we would have to leave that very day.

The weather was crystal clear and it looked like this cold frigid system was going to be around for a while. I did not want his frostbitten toes to warm up and then be susceptible to refreezing which would do even greater damage. After outfitting him with dry wool socks, we packed up and headed for the trailhead.

It was a tough bitterly cold day to travel as we skied our way back to the road. Luckily, snowmobilers had once again packed down the trail when we got back to Bunyan Lake. I hoped that someone on a snowmobile would come by and help us out, but no such luck. We continued to ski down the seven miles of road and reached my Datsun pick-up truck at dusk.

It was extremely cold and the temperature was dropping fast as the first stars came out. We hurriedly loaded my truck with our gear. I hoped that my truck would start in the subzero cold. I put the key in the ignition and turned the key, but nothing happened. Not even a sound.

At the time, I was not sure any residents were living at Lindbergh Lake during the winter but I was willing to walk to the nearest house to get help. But first, I told everyone to push my truck down the slight incline of the road and I would try to

Steve Lamar Camping in 45 below zero weather.

pop the clutch and see if that would work. I was unsure whether it would work but when I tried it, the engine started! I was so relieved.

The four of us crammed into the cab of my little truck and we drove to my house to call the Wilderness Treatment Center to set up the medical help and transport. We later found out that the frostbite on the patient's toes was not as bad as we thought and he recovered completely.

Later, I learned that the temperature had dipped to -45 degrees below zero while we were out in the mountains. And the temperature dipped to -52 degrees below zero in Seeley Lake. It had been a snowy and cold time in the mountains.

A MEMORABLE ELK HUNT
1984

Thinking back, 1983 had been a long winter. Boyd Kessler, a longtime Forest Service employee, kidded me every time he saw me. Every chance he got, he needled me, "You never pass up a good shot for a perfect shot."

His banter started in the autumn at the end of the fall hunting season. While up in the Frenchy Creek area in the Mission Mountains Wilderness, I had passed up a good close shot at an elk thinking that shortly I would get a perfect shot when it stepped into a small clearing between the trees.

But the elk had other ideas. The elk stopped behind a thick spruce tree, then darted off directly away from me using the tree to block my view. It turned out to be my only chance of putting elk meat in the freezer that hunting season. Boyd made sure I relived that fateful moment time and time again the whole year leading up to the next season.

One day in the following summer of 1984 while working for the Forest Service, Boyd and I were at the Owl Creek Packer Camp near Holland Lake. We dropped off a couple of new picnic tables that we had constructed at the Condon Work Center. As we started to drive out of the packer camp, Boyd stopped the truck, looked over at me, and asked, "Steve, do you want to get an elk? Are you really willing to work for an elk?"

I quickly replied, "Yeah, I want to get an elk. You know me, Boyd, I'm willing to hike to hell and back to get an elk."

He looked at me intently for a few seconds, then said, "Okay, then right up there is your elk." He pointed upwards due east to a high mountain basin on the Swan Range. He proceeded to tell a long-ago story of a doctor who hiked up there, sat next to an avalanche chute reading his book, and shot the first elk that came along. He then hiked down and persuaded a packer by the name of Peterson to take his horses up there to pack it out. The packer claimed each year that the country was too rough, that he would never again subject his stock to such torture and physical hardship. But each year when the doctor flashed a little extra money, the packer would relent and pack out the elk.

Boyd said that as far as he knew nobody hunted that area anymore, and he was certain I could get an elk up there. He said, "Hike up to the basin the day before the season starts and camp out. If you shoot an elk, bone it out on the spot, put the meat in bags, strap as much as you can carry onto your pack, and relay the loads down the mountain. Wherever you end up at night, camp close by. Then repeat the process until you get out." Then he laughed and said, "But you might have to take your fork and knife with you and eat your way out." He reminded me that it was a rough country. It would not be a quick or easy trip, especially if I had to pack the elk meat out.

With fresh determination, I set a goal of hunting the high basin and harvesting my first elk. In those days it was legal to shoot either a cow or bull elk the first week of hunting season, but only a bull elk after the first week. I planned to hunt every day of the first week to better my odds of taking an elk.

My seasonal job with the Forest Service was coming to a close for the year. Finding work in the winter was sometimes a challenge, if not impossible. Before winter set in, I wanted to have a woodshed full of firewood, and a freezer full of vegetables from the garden, huckleberries and black-capped raspberries from the mountains, and wild meat from the forest. It had always been reasonably easy to get a deer, but putting elk meat in the freezer had not gone so well for me.

Last season's misfortune had been my closest opportunity to date. I was determined that this year would be the turning point. I left no detail unplanned. I pored over the map and studied the lay of the land. I target-practiced with my rifle. I kept in great shape.

I planned to go reasonably lightweight with only a thin tarp for my shelter, a lightweight pad, and a goose-down bag for sleeping. I did not plan on building campfires or taking a cooking stove. For food, I took a chunk of salami, cheese, and some trail mix. Other than my wool clothing, rifle, ammo, knife, meat bags, water bottle, and emergency items, I had very little else in my aluminum-framed backpack.

As it turned out, I could not hunt on opening day, but on day two I woke early and spent the day working my way up into the high basin. I found the old packer trail at the foot of the Swan Range and followed it. It was not a direct or easy route. Sneaking through rocky, boulder-strewn areas as well as thick brush, the steep trail seemed to wind all over the forested mid-slope of the Swan Range. I went slowly and hunted my way up the trail reaching the bottom of the basin in the late afternoon.

With eight inches of snow at that elevation, I found a level spot on a side bench that afforded a decent view of the open grassy lower basin as well as much of the steep side slopes. I sat with my binoculars glassing the terrain before me. Four mule deer does wandered out across the open basin followed by a huge buck with a wide-spreading rack of antlers adorning his head. Broadside at 80 yards I considered shooting him but reminded myself that I did not come all this way to shoot a deer, even one that big. I watched as the five deer worked their way in a southerly direction up a steep avalanche chute and crossed the ridge.

After satisfying myself that no other game was nearby I quickly set up my shelter tarp and placed my pad and sleeping bag underneath. I then worked my way into the upper basin that is essentially hidden from view down in the valley. Here I found the tracks of six elk that had recently crossed into this upper basin from the Bob Marshall Wilderness. I tracked the elk for some time, but I could see their tracks in the snow up high leading along the rim of a cliff area below the top of a nearby peak heading out of the drainage. By then the sun had set behind the Mission Mountains Range to the west. I figured that they had left the area.

I resigned myself that this would not be the day I got my first elk. I walked back to my campsite in the gathering darkness, stopping to glass the area from time to time. After a cold meal of cheese and salami, I crawled into the warmth of my sleeping bag for a long night's sleep. I was tired and sleep came easy.

The next morning, as I lay in the warmth of my sleeping bag in the early predawn darkness, I heard a bull elk bugle high on a side ridge to the north of my camp. Apparently, the elk that I had been tracking the day before had not left the area. I quickly crawled out of my sleeping bag and headed slowly up toward the elk. The wind was in my favor as the early morning draft flowed down into the valley. As I worked my way up the ridge, the snow crunched noisily with every step I took. It was getting light as I proceeded upward. I jumped three mule deer that made all kinds of noise as they bounded off. I had not gone another hundred yards when I jumped two more mule deer. At that point, I thought that I would never get close to the elk, with the spooked mule deer tipping off my presence. With the arrival of daylight, I felt exposed as I walked through an open area.

Suddenly, the bull elk bugled close by. I strained searching to find its location. He was on the other side of a thicket of subalpine fir trees about a hundred yards uphill and off to the west. Just as I started to take my next step, I spotted the lead cow about 70 yards away, standing broadside looking straight at me. As much as I wanted to go for the bull elk, I knew that the lead cow would shortly sound the alarm and take the small herd out of the area. I could hear Boyd reminding me, "Never pass up a good shot for a perfect shot."

With that thought, I slowly raised my rifle, put the crosshairs on her neck near her skull, and pulled the trigger. The shot hit its mark. The elk rolled down the steep slope, wedging tightly between two subalpine fir trees. I was excited that I finally had harvested an elk. When I got to the elk, I said a little prayer of thanks.

The elk was huge. I had to use my small meat saw to cut down one of the five-inch diameter trees before I could shove the carcass into position to field dress it. I had to tie back the legs to work on such a large animal. After field dressing the animal, I skinned one side, cut the meat off, stored it in the meat bags, then flipped the carcass over and repeated the process. It was my first experience boning out an animal, so I took my time. The whole process took me several hours.

Interestingly, as I boned out the elk, seven mule deer paraded past within 50 feet of me. I was tempted to shoot one of the two young bucks in the group, but wisely realized it was neither the time nor the place.

As I loaded my backpack with elk meat, the bull elk bugled off in the distance. I was surprised that he was still nearby. I thought that after I shot the lead cow, the rest of the elk would leave the area. But apparently, that was not the case. I thought of going toward him to see just how big he was but decided against it. I had my hands full trying to get the elk meat home. I relayed three loads of meat to my camp, took a short break to eat some food, and then packed up my tarp, pad, and sleeping bag.

I spent the rest of the day relaying meat and gear down the trail. The loads were heavy and by dusk I was tired. I still had a long way to go to get down to my truck so I secured the elk meat in a tree, moved off a safe distance, and quickly set up my tarp. It started to snow as I crawled into the comfort of my sleeping bag. As I was lying there happily recounting the events of the day, a bull elk bugled high above me. It sent shivers down my spine. The bugling of an elk has to be one of the most tremendous sounds in nature.

What had started as light snow that first night after I shot the elk turned into a full-blown winter storm. It took me two more strenuous days to get all the elk meat and gear out of the mountains. There were 16 inches of snow at our house in Swan Valley by the time I finally got home. I felt fortunate to get out when I did.

It felt good to be home again with my family as we busily cut up the elk meat. Our woodshed was full of firewood, and now our freezer would be full of vegetables, fruit, and wild meat. It was a good and satisfying feeling.

And by the way, I could not wait to tell Boyd about my hunt.

Elk

CAT AND MOUSE
1984

On the last day of the 1984 hunting season, I had yet to harvest a deer to add to our winter meat supply. Earlier in the season, I had shot an elk up in the high country. But on the last day of the hunting season, I was hunting in the valley near my home.

I was sitting under a Douglas fir tree watching a well-used game trail about thirty feet below me. Below the trail was a frozen pothole with a covering of an inch of snow. My concentration was waning as the day wound down with only 20 minutes of daylight left before the hunting season ended. Nothing seemed to be moving in the area. A quick look at my watch showed only ten minutes of legal light left. It was getting a bit dark, but if a deer came along the game trail, it would be nicely silhouetted against the white background of the snow-covered pond.

As the minutes clicked by, I was getting more discouraged. I was practically resigned to the fact that I would not be getting any venison this season when suddenly I saw something moving slowly along the trail. I checked my watch and still had five minutes of legal light left. I was excited that my luck had changed for the better. It was the large doe that I affectionately called *Mouse* as she was cagey, rarely letting me see more than a glimpse of her. We had often played cat-and-mouse it seemed. She kept turning her head looking back down the trail. I knew that bucks often followed the does as the mating season rut was still in full swing.

Time seemed to be running out. I kept hoping that the buck would show up soon or it would be too dark to shoot. *Mouse* moved up the trail and out of sight. I kept straining to see down the trail, as I was sure that a buck was following her. What a surprise when along the trail came a mountain lion instead of the buck.

Until this moment, I had never seen a mountain lion at close range. No more than forty feet away, the lion moved stealthily along the trail putting the sneak on the doe. It was perfectly silhouetted against the white background. I was mesmerized by the scene unfolding in front of me. Experiencing the sight of a mountain lion was so impressive that I forgot all about the hunting season. The sight put a tingle up my spine and a smile on my face.

When the mountain lion got to a clump of juniper brush along the trail, it stopped. At least I thought it did. The light of the day was almost completely gone. The hunting season was over. On my route home, I needed to head in the direction where the lion had stopped. I hesitated, not knowing what to do. I wondered if the lion knew I was there and had shifted his interest toward me.

Mountain Lion. —Luke Lamar photo

Finally, while there was still some light, I stood up and said in a loud voice, "Well, I'm going home now!"

It was obvious that the mountain lion did not have a clue I was so close. It jumped about three feet straight up in the air, spun around, and raced off. I was amazed at how quiet the mountain lion was as it quickly bounded down the trail.

Talk about an exciting day out hunting! I walked briskly back toward my home, whistling all the way. Even though I did not get a deer that day, I regarded it as one of my best hunting experiences.

DOING THE SAME THING WITH DIFFERENT RESULTS
1985

◆

In March 1985, I was working as an outdoor instructor for the Wilderness Treatment Center in the backcountry of Montana. We were a small group of two students and two staff on that particular trip. We spent sixteen days in a remarkable country with outstanding scenery and wildlife. We had traveled on skis, moving camp and exploring the new country at a regular interval.

The program included a three-day, two-night solo experience where each student camped by himself in a designated area and stayed there until the end of the activity. The students were supplied with ample food, water, and all of their gear for the solo experience. The instructors were camped nearby and made regular safety checks at each student's site.

On the last morning of the solo activity, I made the early morning safety check to see how each student was doing. I skied up to the first student. He was lying partially in his sleeping bag in a small, sunny area free of snow. He had an incredibly small campfire between two small rocks that he fueled with tiny twigs. Sitting on top between the two rocks was a metal cup of steaming hot cocoa. The birds were singing, the student had a smile on his face, and all seemed peaceful with the world.

Next, I skied to the other student's site. Within his designated area he had chosen a low, shaded, cold area for his camp. He had an extremely huge bonfire burning. The fire was eight feet across in its mammoth size. The student was sweating, with black charcoal streaks running down his face. He was attempting to eat a messy glob of pancake dough that was blackened and burnt as well as mostly uncooked. Some of the concoction hung from his chin. The hair on his bare arms had been singed in his attempt to cook his breakfast at the roaring bonfire. He was angry and exasperated with the whole ordeal. He had the look of someone who had been shoveling coal into the boiler furnace of hell.

I was both amused and somewhat astounded that two people, given essentially the same circumstances and resources, could come up with such contrasting results. But when I thought about it, examples such as this are daily occurrences in this world of ours.

A FRIGID TIME IN THE BACKCOUNTRY
1985

◆

As morning dawned, a quiet inaudible hush settled upon the land broken only by loud gunshot-like sounds emanating from the trees. I recognized the unmistakable sound of trees popping from the rapidly freezing sap within. The sky was a crystal-clear cobalt blue. When I inhaled the crisp air, I could feel my nose hairs stand at attention, a sure sign of subzero weather.

At the end of January 1985, I was in Montana's North Fork backcountry near the Canadian border working as a wilderness instructor for the Wilderness Treatment Center (WTC). As part of the therapy regimen, each patient was required to complete a 16 to 21-day wilderness expedition in an attempt to come to grips with their addiction.

In its early history, WTC utilized a US Forest Service special use permit to conduct its winter trips in the upper reaches of the Glacier View Ranger District in the Whale Creek drainage. WTC had access to the USFS Ninko cabin as part of the permit. The cabin was stocked with extra gear and food and was used as a safety valve of sorts. There was plenty of firewood cut and stored underneath the front porch of the cabin. On each trip, the group usually spent a few nights in the cabin but mostly camped out in lightweight tents or snow caves.

Once again our group was small with only three patients and two staff including Alan Orr and myself. The owner and director of WTC, John Brekke, went with us the first couple of days to help ferry some extra food and supplies to Ninko cabin. I found out later that this trip was Alan's first at winter camping. The three patients, Jeff, Jim, and Bob were apprehensive about spending the next two weeks camping mostly in the snow in the dead of winter. During the past dozen years, I worked for several outdoor programs and felt comfortable and confident camping in wintertime conditions.

On the first day, we skied ten miles on relatively flat terrain. Starting at 4200 feet in elevation, we gained only 400 feet along our route that day. A few inches of fresh powder snow had fallen on top of a firm snowpack of several feet. Our backpacks were heavy as we carried the majority of the food and gear we would need for the two weeks. Still, we made good time and arrived at Ninko cabin near dusk. We spent the first two nights at the cabin before moving into the backcountry.

Built by US Forest Service employees between the years 1949 and 1951, the 16 x 20-foot Ninko cabin was constructed with logs. It was originally utilized as an intermediate workstation for the various crews dealing with a spruce bark beetle infestation that had wreaked havoc within the stands of mature spruce trees in the area. The cabin contained a wood stove, propane cookstove, table, chairs, and bunk beds. A lantern provided light at night, and the nearby Ninko Creek provided water. An outhouse down the hill rounded out the facilities. This cabin is currently in the USFS cabin rental program.

Ninko Cabin FNF, 1985.

Each morning after breakfast, the patients read and discussed the message from an inspirational daily reading from the book, *Day by Day*, which dealt with the world of addiction and recovery. Jeff and Bob often related some facet of their lives to the message, explaining how they planned to use the reading to help them with their recovery during the day. Jim, on the other hand, seemed to be going through the motions and not invested in the program. The staff hoped that the trip would help him turn things around for the better.

The rest of the second day of the trip was spent mostly cutting additional firewood. The nearby area had numerous dead lodgepole pine trees that were killed by a mountain pine beetle epidemic that was sweeping through the region. We felled several of these trees and sawed the trees into rounds of firewood. We utilized a plastic sled to haul the rounds of firewood to the cabin where we then split them into smaller chunks. We stored the firewood and kindling both on and under the front porch of the cabin. Afterward, we went for a ski to the nearby Whale Creek Falls, which was mostly frozen with ice draped over the cliff rock.

The next day after we packed up and said goodbye to John as he headed back to the trailhead, our small group skied over seven miles to Whale Lake. The weather for the first three days of our trip had been pleasant by winter camping standards. The temperatures stayed in the low 20s, which in turn, kept the snow cold enough for good skiing, but not too cold to make living in the snowy world challenging.

Unbeknownst to us, things were about to change. As we arrived at Whale Lake, the cloudy weather moved out of the region and was replaced with clear, cobalt-blue skies. As Alan and I were standing in a clearing looking down the Whale Creek drainage, we watched this rapid change of weather. I said, "I don't like the looks of this. It might be 30 degrees below zero by morning."

Alan's anxiety was apparent. He confessed that he had left some of his warmer clothing behind to cut down on weight in his backpack. Then he admitted that this trip was his first winter camping trip ever. I tried to mask my surprise by focusing on the positive. I told him that everything would be okay. I explained that we would build snow caves to sleep in so that we would stay warmer. Snow is a great insulator. The temperature inside a well-built snow cave usually ranges from 32 to 35 degrees above zero. We gathered the group around, explained the weather situation, and went to work building a snow cave.

The snow was not as deep as I would have preferred for building a snow cave but was adequate at over six feet deep. To prevent us from getting completely soaked, we donned our rain gear while digging out the snow cave. As we dug into the drift of snow, we were careful to always keep both the entrance and the sleeping chamber arched for strong structural support. We kept a minimum of 18 inches of snow as a roof between the outside snow surface and the inside ceiling of our snow cave. We used the handle end of a ski pole to poke through the roof to measure that distance as well as to provide air holes for better ventilation. We smoothed off the interior domed wall of the snow cave to prevent any drips of melting snow in case our combined body heat raised the temperature above freezing. We built a snow cave large enough for the five of us to sleep in. We carved a few small arched shelves in the sides of the snow cave to hold candles to light up the interior. I reminded the group to never cook with stoves or use a gas lantern inside a snow cave, as the carbon monoxide buildup could be hazardous.

Later, using our shovels, we sculpted a separate kitchen area outside for cooking. The beauty of winter camping in snow country is that a variety of nooks and crannies can be fashioned from the snow. In our circular kitchen area, we carved a shelf at a convenient height for our stove pad and lightweight cookstoves. We created seats at a comfortable height that we laid our seat pads on when cooking and eating our meals. We dug cabinet holes near the cooking platform to store various pots, dishes, and utensils. We went to the nearby lake, dug down to its frozen surface, chopped a hole in the ice, and got water for drinking and cooking. As darkness overtook us, we completed the finishing touches of a functional winter camp.

By the time we retired to the snow cave that first night at Whale Lake, the sky was perfectly clear with the stars shining bright and sharp. And the temperature was plummeting.

Camping and living in such extreme cold took on a different intensity level. It called for more attention and thought to detail. There was no room for error. We learned to do everything while our gloves and mittens were on so as not to expose our hands to cold temperatures and risk frostbite. It meant that we had to keep moving once we exited the relative warmth of the snow cave to generate body heat. We took turns standing in the kitchen area cooking our meals while everyone else walked, skied, or shoveled snow in an attempt to stay warm. It meant keeping our water bottles inside our jackets so the water would not freeze solid. We made a determined effort to drink plenty of liquids each day as dehydration in that kind of cold could quickly lead to frostbite.

Not knowing how long the cold snap would last, Alan and I made the decision that we would stay at this location until either the weather moderated or it was time to ski back to Ninko cabin to re-supply ourselves with more food and fuel before venturing back out. The snow cave offered us respite from the brutal cold. We estimated that there was approximately a sixty-degree difference between the +32 degrees inside the snow cave and −30 degrees outside. Going from the bitter cold outside into our snow cave felt like going into a heated building, the difference was so apparent.

Although the Wilderness Treatment Center policy and the USFS special-use permit allowed campfires in emergencies, we did not build a campfire. I based that decision on former experience and training. No matter how often people were reminded not to get too close to the fire, they inevitably did. They sometimes ruined critical gear by burning and melting boots, socks, and other gear to try to stay warm. Being miles away in the backcountry without functioning gear in the bitter cold would only make an uncomfortable situation into a dangerous, possibly life-threatening situation. We kept the option of a campfire if we felt we truly needed it. At that point, we had plenty of water, food, clothing, shelter, and activity to keep us out of harm's way.

To keep active, we skied around the Whale Lake area that day. At one point, we skied downhill through the widely spaced trees for approximately one mile. It was incredibly fun to ski through powder snow, carving tight turns with our backcountry skis. We enjoyed it so much that we climbed back up the slope and did it again. Later in the day with an hour or two of daylight remaining, we skied back toward camp. The temperature became even colder as the sun angled toward the horizon, blocked by the mountain terrain to the west of our campsite.

The bitterly cold weather continued as one day blended into the next. We jokingly referred to our campsite as the Whale Lake Snow Hilton. Population 5. Cheap winter rates. Free ski passes with no waiting in line. Just pick up the phone and dial 555-Cold or our toll-free number 1-800- Frostbite. Zip Code −43 degrees F. Meals available, ala-gorp, Gatorade slushes, filet of salami, and flatulence stew, garnished with stellar snowflakes.

On one of our day excursions, we skied up a ridge to the site of the Locke Peak fire lookout. Little sign of the old lookout existed, but the views were exceptional. We marveled at the beautifully rugged mountain scenery of the Whitefish Divide, Glacier National Park, and even Canada. As a bonus, we enjoyed excellent powder skiing on our way back to camp.

By the seventh morning, the brutally cold weather was still holding firm and we were nearly out of food and fuel. We decided to ski back to the Ninko cabin where more food and fuel were stored. We repacked our gear into our backpacks while inside the relative warmth of the snow caves.

Jim complained that he could not make his boot liners fit into his boots. He held them up to show me why he was having difficulties. I was horrified to see that not only had the stitching in his liners come completely apart but it also looked like moths had eaten huge holes in the liners. Luckily, I had an extra pair of boot liners. My foot size was much smaller than Jim's, but we remedied the situation by cutting off the toe portion and forming an extension from his wrecked liners. With the improvised boot liners, I felt better about the seven-plus mile ski back to the cabin in the bitterly cold weather.

Skiing at a steady pace toward the cabin, we stopped only twice to drink water, eat a snack, and warm Jeff's feet on my belly as he was having trouble keeping his feet warm enough. Luckily, his feet re-warmed with no sign of frostbite. We made good time and reached the cabin early in the afternoon.

The first thing we did was to start a fire in the wood stove. The warmth radiating from the stove felt amazing after days in the bitter cold. After huddling around the wood stove for several minutes, we busied ourselves with several tasks. We put our damp gear on nails and ropes to dry out. We got water from Ninko Creek, heated it on the propane cook stove, and made a large pot of hot soup.

Jim still wasn't investing any energy into his recovery. His anger spilled over inappropriately when confronted during group meetings. He threatened to take a club and hurt us, and then he threatened to leave. Eventually, through the group process, we were able to help him work through his feelings. Still, we couldn't get him to make a real commitment to his recovery.

Later in the evening, we prepared for the next leg of our journey as we repacked gear, food, and fuel into our backpacks. We planned to spend the night in the cabin and leave early the next morning. Sleep came early and easy in the warmth of the cabin.

It was hard leaving the security and warmth of the cabin the next morning as the frigid weather continued its dominance over the area. We left the cabin and proceeded up the Ninko Creek drainage for a mile or so before angling west into the basin below Mount Thompson Seton.

Heading to the top of Mount Thompson Seton, 1985.

Mount Thompson Seton, at 7820 feet, was named for Ernest Thompson Seton, a famous author, wildlife artist, naturalist, and storyteller from the late 1880s through the 1940s. His stories were so popular that the Flathead National Forest Supervisor, Robert McLaughlin, named this peak after him in 1913 when the US Geological Survey prepared a map of the Kootenai and Flathead National Forests.

Safely locating our campsite away from any potential avalanche activity, we again built a snow cave shelter for protection from the bitter cold. The frigid weather seemed even harsher that evening. With a slight breeze out of the north coupled with the lack of sunshine blocked by the nearby mountains, conditions became even more extreme. We found the colder conditions very challenging, to the point that we retreated to the snow cave early. Lying in our sleeping bags we discussed the peak climb of Mount Thompson Seton that we planned to attempt the next day. Referring to a map, we planned various route options. We discussed the gear, food, and water that would be needed for the day.

The following morning, we skied through the protection of forest cover to the pass just southwest of the peak. At the pass, we left our skis and walked the final distance to the top of the summit. On top, we found remnants of an old fire lookout cabin with a portion of the walls still standing. An old rusty cook stove was located in one corner.

This fire lookout cabin was built by the US Forest Service in 1931 but had been abandoned in the 1950s. Snow rime encrusted the southwest corner of the cabin. The views were sensational in all directions as a sea of mountains encircled us. We saw the jagged spires of Glacier National Park approximately twenty miles to the east, while the snow-covered Canadian mountains stood less than ten miles away to the north. Immediately around us stood the rugged, snowy mountains of the Whitefish Range.

Mount Thompson Seton Lookout, 1985.

We were blessed that day on top of the peak with more than beautiful scenery. Two very noticeable changes were noted on the summit. The wind was not blowing and the temperature was warmer on top of the peak than down below. We had climbed above the cold-weather inversion that blanketed the terrain below us. For the first time since very early on our trip, it felt comfortable being outside. We soaked up the warm sunshine as we lingered on the summit for more than an hour.

Eventually, we began our descent back to camp and proceeded down the route to our skis near the pass. After skiing a short distance from the pass, we felt the bitter cold temperature return as we entered the layer of cold air that was trapped by the inversion. Regardless of the cold, the ski back to camp was very enjoyable in the excellent powder snow conditions. Once at our campsite, we packed up and headed back to the cabin in the waning light of dusk with a bright moon overhead. It was a cold, but beautiful ski back to the cabin.

The following day was a designated workday. We cut and hauled firewood throughout the morning, as well as doing a thorough cleanup of the cabin. Each patient was scheduled to start his solo exercise the following morning. Later in the afternoon, each patient built individual snow caves in an area that we designated for each of them.

Alan and I built a nearby staff snow cave. All shelters were in proximity to the cabin. For three days and two nights, each patient would be by himself and stay within his designated area of approximately 100 yards by 100 yards. The purpose of the exercise was to reflect and complete a written moral inventory assignment as part of their therapy process in dealing with their addiction problems.

Alan and I planned to do a safety check on each of them hourly throughout the day. As an additional safety precaution each night one staff would sleep in a nearby snow cave. We would bring them hot drinks several times a day when we were doing the safety checks. With the frigid weather refusing to relent, we debated and agonized about whether to conduct the solo exercise, but in the end, felt that the patients were capable and ready for the experience. We decided to monitor the weather and the patients closely. If we felt conditions became unacceptable, we would cancel the exercise.

Later in the evening, we had a good group therapy meeting to discuss the solo exercise and assignment. Secretly, I was hoping that the solo experience would be the impetus for Jim to commit to his recovery. Nothing else had seemed to work up to that point.

After a large breakfast of bacon and pancakes the next morning, each patient went out to his solo site to start his therapy assignment. It was a busy day as Alan and I rotated around the area checking on the patients. All of them appeared to be doing very well as they stayed adequately warm within their shelters and worked on their written assignments.

The second morning of the solo assignment was again very cold as the same frigid system held its grip on the area. Alan and I brought hot drinks when we conducted a safety check just after daylight. All patients were doing well, slept warm, and made good progress on their written assignments.

Later in the morning, Jim walked into the cabin complaining about his feet. He thought maybe he had frostbite. We checked his feet and both were fine. He then confessed that he did not like being alone and did not want to complete the solo exercise. It took us quite a while to convince him that it was important to complete the written assignment. The assignment could be very emotional as it dredged up feelings of how through their addiction, they had wronged various individuals in the past. It seemed as though Jim wanted to avoid what he was finding out about himself as he worked through the exercise. Eventually, we persuaded him to go back to his solo area and complete the written assignment.

By late afternoon the stranglehold the bitterly cold weather had on the area dramatically changed. It clouded up and started snowing. It felt so warm that I half expected the snow to change to rain.

On the afternoon of the third day of solo, we brought the patients back to the cabin where we had a hot bowl of stew waiting for them. We sat around the woodstove discussing the solo experience. It was an emotional time for Jeff and Bob as the assignment had brought out a lot of feelings while completing their personal moral inventory. They both felt the experience had helped them on their journey toward recovery. They were overcome with emotions as they kept talking about it.

On the other hand, Jim did not want to talk much and seemed detached, not invested in the assignment or his experience. He seemed to be just going through the motions without any real investment in his recovery process. None of us knew it at the time, and much to Jim's dismay, his lack of commitment to his recovery from his drug and alcohol addiction only resulted in his time at the treatment facility being extended. He had to completely start the sixty-day process over.

After a big supper, we cleaned up the cabin, packed our gear, and made ready for an early departure the next morning. Storytelling and laughter flowed freely on our last night.

We were up before daylight, ate breakfast, cleaned up, and locked the cabin. By daybreak, we were skiing down the trail. The skies were mostly cloudy, with a few snowflakes falling as we progressed along our route. The temperature seemed very warm to us, to the point that we had taken most of our cold-weather clothing off. We skied in our thin synthetic shirts and wool pants.

A few miles along our route we came across a logging operation that had moved into the area since the beginning of our trip. On the side of a trailer was a large round thermometer that read zero degrees as we skied past. We could hardly comprehend that the zero-degree temperature actually felt warm to us. And we wondered how cold the temps truly were during the past two weeks.

John Brekke was waiting at the trailhead as we arrived. He counted heads, "One, two, three, four, five." He looked up and said, "Thank you, Lord, they are all alive." He then asked us if we still had all our fingers and toes. We assured him that we were just fine. Relieved, he told us that the low temps had been 45 degrees below zero for most of the time we were on our trip. He was thankful that everyone was safe and healthy from the rigorous experience.

We realized our experience camping in adverse weather conditions made us more resilient and resourceful. We endured something that few people in this day and age could lay claim to.

Snow ghosts

THE SILVERTIP MOUNTAIN CAVES
1986

♦

In August 1986, I had the good fortune to spend time in the Silvertip Mountain area in the Bob Marshall Wilderness while working as an outdoor instructor with the Wilderness Treatment Center. On a hot summer day with temperatures in the high nineties, I hiked approximately eight miles from the Meadow Creek Gorge trailhead. I met the group of instructors and patients at Kelly's Point, located a mile south of Black Bear Creek on the South Fork of the Flathead River. One of the instructors was ill, and I came in to replace him for the remaining eight days of the 21-day trip. The plan was to hike to the Silvertip Mountain area for the remainder of the trip.

Previously, I'd heard stories that one of the deepest caves in North America was located somewhere in the vicinity of Silvertip Mountain. Details at the time were sketchy, so we planned to explore the area to see what we could find. Earlier in June, I had been in the same area, but deep snow still blanketed the high basins, and I could not find any of the caves. I hoped that this time would be different.

The first evening was spent fly-fishing the deep holes along the stream. The Joe's Hopper fly, with a pattern that mimicked the grasshoppers found in the nearby meadows, seemed to be the trout's choice as the action was brisk and lively.

We were up early at dawn the next morning in an attempt to break camp and hike a few miles on our route before the hot daytime temperatures became a factor. We hiked north for a mile, then turned off on the Black Bear Creek trail. This trail was in good shape for several miles up the path to an old hunting camp near the junction of Rambler Creek.

Waterfall near Silvertip Mountain, 1986.

From there, the trail became very brushy and overgrown. It was obvious that a trail crew had not cleared this section of the trail in quite some time. We fought our way through the next section, finally leaving the main trail where Rambler Creek veers to the east. We followed a faint hunter's trail for a mile or so until it fizzled out. We bushwhacked through the thick vegetation until we located a suitable campsite on a small knoll just west of a waterfall that poured out of a high basin along the southern flank of Silvertip Mountain.

It was a scenic view from our campsite with a full view of the lacey white waterfall spilling over the lip, cascading down the sheer cliff. I was surprised to see so much water flowing during the late summer hot, dry weather. We had a nice view to the south toward Helen Mountain and Pagoda Mountain.

Closer to camp, it seemed as if all of the plants were loaded with ripe berries. Huckleberries, serviceberries, currants, raspberries, Oregon grapes, mountain ash berries, and rosehips were abundant. We saw fresh bear scat here and there during the day's hike, but no bears were sighted. Clouds moved in that evening and it looked like a thunderstorm might materialize but none did.

Early the next morning, we were on our way. We climbed the steep area just north of the waterfall and entered a high basin that turned in a southerly direction. From below, this basin was wholly hidden from view, thus, we dubbed it Hidden Basin. It was a beautiful green, grassy boulder-strewn basin with many wildflowers on full display with the showy whites of Sitka valerian, bright yellows of arrow-leaved groundsel, vivid blues of explorer gentian, and brilliant reds of Indian paintbrush. At the head of the basin were a few scattered patches of snow.

We continued in a southerly direction over a low pass before turning sharply to the east, where we made our next camp in a high alpine meadow full of brilliant red Indian paintbrush flowers. There were so many hummingbirds flitting about in this area that we nicknamed the place Hummingbird Basin. At one point, we counted 25 hummingbirds from where we stood. From this campsite, we had a grand view, especially to the southeast where Lone Butte at 8475 feet stood as a solitary sentinel over that area. A small stream of clear, cold water flowed through the meadow. This little stream, along with several others in the area, was part of the headwaters of the White River.

Lone Butte as seen from Silvertip Mountain, 1986.

There was evidence that others had camped in this area in the past as we found an old rotted wooden box lying on the edge of the meadow. Nearby I found a hand-forged long-handled kitchen fork, the kind used for flipping steaks over a campfire.

It was still early in the day, so we decided to climb the nearby unnamed peak at 8244 feet. It was an easy walk to the top but afforded an excellent panoramic view of the area, including a good look at Silvertip Mountain a mile to the north.

Later in the evening, after supper, I searched around the area, looking for any sign of caves. I found a few cave holes nearby, but none seemed to go anywhere. Later after returning to our camp, I walked downstream and found a small cave hole exhaling cool air out of its tiny entrance. It would have been hard for even a skinny guy like me to get through its entrance, plus it seemed to drop straight down. I didn't have a headlamp or flashlight with me, so I did not attempt to explore it further. I made a mental note that sometime in the future, I would check it out to a greater degree.

The next day, we hiked along the east side of the south flank of Silvertip Mountain. It was rugged terrain of broken, brown, rocky shelves as we traversed and angled up to the pass that separated Silvertip Mountain and the unnamed peak of 8448 feet. At the pass, we dropped our backpacks and climbed the east ridge to the summit of Silvertip Mountain. At 8882 feet, this peak dominates the area. The view was sensational as we gazed at a sea of mountains and rugged landscapes in every direction. Far to the north, we saw the snow-capped peaks of Glacier National Park.

After spending some time on the summit enjoying the view, I led the group southwest a couple of hundred feet below the summit to a rock enclosure that I discovered on my earlier trip in June. This enclosure was human-made, having been excavated out of the scree slope. Scree rock had been stacked flat in a fashion to form the walls of the bathtub-shaped enclosure. It was large enough for two people to squat or sit in with only their heads exposed above the rock walls. It looked as though it had been there for quite some time, as nothing seemed freshly disturbed.

Earlier, I had asked around inquiring about the history of this structure. Nobody I talked to knew about it. I theorized that its origin was one of several possibilities. Mountain goat hunters could have built it for concealment to hide and blend in well with the surrounding area. Another option might have been that it was made by an early-day Forest Service fire lookout who had climbed up here to scan the area for forest fires. Perhaps the lookout might have built the enclosure to get out of the wind that is often blowing on these high-exposed areas. Another possible use was as a Native American vision quest site as the area certainly had qualities of spiritual power.

Afterward, we hiked back down to the pass, shouldered our backpacks, and continued down into the vast basin north and northeast of Silvertip Mountain. Along the way, we found several cave holes scattered about the landscape.

After quickly making camp, we took off exploring the basin. Unlike in June, when the area was completely covered in snow, it was mostly snow-free. Besides the remnant glacier clinging to the steep north slope of Silvertip Mountain, only scattered patches of snow dotted the area. I found the huge basin an amazing place, as it was literally pockmarked with sinkholes and cave openings. Some of the cave holes were still plugged with snow, but many were snow-free. We found several gaping cave holes that seemed to go straight down, accessible only by rappelling down with ropes. Many of these caves were breathing as I felt the air flowing out of them. The northeast portion of the basin seemed to have the majority of the cave openings.

The limestone rock that made up this basin seemed much different than any other rock that I was familiar with in this region. It looked and felt like hardened concrete that was rough, dimpled, and sharp. I quickly noted that rappelling with ropes would be dangerous if the ropes were not padded when in contact with the sharp edges and lips of the cave holes.

We found several caves that we could explore on a limited basis. We were not adequately equipped for a serious caving undertaking, having only rock-climbing helmets and a few headlamps and flashlights. One cave had a room approximately 30 feet by 50 feet. The formations in the caves that we explored were made of ice instead of rock. We saw stalactites, stalagmites, columns, and flowstone, all formed out of ice. We went several hundred feet in one of the larger caves that we found. We wondered if this was the cave that was supposed to be one of the deepest caves in North America.

We spent the next two days exploring the basin. Even in that amount of time, we did not come close to thoroughly inspecting the whole place. We ended up calling the area Swiss Cheese Basin because of the astounding number of sinkholes and cave openings we found. In some places, we walked only a few yards before encountering yet another hole in the ground.

I wished that we had planned more time to explore the area, but on the sixth day, we packed up and hiked almost ten miles to the Spotted Bear River, where we made camp. It had been a hot day with the temperatures in the high nineties as we first bushwhacked down the Silvertip Creek drainage before finding the old packer trail that eventually led us to the river. It felt good to jump in the water, swim around, and cool off.

We spent the next day swimming and fly-fishing before hiking out the following day.

Silvertip Mountain and the surrounding landscape was a fascinating place to explore. It was one of the more exciting places that I have had the good fortune to visit. It remains a place rich in possibilities for further challenge, adventure, and exploration.

Swiss Cheese Basin near Silvertip Mountain, 1986.

BELLY RIVER OBSERVATIONS
1988

◆

A recipe for nature's best work, the Belly River country is beyond words. The flowing river, scattered grassy meadows, dense willow bogs, and park-like forests are the basic ingredients. Add all kinds of wildlife, sharply carved mountains, dramatic weather moods, and touch off the whole works with plenty of sunshine. This blended mixture of ingredients produced an area of incredible beauty and fascinating interest.

Located in the northeast corner of Glacier National Park, Belly River flows north out of the park into Canada. I've heard a couple of versions of how Belly River got its name. One version comes from the Blackfeet Indian tribe's custom of naming features of the landscape after the anatomy of Napi. They believed that Napi, the Old Man, created the world and the Indian people. To the north, the Bow River at Calgary was Napi's elbow. To the south, the Teton Buttes were his knees. His stomach lay in the middle, thus the Belly River.

In another version, the Belly River was named after the Gros Ventres Indian tribe because they *eat much and have big paunches*. The Gros Ventre's alternate name was the Atsina, which translates to Gut People.

After the survey crews of the United States Northern Boundary Commission of 1872-76 assigned the name Belly River on their maps, the name was officially adopted by the United States and Canada.

The Belly River.

WTC Clients in the Belly River area.

During a series of trips in the mid-1980s, I explored the Belly River country of Glacier National Park when I worked as a wilderness instructor for the Wilderness Treatment Center (WTC). The majority of these trips were in the winter and early spring. Except for WTC clients and staff, we rarely saw another human being.

Getting to the Belly River area in the winter involved a bit of effort because the road to Chief Mountain Customs at the border of the United States and Canada was usually snowed in. We often skied the fourteen miles of snow-covered road from Highway 89 to the trailhead located just short of the border on the United States side. Several miles of the route were open, rolling prairie grasslands exposed to the brutal, strong winds that often characterize that region. It was always a relief to reach the protective shelter that the forest provided.

Despite the biting cold wind, the beauty of the rolling prairie and forested foothills that stacked up against the abrupt jagged mountain terrain of Glacier National Park was incredible. Of particular beauty, seemingly separated from the rest of the range, was the sentinel, Chief Mountain. At 9080 feet, it stood tall and alone on the foothills of the prairie. This prominent peak is of important significance to the various native tribes. One legend told of an Indian brave who spent several days on its summit seeking his medicine vision. It is said that he used a bison skull for a pillow.

In 1892, Henry Stimson and his climbing companions found an ancient, practically decomposed bison skull on the summit of Chief Mountain giving credence to this legend. Chief Mountain takes its name from the Blackfeet Indian name for Old Chief or Mountain-of-the-Chief.

When our WTC group reached the trailhead, we skied a couple of miles down the trail to the flats along the Belly River. As we skied the downhill portion of this trail, I witnessed an amusing and insightful incident involving a young man in the treatment program. The snow was loose and deep making trail breaking slow and tiring. Each member of our group of five took turns breaking trail through the four feet of snow as we slowly worked our way down the trail.

Among our group was an impatient, hotheaded individual who did not take readily to instruction and advice. His boot kept popping out of his ski binding. Earlier, I demonstrated to the group how to adjust their bindings to prevent exactly what he was experiencing. Several times during the day I suggested that he take a minute to adjust his bindings, but he only glared at me and refused to heed my advice.

While we were standing on a steep sidehill portion of the trail, his boot popped out of his binding for what seemed like the hundredth time that day. In his fury, he said a few choice swear words, picked up his ski, and threw it as far downhill as he could. The ski sailed several hundred feet down the hill where it wedged against a couple of lodgepole pine trees. With a beet-red face, the young man swore again and shook his fist, glaring down the hill at the ski.

I patiently waited for him to calm down. Slowly his rage subsided. He stood there staring silently at his ski. After a minute, he turned to me and said, "That was a damned dumb thing to do, huh?"

I replied, "Yes it was. Now you need to go down there and get your ski." If he thought skiing in the deep snow was tough, he found out how much tougher it was without skis. He wallowed down through the deep snow that was chest-deep. He was exhausted by the time he retrieved his ski and got back up to the trail. Only then did he adjust his ski binding so his boot wouldn't pop out. What a learning experience it was for him! This experience drove home how destructive and senseless his anger and impatience were to his well-being.

One day, in an open meadow along the west side of the Belly River, I watched two seven-point bull elk spar with each other. Their massive antlers clanked together as the two majestic animals pushed and shoved each other around. The sparring match didn't have a lot of zest and energy to it as the two behemoths went at it half-heartedly before both would lie down near each other and survey their domain. Later, they rose to their feet and repeated the performance. I had rarely seen a seven-point elk, much less two of them sparring together.

On the last day of February 1984, I was skiing south along the trail toward the Belly River Ranger Station with WTC director, John Brekke. "Do you think we will see any bear sign on this trip," I asked.

He stopped, gave me a withering look, and said, "Come on, it's the last day of February for Pete's sake! You can hardly find a bear in May much less than in February!"

I mumbled, "Yeah, you're probably right." As we proceeded along the trail, we skied no more than a hundred feet when we crossed fresh grizzly bear tracks in the

Lake Elizabeth

snow. As we stared in amazement at the fresh tracks, John sheepishly commented, "Well I'll be damned!"

By glassing the tracks in the snow, We later discovered that the bear came out of its den high above Lake Elizabeth and proceeded to zigzag its way down the Belly River drainage as it gridded the valley for food on its way north into Canada.

During many of the WTC trips, the wind in the Belly River country was astounding in its ferocity. Sounding like a jet airplane coming out of the north, savage gusts roared through the area with an intensity that strained the very fabric of our tents. After a minute or two of sustained blasts, our tents would bend at odd angles, shake, rattle, and make loud flapping noises. Often the wind would die down for a short time before regaining strength and roar down on us again. It was hard to sleep at night as the wind assaulted our tents repeatedly. We pitched our tents in protected areas, but it seldom helped, as the wind seemed to barge its way through the protective forest cover. The fierce winds sometimes lasted for days.

During the early days of March 1985, we experienced extreme winds when we climbed to Bear Mountain Point at approximately 6200 feet. It was so windy that we literally could not stand up straight for fear the wind would pick us up and blow us off the peak. We crab-walked the last hundred yards to the summit and laid on our stomachs while peering over the abyss that dropped abruptly off to the northeast. In over thirty years of mountaineering, I had never experienced roaring winds so strong.

Climbing Bear Mountain Point

One April morning as I sat near the Belly River, the sunshine warmed the face of Bear Mountain. It did not take long until the fireworks began. The direct warmth of the sunshine loosened the grip the snow had on the rugged terrain. With sounds that resonated like gunshots, small avalanches repeatedly released and slid down the mountain. At times, I saw the snow shoot over a cliff area and free-fall some distance before crashing below. At other times, I just heard a loud noise, but could not see the location of the avalanche. I knew that I did not want to be in questionable terrain on that warm, sunny day. The mountains were talking and I was listening.

While camping in the deep snow, our group often dug down and sculpted a kitchen area for cooking and eating. With the fierce winds, we often added a snow berm to block the winds. One cold March morning while we were cooking breakfast, someone exclaimed, "Look, a bear!"

We stood up and looked over the snow berm to see not a bear, but a wolverine. It was about 200 feet away, staring at us and sniffing at the smells. It stayed the same distance as it circled us repeatedly. It definitely liked the smell of our cooking food.

None of us had ever seen a wolverine and were unsure what to expect. Because we planned to climb a peak that day, we were concerned about leaving our food cache with the wolverine around. We approached it, shouting and waving our

Wolverine near Belly River

arms trying to scare it off. It merely retreated to the 200 feet distance between us, but would not leave. We went back to our cooking area to eat our breakfast as the wolverine continued to circle us. We again tried to chase it away. To our dismay, it stayed 200 feet away but did not leave.

We decided that we would stay in the camp that day rather than risk the wolverine raiding our remaining seven days' worth of food. Eventually, the wolverine left. I later tracked it in the snow several miles to see if it was hanging in the area or was moving on. It left the area, heading north toward Canada.

One day as I was exploring along the west side of the Belly River, I discovered a side creek that had a beaver dam built on it. It appeared very old as the wood and sticks that the beaver used were bleached gray with live willow shoots growing up through the dam. I noticed that there was another dam above the first one and then another above that one. I took a detour and walked up the steep side drainage inspecting one beaver dam after another that had been built in successive stages as the water backed up in each to its maximum area where the beaver then built a new dam to flood the area above that one. I did not count how many dams were built, but it must have been dozens.

I was amazed at how much elevation I gained as I worked my way up the steep sidehill. The upper-most beaver dam was freshly built from nearby gathered materials. I contemplated how many generations of beaver had lived and worked this side drainage through the years. From above, looking down on this remarkable scene, it reminded me of a long series of rice paddies or terraced steps advancing up the side drainage of the mountain. It was the first time I had seen anything on that scale and number. I thought that similar extensive beaver dams were probably a common sight here in the West when the fur trappers of the 1800s first came into the region. I knew that I was observing something unique and seldom seen.

On a cold sunny day in March, our group skied to Lake Elizabeth from our campsite near the Belly River Ranger Station. A couple of miles up the trail was the beautiful Dawn Mist Falls. This waterfall, over 60 feet tall, was clad with ice sculptures of all descriptions as the water froze as it poured over the lip of rock at the top. Even in the winter, there was still a fine mist near the bottom of the falls, much of which froze to the surrounding rocks, trees, and shrubs making it a beautiful, but treacherous area. Once called Morning Dew Falls, it was renamed Dawn Mist Falls for the Indian maiden who loved White Quiver, the hero in the novel by H.F. Sanders.

After enjoying the beauty of the Dawn Mist Falls, we continued skiing toward Lake Elizabeth. As always, the view from the outlet of Lake Elizabeth was spectacular. We spotted the location of the 183-foot Ptarmigan Tunnel that exited high up on the northwest side of the precipitous Ptarmigan Wall. This tunnel had been built in 1931.

WTC Director, John Brekke at Dawn Mist Falls

Later, we headed back to our campsite. We had not gone very far when we saw fresh wolf tracks in the snow. The wolf had stepped in our ski tracks as the animal crossed at a right angle from east to west. Wolves were rare in this country at that time. We were amazed at the huge size of the tracks, roughly five inches long and four inches wide. The stride of the wolf was very long, over 50 inches. It was the first time I had seen wolf tracks and it very much heightened my experience and enjoyment of the backcountry of the Belly River.

Steve Lamar in the Belly River Area

SHARING SEPTEMBER SNOW
1989

◆

In September 1989, I decided to climb Holland Peak in the Swan Range. At 9356 feet, Holland Peak is the tallest mountain in the Swan Range. It was named after Benjamin B. Holland, the first settler to homestead in Swan Valley.

Although I had yet to set foot on the summit of Holland Peak, I had been in the vicinity several times camping and fishing at both Lower and Upper Rumble Lakes, as well as exploring and hunting nearby basins and ridgelines.

I knew that it would be a strenuous undertaking. The elevation gain from the Cooney Trailhead to the top of Holland Peak was over 4800 feet. That estimation was based on a straight line of nearly three miles from bottom to top. Like so many routes in the rugged mountains, this climb would be anything but a straight line. It would be a variation of the old mountain saying, *Sometimes you have to go north to get south*. The actual route that I would take was a bit over five miles one-way.

I was planning to attempt the climb in one day so I packed light with adequate clothing, food, water, emergency supplies, an ice axe, and a fishing pole. I decided early in the planning that I would see how I felt when I got to Lower Rumble Lake. If I felt strong and energetic I would keep pushing upward to Upper Rumble Lake. If not, I would fly-fish the lower lake and save Holland Peak for another day. I would repeat my evaluation at Upper Rumble Lake and if I still felt good, I would continue up toward the peak. No matter how the day turned out, it would be a great day in the backcountry.

I woke before dawn on the day of the climb to check the weather. It rained during the night, but the clouds moved out and bright stars were shining in the predawn sky. After a quick breakfast, I was on my way to the Cooney Trailhead at the end of Rumble Creek Road.

In the half-light of dawn, I started up the trail. In less than half a mile the trail merged with the old lower foothills trail running in a north-south direction along the base of the Swan Range. The old trail was built by the US Forest Service in the late 1920s and early 1930s. At one time, the trail went along the foot of the Swan Range from Lion Creek south to the Holland Lake area. The only section of this trail that is still maintained is the stretch from Cooney Lookout to approximately six miles south to the East Holland Connector Trail above the northeast corner of Holland Lake.

According to John Stark, an early-day Swan Valley resident, Rumble Creek was named for an early trapper by the name of Rumble who had a cabin near the creek. The cabin site was included on the 1903 survey map.

The air was crisp and cool as I climbed the steep path to Lower Rumble Lake. The vegetation was wet from the previous night's rain. Making good time and still feeling good, I paused only briefly at Lower Rumble Lake before resuming my climb upward. A few fish were rising on the placid, emerald-colored water as I skirted the southwest corner of the lower lake. I hiked through the scree rock, my route angling upward to the south of the waterfall that poured over the rocky cliff band that held Upper Rumble Lake in its high alpine basin. The waterfall, spectacularly beautiful earlier in the season when the melting snow waters gushed out of the high country, was reduced now late in the season to a trickle of water flowing down the face of the rocky cliff.

Upon hoisting myself over the lip of the rock cliff, I startled a mountain goat that was feeding nearby. It quickly climbed up the sharply angled shoulder of rock to the south and disappeared.

Upper Rumble Lake is a beautiful high alpine lake situated at 7890 feet. Most of the area is rocky with scattered patches of heath meadows. What few trees grow in this area are short and stunted. In the whole basin, there is only one tree tall enough to hang food bags suspended from ropes. A steep snowfield tucked in the cirque headwall at the south end of the lake persists throughout the year.

It was still early in the day, so I continued upward toward Holland Peak. I proceeded up the steep shoulder of rock that the mountain goat had scampered up earlier. Upon reaching the top of the shoulder I hooked around onto the ridge that separated Rumble Lakes from Buck Basin.

Buck Basin is a remote beautiful basin that is not easily accessed. Thinking that I might find some wildlife wandering about the area, I glassed the basin with my binoculars. In the distance, I spotted a black bear feeding in an open meadow. I watched the bear for several minutes before heading up the ridgeline toward what I called Marmot Peak, a bump of a mountain along the Swan Divide at 8852 feet that always seemed to have a hoary marmot on or near its summit.

From the summit of Marmot Peak, I looked north at Holland Peak. The upper elevation of the lofty mountain was covered with snow from the previous night. From where I stood, I could see that a layer of thin ice coated the scree rock. Previously, I planned to climb the exposed and slightly tilted slab rock along the ridge separating the two peaks. With the layer of ice coating my intended route, I changed my plans. Instead of attempting that dicey route, I dropped down east of Marmot Peak into the Bob Marshall Wilderness. I then traversed toward the east ridge of Holland Peak. From the safer and gentler east ridge, I angled up toward the summit.

When I reached the snowline, I found to my surprise that I was not alone that morning on my way to the top of the mountain. In the heavy powder snow that had fallen the previous night were fresh mountain lion tracks. Already excited

Mountain Lion Tracks.
—Luke Lamar photo

about reaching the summit, my adrenaline spiked another notch. I stopped and scanned the slope above me, but saw nothing but white snow and blue sky.

I continued up the route wondering what a mountain lion would be doing up here on the tallest peak in the Swan Range. I followed the mountain lion tracks to the summit. In the snow, I read the lion's story. The mountain lion reached the top, walked about the summit, and then headed down the steep north ridge. With my binoculars, I glassed the route that the lion had taken but saw nothing of the animal. I figured that he was probably hunting the area for mountain goats, but did not rule out that like myself, the lion also enjoyed a good view.

The view was sensational as I turned in a circle to take in the panorama. Almost 1500 feet straight down the headwall of the west face of Holland Peak and directly below me was Upper Rumble Lake. Looking westward beyond the country that I had climbed earlier lay the broad expanse of the Swan Valley and the bordering Mission Mountains. To the north and south stood the rugged chain of mountains that make up the Swan Range. To the east was the vast Bob Marshall Wilderness with its sea of mountains and rugged terrain.

A few feet to the west of the summit, tucked under a rock shelf was a memorial plaque dedicated to a mountain climber who died elsewhere and his ashes were spread on Holland Peak. The plaque indicated that he met an untimely end and simply stated, *Death by Misadventure.*

After spending time on the summit, I retreated down my earlier route. I dropped in elevation to below the snowline where I found a nice ledge to sit, eat lunch, and enjoy the view looking east into the Bob Marshall Wilderness. It was a great feeling sitting in the sunshine and gazing at the wild country as far as the eye could see. Adventures like this reinforced why I loved living in the beautiful Swan Valley with so much wild country nearby to explore and experience. Sharing the September snow on Holland Peak was an experience that I would never forget.

CAT FIGHT
1991

In December 1991, I decided to go skiing up the trail from the Owl Creek Packer Camp near Holland Lake. With the snow firm and granular, my wax-less skis were making an irritating, noisy sound as I skied up the trail. I had gone less than a mile when I thought I heard something. I stopped and listened. I heard nothing for several seconds, then a loud yowl came from below the trail. It was a mountain lion screaming!

At first, I thought that it was yowling loudly at me. I took one step forward to get a better view when I heard another loud yowl. Looking through the yew brush I could see two mountain lions facing each other. One snarled and yowled, and then the other returned the snarl and yowl.

Relieved that none of the commotion was directed toward me, I watched for several minutes as the two mountain lions repeated their performance several times. My vision through the brush was limited, but I assumed that they were fighting over a freshly killed deer as neither was willing to give ground. The face-off continued.

Looking around, I saw that just up ahead the trail turned sharply to the north and if I continued along the trail, I would come very close to the animals. Not knowing if the mountain lions would be aggressive toward me, I decided to play it safe and not disturb them. I slowly and quietly turned around and retreated from the area as quietly as I could. I decided it best for all of us to ski somewhere else that day.

ASBESTOS FOREST
1993

◆

Before years of drought and the subsequent forest fires that became the norm in western Montana, the Flathead National Forest was nicknamed the Asbestos Forest. The ample rain throughout the spring and summer months usually kept the number of forest fires to a minimum, however, the spring of 1993 started hot and dry.

The Flathead National Forest seasonal employees were hired early in the season and sent to forest fire training. Everyone was predicting a forest fire season from hell, as one dry day led to another. I attended the fire training course at the Talley Lake Ranger Station in Whitefish. The day started with clear blue skies, but at noon clouds converged and it started raining, and it didn't seem to stop until October.

Needless to say, I didn't need my firefighting skills that summer, but it was an unforgettable season nonetheless. As a backcountry ranger that season, the daily scenario went something like this: get up, put on my damp gear and clothing, and slog up the trail in the pouring rain. If I got high enough in the mountains, the rain turned to snow. In my journal, I recorded precipitation on 72 out of 77 days. I quit counting after that.

I cleared trees that had fallen over the trails. I picked up a bit of garbage, mostly from the preceding year because no one else ventured out on the muddy trails. And why would they? It was wet, cold, and mucky. I cleared water bars and drainage dips attempting to divert water off the trails. Many trails flowed like small streams. The water bars and drainage dips were overflowing with the amount of water in the trails. The trails were a muddy, wet mess. I recall the Bond Creek Trail flowing with so much water that it would have been over the tops of my hiking boots if it were not for the knee-high gaiters I wore over my boots.

Ironically, people envied my job. When my friend found out that I was working as a backcountry ranger, he commented, "It must be nice, getting paid to hike in the wilderness." He must have thought I only worked on sunny and pleasant days. During the few moments when the rain briefly let up, the mosquitoes came out in force, determined to drain my blood. Very few people would have enjoyed being a backcountry ranger in 1993.

One evening near dusk I hiked my way past Trinkus Lake down to the nearby patrol cabin. Built in 1946, the cabin was formerly used as a shelter for the people who conducted snow surveys at the nearby snow course. It had not been used in years and was in rough shape. I had planned on sleeping in my tent nearby but there was standing water in all the level spots.

Trinkus Cabin, 2009.

With dark approaching and the rain pouring down, I walked into the cabin and looked around. Except for trash and debris scattered about the floor, all that was in the cabin was a rusty metal bed and a rickety table. But everything was dry and that was not something I was used to experiencing that season. I decided to spend the night.

After a quick supper cooked on my backpack stove, I rolled out my sleeping pad on top of the rusty metal springs that would become my mattress for the night. On top of it went my damp sleeping bag. For light, I had a stub of a candle and my headlamp. As I snuggled into my sleeping bag, I listened to the sound of pouring rain as it hammered on the roof. I blew the candle out and started to drift off to sleep.

Suddenly, the whole world inside the cabin came to life. Mice were everywhere, scurrying about. One ran across my chest. I jumped up and turned on my headlamp and quickly lit the candle. Complete silence followed with not a peep. I turned off the headlamp and blew out the candle. Within seconds total bedlam ensued as the mouse reunion was back in full force.

Again, I jumped up, threw a boot, turned on my headlamp, and lit the candle. I was about ready to vacate the Hantavirus Hilton for my rain-soaked tent but decided to see if there were any mouse traps in the cabin. Surely, there was one somewhere. I looked through the cabin and didn't find one. I went outside and looked around and finally found an old weather-worn trap under the cabin. I didn't have any peanut butter for bait but I had some peanuts. I crushed a few, made a thick paste, and baited the trap. I set it in the cabin and blew out the candle.

Within seconds, *snap* went the trap. I turned on my light, tossed the dead mouse out the door opening, and put bait on the trap again. I repeated that scenario twelve times. Finally, when I had just about given up hope, silence reigned inside the cabin while Mother Nature provided thrumming rain that eventually lulled me to sleep.

Day after day, the rain and snow continued. It got to the point that I joked that I had webbed toes and mold growing on my skin.

In early September, the weather cleared up for four days straight. Hoards of hikers, backpackers, and horseback riders invaded the mountains to camp and get outdoors. It was great to feel the warmth of the sun again and to wear dry clothing and gear.

The reprieve from the rain was fleeting, and the wet weather soon returned. Usually, I dreaded getting laid off at the end of the field season but that year it came as a welcome relief.

L to R: Al Koss, Steve Penner, and Steve Lamar clearing trail at Smoky Creek, 1993. —Russ Owen photo

A SKI THROUGH THE HEART OF THE BOB MARSHALL WILDERNESS
1993

◆

Inhaling the delicious cold crisp air, I stood motionless, surrounded by the silent winter scene before me. Except for my breathing, not a sound could be heard, nothing at all. Along with the layers of snow, winter's hush blanketed the landscape. What a rarity in today's world. I smiled as I thanked my lucky stars, soaking up this moment deep in the serenity of the wilderness.

Several months earlier, my friend Rusty Wells asked if I was interested in skiing through the heart of the Bob Marshall Wilderness. I jumped at the chance to join the venture. He knew three others who wanted to join us. We agreed to meet as a group several times to plan and work on the many details of the trip from the route we would travel to the gear each of us would carry. It was at these pre-trip meetings that I first met the other members: Barb Bennetts, Dale Sweetser, and Greg Ontiveros. All of our crew had outdoor experience and were eager to participate in this adventure.

For twelve days in the winter of 1993, we skied through the heart of the Bob Marshall Wilderness Complex, one of the finest wild areas left in this country. Our route took us from the Meadow Creek Gorge trailhead near the northwest corner of the Bob Marshall Wilderness to the vicinity of the Whitetail Ranch near Ovando, 82 miles to the south.

Rich in cultural and natural history, the Bob Marshall Wilderness Complex is immense, comprising over 1.5 million acres of wilderness that includes the contiguous Bob Marshall, Scapegoat, and Great Bear Wilderness Areas. The area got its name from Bob Marshall, an explorer and forester, who was a leader in the conservation movement in the 1920s and 1930s. He championed the preservation of the last remaining wild areas in the United States.

The sixty-five-mile-long road from the Hungry Horse Dam to the Meadow Creek Gorge trailhead is usually snowed in during the winter months. Due to time constraints, we decided to ride snowmobiles to the starting point of our ski trip. The US Forest Service provided the snowmobile shuttle in exchange for our volunteer services in conducting a snow survey deep in the wilderness.

The trailhead is several miles south of the Spotted Bear Ranger Station, a rustic facility with a long history that began in 1906. Along with the nearby Spotted Bear River, it derived its name from an incident in 1861 when Baptiste Zeroyal guided two miners through the area and they observed a black bear with unusual markings of white on its chest and undersides, hence, the name Spotted Bear.

Because of mechanical problems with the snowmobiles, we got a late start on the first day of the trip. Eventually, after a bone-jarring ride over the sixty-five miles of uneven road, we arrived at the trailhead late in the afternoon. We decided to ski a couple of miles while there were still a few hours of daylight left. We enjoyed the open view as we skied across the spectacular Meadow Creek Gorge via a footbridge. The view of the multi-hued canyon of winter ice was impressive.

Skiing in the Bob Marshall Wilderness

After crossing the gorge, we entered the snow-clad forest. With six inches of fresh powder on top of a three-foot base of snow, the skiing conditions were excellent. As the sun broke through the clouds for the first time that day, we continued on our route in silence, each of us lost in our own thoughts. We soaked up our surroundings. After all of the dreaming, anticipating, and planning, we were actually on our way.

We made camp near Mid Creek with only an hour or so of daylight left. By this time the weather had changed and it began to snow. We hustled to get our camp chores completed in the waning daylight. Our camp consisted of three lightweight tents scattered about the area with a nearby cooking area sculpted from the snow with our small, lightweight shovels. We obtained our drinking and cooking water from the nearby South Fork of the Flathead River. Dinner and breakfast fare consisted of basic one-pot meals cooked on camp stoves.

It continued to snow the next morning as we broke camp and skied down the trail. The falling snow, as well as the dense forest, blocked our view of any distant scenery. Unseen to the east of us was Silvertip Mountain, which at the time contained what was thought to be the fourth deepest cave in the United States. This cave had been mapped at a depth of 1,052 feet and was considered the fourteenth deepest in the U.S.

According to our itinerary, we were to ski to the Black Bear cabin area, one of several historic administration cabins that are scattered about the Bob Marshall Wilderness Complex. These cabins were built to house employees while conducting work within the backcountry. In 1925, Forest Service employee Everett Hart built the Black Bear cabin. Using the intricate compound dovetail notch in the corners, the well-constructed log building was still in good shape.

Later that afternoon, Rusty commented, "The side hills from hell are coming up." The terrain between the Mid Creek area and the Black Bear cabin area was rugged with the trail located along steep sidehills. A warm, wet weather system moved through western Montana the week before our trip and crusted over the snow on these sheltered, steep sidehills. Some of the areas avalanched, leaving the trail covered with rock-hard avalanche debris.

In our pre-trip planning, we decided to pull mountaineering sleds loaded with gear to reduce the weight in our backpacks. We were experiencing tough going as the sleds kept sliding off the trail and swinging downhill throwing us off balance. It was frustrating wrestling with the cumbersome sleds through these areas. Because our progress was very slow, we did not reach our intended destination. Instead, in the snowy twilight, we camped in the Hodag Creek area. We set up our tents, gathered water from the nearby stream, and cooked our evening meal.

Waking before daylight, we ate breakfast and broke camp in the predawn darkness. We started down the trail when we could see well enough to make out our intended route. The snow was still coming down, making trail-breaking a bit more difficult each day. We were beginning to wonder if we would be able to complete our trip in 12 days. We were well aware that our options were limited. We estimated that we would be able to make up for our slow progress by traveling on our scheduled layover day.

Later in the day, I saw a large tree that had been notched in such a manner to form a flat alcove into the tree trunk. It was the work of someone who had used the area for trapping purposes, in this case, pine marten. The tree notch looked old but no trap was present. One of the first recorded accounts of fur trapping in the area took place in the winter of 1896-97 when six French Canadians trapped the South Fork of the Flathead River and brought out 2,700 pine marten pelts. The trappers built log rafts and floated out during spring runoff. Tragically, one man drowned when a raft overturned.

The snow was still falling as we set up camp at the Independence Park area on the third night. Setting up camp was becoming routine as two members sculpted a kitchen area out of the snow to place the stoves for cooking the meal, while the other three people set up the tents, got water from the stream, and did any repairs or other chores. We were becoming more of a team with each passing day.

The challenging journey continued on the fourth day as we skied toward the Salmon Forks area. The fresh snow was heavy, sand-like, and fifteen inches deep. Our group had to negotiate plenty of steep side hills with our mountaineering sleds. We encountered many fallen trees that slowed us down as we maneuvered around the obstacles. It was a tough, energy-draining day.

As we neared the Salmon Forks area, the terrain flattened out in places making the traveling trouble-free as our sleds glided across these gentler areas with ease. We began to see a few elk in this area.

In 1872, approximately a mile northeast of this area, near Mud Lake the U.S. Army conducted an exploratory trip seeking a possible route for a railroad site. Luckily, no development ever came from that exploratory foray.

Our campsite was near the Salmon Forks cabin. Newer than most of the other USFS administrative cabins found scattered throughout the wilderness, it was built just before the 1964 Wilderness Act was enacted.

The fifth morning dawned cold with clear skies. We estimated the temperature at 20 degrees below zero. Although the weather was cold, the scenery was incredibly beautiful with the snow-draped terrain backed by a sharp, brilliant blue sky. The sunshine and scenery lifted our spirits. We traveled at a much faster pace. Although the country was thickly forested in places, the area was scattered with open meadows, allowing us to see the distant mountains.

After several miles, we entered the area known as Murphy Flats. This area was named after Joe Murphy, an outfitter and rancher from Ovando who used this area beginning in 1919. At one time Murphy had several cabins and a lodge in this area, but after his special permit expired in 1937, the buildings were removed. This area is park-like with grassy meadows and scattered with large, old ponderosa pine trees. Several of these culturally modified trees had evidence of former Native American use. The oblong scars resulted when Indians peeled off the strips of bark to get to the sweet, inner cambium layer. This layer was used as a food source during times of scarcity, as well as a sweetener that was dried, broken up, and added to meals.

Later in the day, we arrived at the Holbrook patrol cabin. This cabin and nearby creek were named after Fred Holbrook, an early-day ranger at the Big Prairie Ranger District in 1913 and 1914. Holbrook was a Mormon, raised by one of Brigham Young's wives, Amelia. This cabin later burned down during the forest fires of 2003.

We were allowed to use the cabin in exchange for volunteering to do the annual snow survey for the U.S. Forest Service. Inside the cabin, we found the needed snow survey equipment. Three of us proceeded to the snow course just to the north of the cabin while the other two members put things in order in the cabin.

Steve Lamar at Holbrook Cabin in the Bob Marshall Wilderness.

This snow course, one of thirty scattered in and near the wilderness, was at 4,530 feet. Since 1951, snow surveys have been taken annually at this site. The data from all the scattered snow survey sites were used to forecast spring and summer runoff of the various watercourses that exit the wilderness.

From the snow survey kit, we screwed a couple of lengths of two-inch diameter hollow aluminum tubes together. At the first of ten stations along the course, we pushed the tube vertically down into the snow until it struck the bare ground. Then we recorded the depth of the snow. The tube with its core of snow was carefully lifted out and weighed. The difference between the weight of the empty tube from the total weight gave us the water content in inches. A chart of snow depth and water content showed the percent of water or density in the snow sample.

After completing the ten stations we did the math to average the findings. The average snow depth was approximately 30 inches with water content only 75% of normal. Usually, at this time of the year, this site averages around 35 inches of snow with a water content of approximately 11 inches. The maximum snow depth ever recorded at this site was 58 inches in 1978. Snow depths can vary widely from year to year and from place to place. There is also a snow survey site near Upper Holland Lake in the Swan Range that is 6200 feet in elevation. The maximum snow depth ever recorded at that location was 135 inches in 1971.

Located along the edge of a huge, beautiful open meadow, the Holbrook cabin offered fantastic views of the mountains. Because there was not much firewood at the cabin, we took a crosscut saw and replenished the firewood supply. For several members of our group, this was the first time they had ever used a crosscut saw. Nicknamed by old-time lumberjacks as the *Misery Whip*, the crosscut saw offered a good vigorous workout.

Each of us, in turn, pulled on the wooden handle attached to the end of the sharp-toothed metal saw blade. Our two-person team worked together in a synchronized rhythm sawing through the wood. We took short breaks from time to time to rest or trade off to let someone else try their hand at sawing with the crosscut saw. After cutting enough firewood, we hauled the firewood rounds back to the cabin in our sleds. We took an ax to split some of the rounds into smaller sizes and stacked them in the cabin.

Knowing that we would be cooking on an old wood stove, I brought out two packages of elk steaks that I had packed just for this occasion. Spirits ran high as we soaked up the wood heat, ate a hearty meal, dried out damp gear, and figured out how to fit five people into such a small cabin.

Later that night I stepped outside to look at the multitude of stars glistening above the cold, beautiful panorama that lay before me. Except for the distant howling of a coyote, the only sounds to be heard were the popping of trees from the intense cold. It was an incredibly rich moment for me. Deep in the wilderness, it was like experiencing a scene straight out of a Jack London story.

Except for our small group, the closest humans were twenty miles away to the west up and over the mountains of the Swan Range. The distance was even farther in any other direction. I was standing in the middle of a huge wilderness area in the wintertime, soaking up the serenity and the beauty, and loving every bit of it.

The morning dawned clear and cold with frigid temperatures in the range of 25 to 30 degrees below zero. The gear we left outside the cabin was covered with a thick layer of frost crystals. It was tough to leave the warmth of the cabin, but at daybreak, we were on our way down the trail. The cold was numbing even though we were exerting a great deal of energy as we skied along pulling our sleds behind us.

My right foot was so cold that I had no feeling it. I voiced my concern that I might develop frostbite. At that point, Rusty suggested a quick surefire remedy for warming cold feet. I stopped, took off my boot, and warmed my foot on Rusty's belly. That helped bring back the sensation to my toes. Afterward, my foot stayed warm as long as we kept moving. The temperatures had continued to drop for the past three days. We hoped that the cold would not continue to deepen. We knew that this area experienced record cold in the 1930s when the Spotted Bear Ranger Station recorded a frigid 57 degrees below zero.

Almost due east of the Holbrook ranger cabin and the South Fork of the Flathead River was the White River Park area. Much of this area burned during the large forest fires of 1910. The elk herds grew dramatically in the following years with the increased lush vegetation. This upward spiral continued until the harsh winter of 1933 dealt a lethal blow to the elk herd. Over 500 elk carcasses were counted in a ten-mile stretch from the White River area south to the Cayuse Meadows area that winter.

By the afternoon of the sixth day, the cold did not present as much of a challenge as the temperatures were moderating. The skiing became easier and the terrain was much flatter than the country that we had previously traveled across. We spotted elk tracks all across the open meadows. As we approached the Big Prairie area we saw a couple of small herds of elk. We skied near the Big Prairie Ranger Station and made camp in a protected area.

The Big Prairie Ranger Station is a collection of old rustic log buildings. Construction began in 1917 and continued for the next couple of decades. Several Forest Service employees live and work here in the summer but no one spends the winter here anymore. Late in the evening, we skied around looking at the buildings. What a contemplative setting with the rustic log buildings, the elk feeding in the nearby open meadows, and the distant mountain scenery with the half-frozen river meandering below. The scene reminded me of a painting, only this was better for it was real.

Although this area seemed serene and peaceful, we saw signs of past hardship and sorrows. The heavy peeling of many of the old, large ponderosa pine trees by Indians may have indicated struggles to find food in the past. Just northwest of the

One of the cabins at Big Prairie Ranger Station.

Big Prairie Ranger Station next to the river were two Indian graves. According to Charlie Shaw, an early-day US Forest Service employee, these graves had been there for many years. According to a 1940 story told by Forest Service employee Henry Thol, the graves are those of an Indian woman and a small boy who died while an Indian party was camped in the Big Prairie meadows.

Another sad story occurred in January 1924. Clayton Roush, his wife, and young daughter were spending the winter at the Big Prairie Ranger Station caretaking the Forest Service facilities and stock animals when their daughter became very ill. Donning snowshoes, Roush walked over one hundred miles to get medicine for his daughter. Sadly, his daughter died before he could return. She is buried nearby.

The cold weather continued the next day as we left the Big Prairie area and skied along the trail. The earlier snows in the northern area of the Bob Marshall Wilderness had not reached this far south. We experienced our best traveling thus far as our skis and sleds glided with ease on the firm base of snow. Most of the terrain was reasonably flat and rolling. By the afternoon, the weather had warmed and we found ourselves taking more breaks to enjoy the scenery. We were now over halfway through our trip and had not seen another sign of anyone else.

Late in the afternoon, we camped near Camp Creek, a former site of a major battle between the Salish and Blackfeet Indians in the 1840s. The Salish had been in the Augusta area hunting bison and were on their way back home when their scouts alerted the group that the Blackfeet were following them. The Salish set up an ambush and completely surprised the Blackfeet, nearly wiping them out in the ensuing battle.

Less than fifteen minutes into our ski on the eighth morning, we came across fresh wolf tracks. We were amazed at how large the tracks were, measuring five inches long and four inches wide. We were very intrigued by this sight and wondered if we would get a glimpse of the wolf, or hear it howl. Of our group, only Greg had ever seen a wolf in Alaska.

We later found out that a wolf researcher had been tracking a breeding pair of wolves to the east of these tracks. We had barely contained our excitement and started skiing again when we met three skiers coming down the trail toward us. It was an ambivalent feeling meeting someone else after seeing no one for over a week. It was amazing that our groups even crossed paths as their group was traveling east to west across the Bob Marshall Wilderness. They were on the north and southbound trail for a very short jog before heading west again. Unknowingly, our respective groups camped less than a quarter-mile apart the previous night. The wolf crossed between our camps. After a few pleasant exchanges, each group continued on its way.

By the time we got to the Basin cabin area, the weather warmed up considerably. It was now above freezing and we found ourselves peeling off layers of

Basin Cabin in the Bob Marshall Wilderness.

clothing to regulate our body temperatures. We stopped to look at the old, historic cabin that was built in 1925. The weathered cabin seemed to blend into the surrounding landscape harkening to a bygone era. Instead of intruding upon the wilderness character of the land, this relic of the past seemed a part of it.

The weather became so warm in the afternoon that the snow started to stick to the bottom of our skis. We tried different types of wax, but nothing seemed to work very satisfactorily. Our pace slowed considerably. Luckily, by late afternoon the temperatures had cooled just enough to change the snowpack characteristics making the skiing pleasant once again. We skied until we came to the north end of the Danaher Meadows where we decided to make camp for the night.

Named after Thomas Danaher, this broad upper basin of the South Fork of the Flathead River was homesteaded by both Danaher and A. McCrea in 1898. The homesteads were too isolated, and the climate too harsh, leading McCrea to abandon his land. In 1907 Danaher sold his land to the Missoula Hunt Club. The land eventually came under the ownership of the Forest Service. We saw the remnants of the homestead attempt. A rusting horse-drawn hay rake lay near the site. The remnants of an old root cellar could be seen dug into the side hill. Also, along the eastern side of the Danaher Meadow area was the Danaher cabin, a Forest Service patrol cabin that was originally built in 1910 and later replaced in 1932.

As we skied across the Danaher Meadows, we noticed a metal box mounted on a tree. Looking inside revealed an old crank telephone. This system of communication was a working relic that was once commonplace throughout the Forest Service lands. In the past, there was an extensive system of telephone lines connecting the fire lookouts with various patrol cabins. At the time of our trip, there

Steve Lamar with the USFS crank telephone in Danaher Basin.

were about 45 miles of phone lines stretching from the Danaher cabin north to the Black Bear cabin still in working order. One of the earliest telephones in the area was installed at Big Prairie Ranger Station in 1912. In jest, I picked up the phone receiver and said, "I'd like to order a large pizza to be delivered to the Danaher Meadows!"

We saw a lot of elk sign in this area as we skied along, but did not see any of the animals. Taking a short break, we left our backpacks and sleds along the trail and skied to the top of a small hill. The view was outstanding as we looked over the large expanse of the Danaher Basin and the surrounding mountains. After a few minutes of gazing at the scenery, we skied back to our packs and sleds. The snow conditions were just right for carving a few telemark ski turns on the way down. We enjoyed it so much that we repeated the downhill ski run several times. It was fun just to play around before donning our backpacks, hooking up the sled harnesses, and proceeding along the trail.

Later in the day, we crossed over the Dry Fork Flathead Divide. At 5,400 feet, this is the lowest pass in the Bob Marshall Wilderness. Upon crossing this watershed divide we entered the southern portion of the Bob Marshall Wilderness Complex called the Scapegoat Wilderness. This portion of the federally designated wilderness was added in 1972.

Nearing the origin of the huge 1988 Canyon Creek Forest Fire, we were awestruck by the change the fire made upon the landscape. The landscape now seemed to take on only two colors, black and white. The Canyon Creek fire perimeter included over 240,000 acres. It started as a lightning strike on June 25, 1988, and was allowed to burn under the prescribed natural fire policy of the U.S. Forest Service. The fire smoldered for about a month, but with exceptionally dry weather and several wind events, the fire made dramatic runs in August and early September. Finally, on September 10th a snowstorm halted the fire's momentum approximately 35 miles from where it had started.

Because the burnt trees posed a hazard, we searched for a safe place to camp where the wind would not topple a tree snag on us. Luckily, we found a small island of live trees near Dwight Creek that had been spared by the forest fire.

The next day gave us an even greater awareness of the immensity of the Canyon Creek fire as we skied all day, rarely witnessing anything but a burned-over landscape. We knew that we were only seeing a fraction of the whole burned area. The evidence of the incredible power of nature was very humbling as we skied through this area. Even though this country had taken on a stark appearance, I found the contrasting black trees and white snow picturesque.

In the early afternoon, we came to an avalanche chute that intersected the trail. There was no way to skirt around this potentially dangerous area due to the existing cliffs above and the river below. The snowpack seemed reasonably stable, but we took precautions just in case. We checked our avalanche transceivers to make sure they were working properly, zipped up our jackets, pulled on the jacket hoods, and talked over our strategies. We posted lookouts and had rescue equipment handy. We crossed the avalanche chute one at a time.

The mountaineering sleds made crossing a challenge, as the chute was steep with a hard snow base and only a couple of inches of fresh snow on top. I started first and was about halfway across when my sled slid downhill and flipped over. I lost my balance and almost fell. I didn't want to stay on the exposed slope any longer than possible so with my adrenaline running high I hurriedly struggled to drag the upside-down sled along with me as I worked my way to the safety of the other side. I was very thankful when, one by one, each of our group made it safely to the south side where I stood positioned as a lookout. Everyone breathed a little easier.

Later that afternoon, we skied past the North Fork cabin. Built in 1931, this old log structure had been spared from the Canyon Creek fire because of protection measures put in place by firefighters. A sprinkler system was set up and the cabin was covered with aluminum fire shelter material. Amazingly, that effort was successful as the surrounding burned-over landscape would attest.

We made camp on the edge of the North Fork of the Blackfoot River in the Sourdough Flats area. It was the only place where we could safely set up camp out of range of possible falling tree snags. This area had extensively burned during the Canyon Creek fire.

On the eleventh day of our trip, we skied along the North Fork of the Blackfoot River. The stream through this section was frozen over with several inches of snow on top. We made good progress along this flat route for a couple of miles until we came to the pack bridge where we left the river and got back on the trail. By early afternoon we were at the North Fork trailhead. The road to this trailhead was not plowed in the winter so we continued to ski for another mile or so before making camp for the night. This was to be our last night out. With clear skies and a half-moon overhead, we decided to forego setting up the tents and slept out under the stars.

Imagine our surprise when we woke at daybreak with an inch of fresh powder snow covering us. The sky had clouded up during the night, and it was snowing. We shook the snow off our gear, had a quick hot drink, packed up, and skied the final six miles to our prearranged pickup point.

Everyone was in a euphoric mood knowing that for the past twelve days, we had endured something that most people would never get to experience. Bob Marshall summed it up best when he said, "Toting a 50-pound pack over abominable trail, snowshoeing across a blizzard swept plateau or scaling some jagged pinnacle which juts far above the timber, all develop a body distinguished by a soundness, stamina, and élan unknown amid normal surroundings."

The end of the 12-day trip through the Bob Marshall trip.
L to R: Greg Ontiveros, Barb Bennetts, Rusty Wells, Greg Sweetser, and Steve Lamar

THE INSPIRATION POINT GRIZZLY
1995

◆

In July 1994, I was working as a backcountry ranger for the US Forest Service. After a week of fighting forest fires in the Plains area, I needed to get caught up on my duties along the Swan Range. I had yet to clear the trail from the Napa Point Trailhead to the Bob Marshall Wilderness boundary near Inspiration Point.

It was already hot and dry as I left the trailhead early that morning. It appeared that this season could be a busy year with forest fires if conditions did not change.

I carried a one-person cross-cut saw, a pulaski, and a shovel to complete the anticipated work on the trail. I shoveled rocks out of the trail while cleaning out water bars and drainage dips as I moved along. Fortunately, only a few trees were over the trail that needed cut out as I worked steadily toward the pass.

Within half a mile of the pass, I encountered two boulders in the trail. I rolled both rocks down the brushy hillside. I immediately heard a large creature moving in the brush below me. I strained to locate the source of the noise, but the brush was too thick where I was standing.

As I moved up the trail a few steps to get a better view, I realized a grizzly bear was slowly walking toward me. It did not appear to know I was standing there as it moved its head from side to side. It suddenly occurred to me that I awakened the bear by rolling the rocks down in its direction where it had been bedded down in the brush. The other thought that simultaneously occurred to me was that he was getting too close. I quickly looked around for a tree to climb but found none nearby. I drew my can of bear spray and started to back away. Finally, I said in a calm, mild voice, "Whoa, boy, that's close enough." He jerked his head up with his eyes wide open in surprise, woofed, spun around, and ran off in the opposite direction. I let out a sigh of relief. The bear had been within 60 feet of me, close enough that I could see his raccoon eyes, rounded ears, humped back, and long claws. I was relieved that it had only been a close encounter.

After a few minutes, I continued toward the pass completing my trail work. After finishing up, I headed back toward the trailhead. When I got to the place where I had earlier seen the grizzly, I stopped to look the area over before proceeding.

Suddenly, out of the corner of my eye, I saw something furry running directly toward me. I jumped and spun around, pulling my bear spray out. It wasn't the grizzly bear but a Chow dog. I laughed at myself for letting my excitement nearly get the best of me. The dog was friendly and wanted to be petted. Then around the bend came his owners, a couple in their 30s. They stopped to talk. I laughed, telling them my bear story and how I almost sprayed their dog. They were headed to the top of Inspiration Point, where an old fire lookout once stood. After talking, we parted ways as I continued on my way to the trailhead.

I stopped for a while to rehab a few campsites along the way back, as well as finish a bit of touch-up work on the trail. It was late in the evening when I made it back to the trailhead. I was sitting in my truck writing up some ranger notes to post on the bulletin board when the couple I met earlier on the trail came strolling into the parking lot. They asked me if I had seen their dog. I replied that I had not. They explained that when they reached the top of Inspiration Point, their dog took off running down the northwest ridge. I did not tell them that it was in the same direction that the grizzly bear had run after my encounter.

The couple further explained that they searched for the dog, and called its name, but it never returned.

I thought there was a strong possibility that the dog had met an unpleasant and violent end if it had crossed paths with the grizzly bear. I wrote the couple's names and phone numbers down and promised to call if I found the dog or heard any news. I also posted it on the bulletin board. I stayed around for a while, but the dog never showed up.

The owners called me regularly for the next few weeks, but there had been no sign of the dog. At that point, I figured the dog was a goner.

A month later, when I got to the Condon Work Center office after a long day on the trail, the phone rang. When I picked up the phone, a guy asked me if I was still looking for the Chow dog up in the Napa Point area. Surprised, I said, "Yes."

He went on to say that he saw the dog walking slowly down the Napa Point road toward the highway. He said the dog appeared to be a bag of bones and that it looked malnourished. I thanked him and immediately called the owners. The next day I received word that the owners had found their dog.

Thankfully, my hunch about the grizzly bear getting the dog had been wrong, but I wondered what the dog had subsisted on for that past month to stay alive. If only the dog could talk, what a tale it could tell!

A SNOW SURVEY IN THE BOB MARSHALL WILDERNESS
1994

◆

"I stopped to listen to the sounds of wilderness that I have grown to cherish – the wind whispering through the trees, the gusts of wind charging through the higher terrain of the nearby mountains, the muffled sounds of distant ravens, the squawk of a Stellar's jay in the nearby brush, the gurgling sounds of the river on its long trek to the Pacific Ocean," I wrote in my journal after a solitary ski in the remote Bob Marshall Wilderness.

In February 1994, Russ Owen, Barney Jette, Joe Flood, and I went on an eight-day trip to the Bob. We volunteered to conduct the first of two winter snow surveys taken annually at the snow course near Holbrook Cabin located deep within the wilderness. It was over thirty miles from the trailhead to the snow survey site. Also, we were to inspect the patrol cabins and depending on the snow depths, shovel the snow off the roof of the Salmon Forks cabin.

We parked our vehicle at the Owl Creek Packer Camp near Holland Lake in Swan Valley, hoisted our backpacks, and headed up the trail. Due to the lack of deep snow in the lower elevation terrain, we hiked several miles up the trail toward Upper Holland Lake until we found snow deep enough to don our backcountry skis. Our backpacks were reasonably light as we carried only sleeping bags, some food, clothes, and emergency items. We planned to stay in the old patrol cabins strategically located along our route. As a precaution, we carried enough basic gear to spend the night out if necessary.

The first day's travel went quickly as the snow conditions in the high country were favorable with a firm base overlaid with three inches of fresh powder snow. We made the eleven miles to Pendant Cabin in good time. We utilized the remaining daylight to remove the snow from around the cabin. We had to dig down to the cabin door to unlock it and gain access. Only the very top crest of the outhouse appeared above the level of the snow. We estimated that the snow was seven or eight feet deep at this location. After shoveling out, we took the shutters off the windows, built a fire in the woodstove, hooked up the propane line to the cookstove, and started cooking supper. We melted snow in a large cook pot for water.

A small building, the 16 x 20-foot Pendant Cabin, was built in 1954. The furnishings included a table, kitchen counter, pantry cabinet, woodstove, cookstove, a set of bunk beds, and several wooden chairs. A lantern hung from a nail on a crossbeam. I was mildly disappointed to find the cabin built from lumber instead

Pendant Cabin. —Russ Owen photo

of logs. There's just something about a log cabin tucked back into the forest that appealed to me.

After years of camping in tents and snow caves in the winter, I found staying in the cabin almost luxurious. Even though the cabin was a bit cramped with the four of us inside, the amenities more than made up for any inconvenience. Drying out any damp gear or clothing was a cinch. The light from the lantern allowed us to cook and wash dishes with ease. The propane cook stove made cooking and melting snow for water very convenient. An ample supply of firewood stored under the lean-to shed at the back of the cabin kept us warm and dry.

We were up early the next morning as we had a long day ahead of us. It was fifteen miles to our next destination at Salmon Forks Cabin. Again, the skiing was good as we were blessed with three to six inches of fresh powder snow over a firm base of settled snow. Also in our favor was the fact that the route gradually headed downhill. We dropped in elevation from 5,800 to 4,400 feet by the end of the day.

By afternoon we arrived at the head of the frozen, snow-covered Big Salmon Lake. At that point, we left the trail and skied the length of the lake. This large wilderness lake is approximately four miles long and half a mile wide. We enjoyed the open vistas after skiing in the closed-in forest canopy for much of the day. We saw Charlotte Peak, at 8065 feet, standing sentinel to the south of the lake. To the northwest and north stood the mostly forested Garnet Peak and Salmon Point, at

Barney Jette and Joe Flood.
—Russ Owen photo

8,121 feet and 6,965 feet, respectively. To our surprise, 17 elk were standing in the middle of the lower half of Big Salmon Lake. The herd stared at us for several minutes until the lead cow had seen enough, and led the herd off to the cover of the forest along the south shore.

We arrived at Salmon Forks cabin near dusk. Newer than the rest of the cabins in the Bob Marshall Wilderness, this cabin was built out of logs just before the Wilderness Act of 1964 was enacted. It was much larger than the Pendant Cabin where we stayed the night before. It had several bunks and beds along with the usual complement of wood stove, propane cookstove, chairs, table, and all the rest. I built a fire in the woodstove as Joe and Russ got the propane stove hooked up and functional. Barney, whose skills at cooking far outweighed the rest of us, took over as the camp cook.

Later, with the combination of the warmth of the cabin, a full stomach, and the day's exertion, sleep came easy.

The next day was a scheduled layover and maintenance day. Russ was having a problem with his boot and a broken ski binding. At first, it did not look fixable, however Barney, being an artist and craftsman, studied the problem for just a few minutes. He dug through the trash can and other storage areas. He found a tin can and a metal hinge, grabbed what tools were available, and went to work. He fashioned an ingenious new ski binding for Russ's boot that saved the day, and possibly the trip.

Afterward, Joe and Barney decided to try their hand at ice fishing in Big Salmon Lake. After cutting a hole in the ice, they lay on their stomachs with a jacket over their heads and the hole. In that fashion, they could easily see the fish swimming around under the ice. Both brought fishing lines and the needed lures.

Later in the day, I skied to the lake to see how they were doing. When I looked through the hole, I was amazed at how well I could see in the aquamarine-colored water. A large number of fish were swimming around in that area. Joe and Barney would easily catch their limit that day.

While they continued to fish, I skied back to the cabin to help Russ shovel the snow off the roof. This cabin did not have as steep a roof as many of the other cabins and sometimes needed to have the snow removed to keep the cabin structurally sound. The snow was four feet deep on the roof and was bonded by four distinct ice layers. It was a good hearty workout.

Later in the evening, Barney treated us to a delicious fish and rice dinner that was nothing short of sensational. He had brought along a complement of fresh spices on the trip that turned our meals into gourmet extravagances.

As we ate breakfast the next morning, we decided to ski to the Big Prairie Ranger Station. We would bypass the Holbrook Cabin and the snow survey until our return trip. Getting a good start, we were on the trail by daybreak. The clouds and snow squalls moved out of the area. We were greeted with clear skies and colder temperatures hovering around zero degrees. We moved at a steady pace as the snow continued to be good for skiing. We glimpsed several nice views of the distant mountains from time to time as the rolling forested terrain was scattered with open meadows and park-like areas.

Murphy Flats was one such park-like area with its old, large ponderosa pine trees scattered about the open terrain. We also noticed the elk had pawed up the snow to get to the grass underneath. We surprised several elk in this area as we glided along the trail.

We came to the South Fork of Flathead River in the White River Park area. Unfortunately, the river was open water and necessitated us wading across. We took off our skis, boots, socks, and pants, and put them in or on our packs. We rolled up our long underwear and using our ski poles for balance waded across one at a time. The water was so cold that my legs were numb almost immediately. The pain was similar to that of eating ice cream too fast. Instead of the pain being in my head it was in my legs. There were more than a few discouraging words hollered that mid-morning, breaking the calm, quiet of the vast wilderness.

We continued to see elk as we skied toward Big Prairie Ranger Station. Some were in White River Park, some along the route, and some in the meadows of Big Prairie. We counted 64 elk that day.

Skiing around the buildings the Big Prairie Ranger Station was like stepping back in time. The structures were old, rustic, and mostly made of logs. Although this was a busy place with many people and stock coming and going during the summertime, no one had been there that winter except for us.

We did a quick inspection of the buildings and found everything satisfactory. We then settled into one of the cabins while Barney and Joe went to work preparing supper in the cookhouse.

Although the skies were cloudy in the afternoon, by late evening it cleared off. Skiing in the open meadow above the group of buildings, I watched as the end of the day came to a close. Both the buildings in the foreground and the mountains in the background were silhouetted in the fading light. Overhead, the three-quarters moon shone sharply in the gathering dusk. Coyotes sang in the distance while elk fed in one of the nearby meadows. I stood soaking it all in, thanking my lucky stars that I was able to do so.

Even though it was a scheduled layover day we were up early the next morning. With time on their hands, Barney and Joe joined forces and cooked one heck of a delicious breakfast of homemade biscuits, ham, and scalloped potatoes. Russ and I took care of the dishes and cleaned up afterward.

Later, with my journal tucked in my daypack, I went for a long ski around the area. I thoroughly enjoyed the day as documented in my journal entry:

> "What a glorious day to be in the wilderness! Skiing alone along the South Fork of the Flathead River across the open flats near Big Prairie Ranger Station with the wind blowing against my face, the sun alternately shining upon the land and then being blocked off by rapidly moving snow squalls make me feel very much alive and living life to the fullest. Being in the center of the Bob Marshall Wilderness is an indescribably good feeling. I feel extremely fortunate to experience such grandeur in the middle of winter. The distant peaks in every direction are either bathed in sunshine and stunningly beautiful or veiled in a hazy shroud of falling snow. Occasionally, the peaks are completely engulfed in a temporary snow tempest only to later reappear in all of their magnificent glory."

As I skied through a dense thicket of lodgepole pine trees near the river, I inadvertently startled a herd of 15 cow elk. They bolted and ran off seeking safe refuge in the dark forest to the west. I continued skiing along the river, occasionally stopping to look and listen at something of interest or to take a photo.

Later as I returned to the Big Prairie Ranger Station, a coyote came running across the open meadow in front of me. It kept looking at me as it ran off. The song dogs are a favorite of mine as I love to listen to their yelping and howling, especially when one starts and the rest of the pack joins in.

Barney rummaged through the supply cache and discovered a can of apple pie filling. He baked a delicious homemade apple pie for dessert that evening as we gathered in the cookhouse for supper. It was an enjoyable time as we sat around telling stories, laughing, and eating leftovers far into the night.

We were up by 5:00 am, ate breakfast, cleaned up, packed, and out on the trail by 7:00 am. Skiing conditions were excellent as we backtracked toward Holbrook Cabin to complete the snow survey before traveling on to Salmon Forks Cabin for the night. The temperatures were getting colder, barely above zero, as the skies were alternately clear and then cloudy with fast-moving snow squalls moving through. Again, we waded the numbing cold river. It felt good to get moving and warm up afterward as we skied the remaining distance to Holbrook Cabin.

Holbrook Cabin, along with the nearby Holbrook Creek, were both named after Fred Holbrook, an early-day ranger for the Big Prairie Ranger District in 1913 and 1914. The cabin was similar to the Pendant Cabin both in construction and size.

Inside the cabin, we found the needed snow survey equipment. We skied to the snow course just to the north of the cabin. This snow course, one of thirty scattered in and near the wilderness, was at 4530 feet. Since 1951, snow surveys have been taken annually at this site. After completing the ten stations we did the math, averaging the findings. The average snow depth was 29 inches with water content only 73% of normal. The maximum snow depth ever recorded at this site was 58 inches in 1978. Snow depths can vary widely from year to year and from place to place.

Joe Flood, Steve Lamar, and Russ Owen doing the snow survey near Holbrook Cabin. —Russ Owen photo

After completing the snow survey, we continued down the trail to Salmon Forks cabin. We saw 13 more elk along the way, bringing the total of elk I saw on the trip to 109. We made good time and reached Salmon Forks cabin by mid-afternoon.

The next day, we were up a couple of hours before daylight, because we had a long day of skiing to Pendant Cabin. Even though the fifteen miles were gradually uphill, we thought we would make good time because the trail was already broken. Or so we thought.

We opened the door that dark morning to six inches of new snow with more falling thickly to the ground. Unfortunately, the snow was not a loose fluffy powder but heavy dense snow. We quickly realized that if the snow kept falling at the same rate and consistency, we would be in for a very long day.

It indeed proved to be a long, tough day as the snow continued falling at a fast rate. By the time we got to Big Salmon Lake, the snow was 12 inches deep. When we reached the end of the lake, the snow was pushing 15 inches. By dusk, still several miles from the cabin, the snow was over 20 inches deep. We debated whether to make camp instead of venturing further. But the lure of the cabin with its wood stove to dry us out kept us going.

We donned our headlamps when it became too dark to see the trail corridor with the distinctive faint groove indicating the buried trail tread below the snowpack. As we gained in elevation the wind and the swirling snow made the conditions even tougher. Several hours after dark we continued to push on. Within a mile or so of the cabin, the wind drifted the snow so badly that it was becoming hard to determine where the trail meandered through the forest. The wind gained strength, as the swirling snow reduced visibility to less than a few yards.

Again, we debated about holing up for the night but decided to keep pushing toward the cabin. Our clothes were damp from the exertion. The blowing snow seemed to find its way inside our clothing. I strained my right knee while pushing through the deep, heavy snow, making me wince in pain with every step forward.

Russ seemed to have the nose of a bloodhound, sensing the trail as he led us on the last leg of the journey. When we could finally see the outline of the cabin several hundred feet away, we paused for a minute to rest and catch our breath. We were physically exhausted from the effort but slowly came back to life when we were inside the cabin. It felt good to warm up and dry off near the woodstove as we shoveled hot food and drink into our tired bodies that night. Later, sleep came easy.

The new heavy snow was 26 inches deep in the wind-protected areas near Pendant Cabin when I measured it the next morning. The storm had blown itself out during the night. With the clear skies, the temperature dropped to at least five degrees below zero, maybe colder. Ice crystals readily froze on our mustaches and beards.

Russ Owen, Steve Lamar, and Joe Flood at Pendant Cabin.
—Russ Owen photo

After a prolonged breakfast of pancakes, we repacked our gear, cleaned up, then closed the cabin, and headed out on the trail.

We knew that the avalanche danger was very high with yesterday's heavy snowfall and high winds. Of special concern were several small avalanche run-out zones we had to cross. We turned on our avalanche transceivers. We each had a shovel and probe poles. We discussed our strategy. If possible, we would avoid any areas of concern by going down and around rather than exposing ourselves to possible danger. If the danger was too great, we would retreat to the cabin and wait for conditions to stabilize. If we felt that the conditions were acceptable, we would stay spread out in areas of concern, posting lookouts, and only exposing one person at a time.

As we skied along, we found that some of the avalanche zones had already slid. One larger zone appeared to have avalanched two times. We avoided most areas of concern by skiing down and around. A few areas seemed reasonably safe and we quickly crossed one at a time. Cautiously, using stringers of trees for protection as we traveled up our route, we safely made it to Pendant Pass. It was slow going in the deep snow. It took us several hours to travel a little over three miles. The rest of the route was mostly downhill from this point, although the deep, heavy snow prevented us from going very fast. We stayed in the safety of moderate terrain with stringers of trees for protection as we worked our way toward Upper Holland Lake.

At one point we were standing on a small knob looking down at the lake, when on impulse Joe said, "I'm gonna ski this slope." Just as we were beginning to protest, he took off down the slope. He only went about twenty feet before falling headfirst into the deep snow. At that moment, there was an audible "Whump" sound that emanated from the snowpack. An avalanche about a hundred yards away to the west released and slid down the slope coming to rest on Upper Holland Lake.

As Joe struggled and finally stood upright, the three of us hollered to him, "You just touched off an avalanche!" He immediately came back up to where we were safely standing. After regrouping, we continued down to the lake in a gentler, safer location.

The pace of our skiing remained slow until we got a mile or so below Upper Holland Lake. At that point, the snow depth lessened and we made better time. When we reached the trailhead at dusk there were only 3 or 4 inches of snow on the ground. It was amazing that the winter storm dumped so much snow in the Pendant Cabin area and so little in the valley. It was another reminder that life inside the wilderness was often a much different world than life on the outside.

Steve Lamar on a Bob Marshall Wilderness snow survey, 1994. —Russ Owen photo

BEAR DREAMS
1995

◆

It had been a long, hot, dusty day on the trail as I went about my duties as a backcountry ranger for the U.S. Forest Service. I spent the day in the Bob Marshall Wilderness cleaning up and naturalizing campsites at Lick Lake as well as doing some much-needed trail work on the upper reaches of the Gordon Trail.

It was late summer of 1995 in the high mountains of the Swan Range. The huckleberries were ripe but not particularly numerous in that general area. Even so, there were plenty of bear sign. I jumped a black bear near Lick Lake and saw numerous tracks and scats of both black and grizzly bears.

Named for the numerous saline deposits found in the area, Lick Lake is an incredibly beautiful, high-alpine lake. This lake, at almost 6000 feet, is nestled in a classic cirque basin that is bordered by a fortress-like headwall that arcs around the lake from the northwest to the southeast. As I stood on the shore of the lake, I spotted two mountain goats climbing on a narrow ledge high on the rock face of the cirque wall.

The sun was low in the western sky when I crossed Gordon Pass on the Swan Divide, heading toward Upper Holland Lake. I planned to spend the night at a quiet out-of-the-way campsite about a quarter of a mile above the lake. It was a spot that most people were not aware of and was seldom used.

With less than an hour of daylight left, I arrived at the campsite only to find that the site had indeed been used the night before. The previous campers had left a monumental mess. The scene before me was a classic good example of a bad example of backcountry camping. A two-foot pile of potato peels was smoldering in a fire pit. Cooked, uneaten beans were dumped on the shore of the small stream flowing near the campsite. In the water itself, were fifteen cooked but uneaten fish. There were several broken whiskey bottles and numerous beer cans scattered all about the area. The campers had tied their horses directly to the trees adjacent to the creek and the ground was rototilled and pawed so deeply that I doubted the trees would recover. Horse manure was in the stream. Many tree branches had been cut for bedding, heavily scarring the site. Garbage was strewn everywhere.

Disgusted with the campers' obvious lack of respect for both the land and the people, I took off my backpack and proceeded to clean up the mess. By the time I finished the task, it was well after dark. Using my headlamp to see, I hung the thirty pounds of garbage in a tree to keep the bears from getting it.

With all the bear sign in the general area, I decided not to camp at this site with the smell of food all around. The popular campsites at Upper Holland Lake were probably occupied by that late hour, so I walked back up the stream quite some distance until I found a level spot for my tent. I went to sleep late that night thinking about bears. I was sure one would visit the trashed-out site that I had cleaned up. I drifted off to sleep dreaming of bears.

In the middle of the night, I was abruptly awakened when a large animal tripped over the guy line on my small tent and fell up against me. I awoke from a deep sleep to a thrashing animal pressed up against me. I had gone to bed thinking of bears, went to sleep dreaming of bears, and awoke to a bear trying to claw its way into my tent!

I desperately groped for my bear pepper spray when suddenly, the animal stood up and bounded off toward the nearby beargrass slope. I breathed a sigh of relief when I heard the distinctive bounding gait of the animal. I realized it was not a bear, but a mule deer that had tripped, falling up against me in my tent. I had to laugh, although it took me a while to calm down and drift off to sleep again.

I woke peacefully the next morning to the singing of a nearby varied thrush. As I sat on a log eating my breakfast, I watched the early morning alpine glow spread across the tops of the mountains. I drank in the cool morning air as I contemplated my night of bear dreams and the ensuing excitement.

Later that day, I retrieved the wayward campers' garbage, visited with other campers down at Upper Holland Lake, and cleaned the water bars along the trail as I worked my way out of the mountains. Again, the backcountry did not disappoint, as it had been another memorable trip into the mountains.

Grizzly bear

WINDY TIMES ON THE TOO MUCH FUN TRIP
1995

◆

In August 1995, my son Luke and I backpacked to Pyramid Lake on the Swan Range just inside the Bob Marshall Wilderness boundary. Twelve-year-old Luke strapped his fishing rod to his new backpack. We planned to stay for a couple of days, hoping to climb a peak or two while getting in some trout fishing.

We hiked the four-plus miles to Pyramid Pass in good time. Even though his backpack was full of gear and food, Luke flew up the trail. I tried to talk to him about pacing himself and not tiring out early in the day. He would have none of it as he was young and full of energy. He probably would have trotted up the trail if left to his own devices. As it was, we got to the lake in what seemed like no time at all, found a level spot away from the lake, and set up our tent. Once we set up our simple camp with our food bag safe from bears hanging high in a tree, we strung our fishing rods and walked down to the lake.

Up to now, Luke had not been too keen on learning to fly fish. He had only cast lures with his spinning rod. That was about to change.

A hatch was on as we proceeded to fish our way around the lake. At times, the lake looked like it was raining as the trout were feeding on emerging insects on the water's surface. Using handmade flies that I tied the previous winter, I caught and released fish on practically every cast with my fly rod.

Luke Lamar with Pyramid Lake in the background.

On the other hand, Luke, with his assortment of store-bought fishing lures, caught only a few. He did not like the fact that I was having all the fun. Finally, I asked him if he would like to use my fly rod. He readily agreed, and after a quick lesson, he went about it tenaciously. The action was fast and furious as he caught fish after fish. In two partial days of fishing, he caught and released over 65 trout.

From that point on, he became a dedicated fly fisherman. It was so much fun watching him as he wore a huge nonstop smile while intermittently hollering, "I got another one!" From time to time, I showed him how to tie on a new fly as the old fly got chewed up to the point that nothing much was left but the hook. An occasional fly ended up snagged in a high tree branch. He quickly learned the fly-tying knot to the point that I no longer needed to hover nearby to help out.

He tried several flies, Royal Wulffs, Joe's Hoppers, Gray Hackle Peacocks, Yellow Humpy's, and Stimulators. They all seemed to work just fine. Occasionally, the natural insect hatch would abate only to pick up again a short time later. With practice, Luke became better and better with his fly-casting. He learned to drop the fly on the surface of the water in such a manner that brought an immediate strike from a rising trout.

Later, as the day wound down, we stopped fishing long enough to cook supper and watch a beautiful sunset bring to a close the first day. It felt great to be in the mountains enjoying the experience with my son.

We got up early the next morning, ate breakfast, and hiked up the ridge to the top of Pyramid Peak. It was an easy climb. At 8,309 feet, the summit offered a

Luke Lamar on the Summit of Pyramid Peak.

beautiful view of the surrounding country. We looked far into the Bob Marshall Wilderness with wave after wave of mountains seemingly going on forever.

We watched the early morning shafts of golden light playing on the mountainous terrain contrasting with the dark blue shadows of the landscape that had yet to feel the light of day. It was an incredibly stunning scene. We gazed at the northern and northeastern peaks with names like Marshall, Leota, and Crimson. We saw parts of the twisting Young Creek drainage to the east. To the southeast and south, we saw Devine Peak and Morrell Mountain. We looked southwest into the valley bottom toward the community of Seeley Lake. We stood on top of the peak, breathing in the cool morning air, and marveled at the scenery for quite some time before slowly walking down the ridge to Pyramid Point and back to camp.

Upon reaching camp, Luke immediately picked up my fly rod and went back to fishing while I sat on a rock and watched.

Until the second afternoon, the weather had been excellent with warm temperatures and clear skies. As I walked to the lake and explored the area a bit, I noticed a huge strange-looking thunderhead cloud quickly moving our way across the valley to the southwest. I hollered to Luke, who was fishing on the other side of the lake, "Let's head to the tent before the storm hits."

As the sinister-looking cloud quickly moved toward us, it looked as though it would mostly just miss us to the north. But the south edge of it hit us. It was on us in no time at all. We dove into the tent just as the brunt of the storm hit.

I was amazed at the storm's ferocity. The wind was so strong that I thought my mountaineering tent which had survived numerous stormy weather events, would be ripped to shreds. I expected it to either collapse or come apart at the seams at any moment. Luke sat on one end while I sat at the other end, trying to keep it anchored down. The wind pushed, pulled, and buffeted the tent to the point that I thought it might disintegrate any second.

We heard several trees crack and crash to the ground. With the wind came hail the size of small marbles. It pelted the tent in a deafening roar to the point we could hardly hear each other speak without hollering. After a long and agonizing fifteen minutes or so, the storm passed into the Bob Marshall Wilderness to the northeast. When we got out of the tent, there were two to three inches of hail covering the ground. The skies cleared, the summer-like temperatures returned, and the hail quickly melted.

In my many years working in the outdoors, I had never endured anything quite like what we just went through. I had experienced many weather events that moved in quickly, but this storm seemed quicker. I had witnessed my share of violent thunderstorms, but somehow this one had more intensity packed into a shorter time. I had endured extreme winds at various times, but this one had a violent edge to it.

Later that day, we packed up for our return home. Many fallen trees were over the trail as we hiked toward the trailhead. I was concerned that once we reached the truck, we might have to cut out our way back home. Luckily, someone with a chainsaw had cleared the roads by the time we hiked out.

Upon reaching home, we heard the news that a tornado had ripped through the area, touched down from time to time, and flattened swathes of trees as it went. Most of the damage occurred north of our campsite. We only experienced the southern edge of the storm.

We heard later that someone with a video camera had filmed the tornado funnel. We also learned that forested areas were flattened in the Pierce Lake area near the Summit Divide and in the Big Salmon Lake area of the Bob Marshall Wilderness.

I was thankful we were spared from a direct hit. If we had been in the direct path of the storm, the outcome might have been much different. We had excellent fly-fishing, climbing, and camping, with a different kind of excitement coating the experience. As it was, we called our trip *The Too Much Fun Trip*.

Indian Paintbrush

FIELD NOTES
1991-1996

◆

It was late in the evening as I went for a walk in the fading sunshine. The January air was a crisp 10 degrees and felt refreshing to breathe. The mountains on both sides of the valley were stunningly beautiful. The alpenglow on the Swan Range was a vivid pinkish-orange bordered by a bright clear blue sky. A few ravens squawked in the distance to break the silence. Across the open meadow, a deer fed along the forest edge. It was one of those contemplative serene evenings in Swan Valley.

When it snowed 12 inches overnight one January, Luke and I got out our cross-country skis and headed to the old Smith Creek School. The schoolhouse was built with logs back in 1918 but was in sad shape.

A bald eagle flew by as we skied across the snowy meadow. Near the schoolhouse, we found a dead deer that had been killed by a mountain lion. The ravens were finishing up what was left of the carcass. Mountain lion tracks led to the lion's bed. All the snow had been scratched away and the forest duff had been fluffed up. A well-worn trail with numerous lion tracks led away from the bed. We didn't see the mountain lion but figured it wasn't far away.

Smith Creek School, 2004.

The powder snow was some of the best snow that we'd had in a couple of years. It was a pleasure to be out skiing. Gliding along in the fluffy powder was pure joy. Part of the joy was the tranquility associated with skiing in powder snow. It was serene and refreshing to the soul.

We continued to ski in an easterly direction. Many deer tracks were heading all over the place as well as a few elk tracks. We were hoping to find some fresh-shed deer antlers but knew it was early in the season. Our dog, Kirby was along and was good at finding antlers. Kirby didn't find any fresh antlers but he did find a huge six-point antler that was buried under the snow. It was the match to another antler that he found last year.

One February weekend, Sharon, Luke, and I met friends Rod, Camille, and Rachel Haynes at Polebridge in the North Fork. We rented two old cabins behind the historic Polebridge Mercantile store. We crossed the North Fork River to Glacier National Park to do some cross-country skiing. We were hoping to see one of the wolf packs that relocated from Canada into the area. We saw about 50 elk, a moose, six bald eagles, and lots of ravens, but no wolves. We did discover a fresh elk calf carcass that the wolves had killed earlier in the morning or the night before. We spotted wolf tracks in the snow that led to the carcass. By following the tracks, we found the site where the chase began, tell-tale hairs where the wolf first bit the elk, drops of blood from the wound, and finally the elk carcass itself. By the time we arrived on the scene, the wolves were gone and the bald eagles and ravens were picking at the scraps.

On a sunny day, I was walking with the dog several miles from our house when we came across a fresh deer kill. The whitetail doe had a large hole eaten out of its side near the heart area. It was so fresh that the blood pooled in its chest cavity hadn't coagulated yet. The carcass had moss and sticks scraped up around it. I immediately thought, "Mountain lion!"

I quickly looked around to see if the animal was still close by. I didn't see it but figured that it must be nearby. A large old ponderosa pine stood a few feet away and I scrutinized its branches closely but didn't see the lion. I decided that it would be best if I took the dog and left the immediate area.

A couple of weeks later, I was driving down a road near the area of the deer kill when a large mountain lion came out of the brush and crossed the road in front of me. It didn't seem in any hurry and I got a good look at it. The size of the animal with its big paws and long tail, was striking. I'd guess that this lion was the same one that had preyed on the deer. Both events made each day memorable.

As I stood on our front porch on an early April evening at dusk, I saw 21 whitetail deer feeding in the wet marsh to the east of our log house. The water level was halfway up the deer's legs. A few mallard ducks and a green-winged teal were swimming and feeding among the scattered deer. The fresh snow, silently falling, added a peaceful mood to the scene before me. The sound of Canada geese could be heard coming from the nearby ponds and marshes as the waning light gave way to darkness. I breathed in deeply and relished the crisp taste of the air.

On a bright day in May, I spotted a northern pygmy owl in a tree next to our west boundary. It was the first one that I'd seen around here. A bit later I jumped a cow elk. The following day a moose ambled through our property. I cherish these precious moments here in the proverbial wild kingdom.

In June, while hiking in the Upper Holland Lake area, I came across fresh wolverine tracks in the snow. It was the second time that I had seen its tracks. Last year in June I just missed seeing a wolverine in the same area. I could tell by its tracks in the snow that I had startled it. I tried tracking it, but never caught up. I'd only seen one wolverine in all my years in northwest Montana.

While near the Cat Lake trailhead, I jumped a grizzly bear. It had been feeding in a ripe huckleberry patch. Luckily for me, it ran off in the opposite direction. The ripe berries were abundant that July, along with a lot of bear activity.

September has always been a favorite time of mine as the weather can be very pleasant during the day, yet cool at night. I saw a mountain goat while up in the Pony Lake area. The bugs were gone as well as most of the people. Life had slowed down a notch after a busy summer.

Autumn in the Swan Valley

Autumn in the Swan Valley.

The fall colors were vivid in Swan Valley with rich yellows of the birch, cottonwoods, aspen, and larch trees. With the colorful trees bracketed by snow-covered mountains and deep blue skies, the beauty was breathtaking. The fall air was crisp with a hint of wood smoke. The sounds of fall included geese honking overhead, an occasional elk bugling in the distance, and ravens squawking loudly as they flew by looking for a meal. The absence of songbirds was conspicuously noticeable as most had departed for more favorable winter climates.

In the fall, Annie and Luke often helped me gather firewood. Our goal was to fill our woodshed before the winter snow arrived.

Luke and I were out looking for birds during the Audubon Christmas Count when we jumped a herd of elk just west of our land. The elk filed by in a single line. All 29 were cows and calves, no bulls. These elk had been hanging around the area for several weeks.

During the bird count, we saw 15 species of birds. Most notable were two robins that we saw in our front yard. With the lack of snow and the abundance of natural food available, some birds were hanging around that normally would have migrated by this time of year.

RINGS OF TIME: A HISTORICAL JOURNEY THROUGH THE BOB MARSHALL WILDERNESS
1996

◆

It had been a long day on the trail in 1996 as I slowly worked my way toward the top of the ridge while clearing the downfall from the trail. When I reached the top of the ridge, the land opened up and the views were especially beautiful as the late evening sunshine cast a golden hue across the landscape. Overhead, a few reddish, wispy clouds contrasted the deep, cobalt blue sky. A nearby hermit thrush began its melodic song. I was less than a hundred yards from a trail intersection that would lead to my camp. I came around a slight bend in the trail and to my dismay, found that a large whitebark pine tree had fallen across the trail. In an instant, I knew that my day as a Forest Service backcountry ranger would be a bit longer.

As I took out my one-person cross-cut saw and began cutting through the large tree, I wondered about its age. I inhaled a mixture of evening coolness and the aroma of fresh-cut wood as I worked the saw rhythmically back and forth. As I sawed through the growth rings of this majestic tree, I speculated about the history of the surrounding land.

Although the tree succumbed to the white pine blister rust that plagued this region, it survived the historic forest fire season of 1988. It stood proud during the 1964 signing of the Wilderness Act that gave areas like this formal protection. The tree also survived the 1964 floods that wreaked havoc on the lower-elevation lands below it. This tree was still thriving in the winter of 1954 when the coldest temperature ever recorded in the Lower 48 registered an incredible -70 degrees below zero near the southern edge of the Bob Marshall country near Rogers Pass. It survived the severe windstorms of 1949 that toppled so many trees in this area of Montana.

In 1940, this whitebark pine was in all its glory when the Secretary of Agriculture established the Bob Marshall Wilderness, named in honor of the man who championed the cause for areas like this to remain forever wild. Sadly, Bob Marshall died the year before in 1939 at the young age of 38.

This tree survived the severe winter of 1933 when snow depths were great and temperatures were frigid. That spring, over 500 elk carcasses were counted in a 10-mile stretch along the South Fork of the Flathead River, between the White

River and Cayuse Meadows. In 1929, fortune was again on its side as it avoided the potential destruction of yet another historic forest fire season.

Human tragedy struck in 1925 when forest rangers found the frozen body of a trapper named Marshall in his cabin near Cabin Creek. The trapper had apparently committed suicide. Tragedy also struck in the winter of 1923-24 when the young daughter of the caretakers at Big Prairie Ranger Station fell sick and died before her father could return from his 100-mile snowshoe trip to obtain medicine for her. She is buried nearby.

In 1923, the Forest Service attempted to use dog sled teams as a means of winter travel in the backcountry but found this method unsuitable because of the steep, side-hill trails. The year 1919 was once more a historic forest fire season. That same year Joe Murphy of Ovando, Montana began packing hunters into the South Fork of the Flathead River. Murphy Flats now bears his name. In 1914, the first permanent fire lookout building in the Flathead National Forest was erected on Spotted Bear Mountain.

Once again, this whitebark pine was spared during the 1910 forest fire season when large areas of the Bob Marshall backcountry burned. In 1903, over 21 miles of Forest Service trail was built from the Ovando area into Danaher Basin. In 1898, this whitebark pine had lived over half of its life when Tom Danaher and A.P. McCrea each homesteaded 160 acres in the upper reaches of the South Fork of the Flathead River drainage. Neither man experienced success, and the land eventually came under Forest Service ownership.

In the winter of 1896-1897, six French Canadian fur trappers spent the winter trapping in the Big Salmon Lake and the South Fork of the Flathead River area. They brought out 2700 pine marten pelts and other furs that spring. From 1886 to 1889, Charles Biggs and a few others built a wagon road from Hanna Gulch up the Sun River to the Gates Park area. They cut 200,000 railroad ties and 25,000 cords of fuelwood from Headquarters Creek and Biggs Creek drainages before abandoning the venture.

Legend has it that the U.S. Army made a trip through the South Fork of the Flathead River area scouting a possible route for a railroad when the whitebark pine reached middle age in the 1870s. Around 1840 a major battle between the Salish and Blackfeet Indians took place near the Camp Creek area. The Blackfeet were ambushed and suffered heavy losses.

The tree was at least 50 years old in 1806 when the Lewis and Clark Expedition traveled through this country along its southern and southeastern edges. The whitebark pine was a mere teenager of 15 when the United States declared its Independence from Britain in 1776.

After I finished making cuts, I rolled the bulky log sections off the side of the trail. While I sat down to rest, I counted the rings of time on the remaining uprooted tree stump. It was approximately 245 years old when it died. Its life began around 1750 when guns and horses reached the Montana Indian tribes, forever changing their culture and way of life.

The hermit thrush quit singing, and darkness had settled in when I finally put my cross-cut saw away and headed for camp.

Steve Lamar as a backcountry ranger on the Holland Ridge Lookout Trail, 1993.

A TRIP TO THE NORTH WALL
1999

Although some say it's less spectacular than the famed Chinese Wall in the Bob Marshall Wilderness, the North Wall is nonetheless extremely beautiful and grand. Somewhat shorter in length than its famous counterpart, the North Wall is still an imposing escarpment of cliffs running several miles roughly north to south, and in places up to a thousand feet in height. Access through this fortress-like barrier is limited to steep scrambles in only a few locations along its length. The North Wall is part of the Northern Rockies overthrust belt where the older Cambrian sedimentary rock tilted and slid eastward, up and over the younger geological rock formations.

In September 1999, I backpacked into the Bob for an 18-day trip as the wilderness instructor for the Wilderness Treatment Center. Along with getting a taste and feel of this wild area of the Bob Marshall Wilderness, one of our group's objectives was to do some volunteer work for the US Forest Service on the trail system below the North Wall.

A large portion of the area had burned during the Gates Park Forest Fire in 1988. Numerous burned tree snags had fallen over the trail and some sections of the trail had serious soil erosion problems. We planned to clear the fallen trees from the trail, as well as perform some much-needed drainage and tread work along the steeper grades of the trail.

It was a magical trip of wondrous sights and sensations. Early in the trip, the weather was summer-like with daytime temperatures in the mid-eighties. The deep aroma of pine needles baking in the hot afternoon sun permeated the air. The lofty peaks of the majestic Rocky Mountain Front stood sharp and jagged against the bright, blue sky. A few chickadees, golden-crowned kinglets, and other birds gave muted musical notes from within the forest while overhead the Canada geese echoed goose music as they passed on their way south.

The fall colors became brighter and more beautiful with each passing day as the leaves of the aspen and cottonwood changed from green to shimmering bright yellow. The huckleberry bushes were a brilliant red, while the spirea and mountain spray were vivid orange. Fireweed, a personal favorite, was often multi-colored with various shades of green, yellow, orange, and red all on one plant. The grasses became various shades of greens, yellows, and browns. As the evening sun dipped behind the mountains to the west the air became crisper and cooler.

We accessed the North Wall from the Lick Creek Trail via Route Creek Pass and the Middle Fork Teton Trailhead. We surmised that Lick Creek got its name from the numerous mineral licks located in that area.

As we neared the North Wall, located along the Continental Divide some twenty miles from the trailhead, the signs and sounds of elk became more and more frequent. The bugling, grunting, and fighting bull elk came so close that we could smell the elk as well as see them. The full moon shining brightly above us at night seemed to entice the competition among the bull elk.

The elk seemed to be all around us while we were in our tents attempting to sleep, often as close as a hundred feet as they crashed around through the forest, bugling challenges steadily throughout the night. We heard the sharp sound of colliding elk antlers as each opponent pushed and shoved in their zeal to prove dominance over the other. The noise was so great that we often had a hard time sleeping at night.

We spent several days working on the trail system. It was hard, dirty work cutting out the burned trees that had fallen over the trail. We installed water bars diagonally across the trail to divert water off the tread and grubbed out a new trail to replace the badly eroded older trail. We looked like coal miners with black soot covering us from head to toe at the end of the workday. Luckily, there was a small stream nearby where we dipped buckets of water to clean up.

On the ninth day of our trip, we were re-supplied with food by the Forest Service wilderness ranger stationed out of Gates Park guard station. As it turned out, he was the only other person we saw in the 18 days that we were in the Bob Marshall Wilderness. After re-supplying our group with food, he returned to Gates Park to finish closing down the old administrative cabin before packing out for the winter.

After earning a much-needed day off from the work schedule, we decided to explore more of the area. On the tenth day of our trip, we clambered through a notch of the North Wall into a high basin and climbed higher to the top of a prominent peak. It was a beautiful, sunny afternoon without a cloud in the sky. The wind, however, was blasting across the summit ridge making it hard to stand up when we reached the broad summit of Hahn Peak at 8310 feet. The mountain was named for Tom Hahn who was a trapper in this area in 1908.

We could see for many miles in the distance with mountains stacked up to the horizon in every direction. The afternoon sun cast a dazzling effect upon the landscape as the blue-hued shadows sharply contrasted with the mellow, soft browns and greens of the rocks and trees. Viewing the incredible beauty of the wild country, I felt fortunate to be standing on this peak in the middle of the vast wilderness. As far as the eye could see was nothing manmade, only natural landscapes. A sense of freedom, an appreciation of beauty, and a tingling of excitement washed over me as I stood gazing at the surrounding scene, soaking up the experience.

After ten days of beautiful, sunny weather, we awoke on the eleventh day to three inches of snow. The skies were leaden with the snow falling steadily. As we were packing up camp that snowy morning, a large section of limestone rock split off the North Wall and came crashing down toward us. Instantly alert, I shouted a warning. The large house-size rock bounced several times, broke up into smaller boulders, and eventually stopped a couple of hundred feet from our camp. The constant freeze and thaw action of moisture in the cracks of rock loosened the rock until gravity took hold, bringing the boulder falling down the steep slopes.

Throughout my life, I had often seen and heard smaller rocks falling down various mountains, but this was by far the largest I ever witnessed. We decided that a new campsite with less exposure to rockfall would be welcome.

Due to the heavy snowfall muting both the sounds of our movements as well as our scent, we saw over 100 elk while hiking. One bull elk lay in the trail with his back to us as we approached through the thickening snowstorm. He had a thin layer of snow coating him. We were all startled as the bull elk jumped up and disappeared into the curtain of falling snow.

By late evening, the wet, heavy snow accumulated to 14 inches in depth, the skies cleared, and the temperatures plummeted. The stars were bold, bright, and twinkling in the crystal-clear night sky. Half chilled from the dampness of the earlier snowstorm, it felt good to crawl into the warmth of my sleeping bag.

By daybreak the next morning, the temperature hovered around zero degrees. It seemed as though the weather abruptly made the switch from summer to winter without the pleasant Indian summer autumn of warm days and cool nights sandwiched in between. Although the trip now became more physically challenging while dealing with the cold weather, the beauty of the white, snow-draped mountains and forest was breathtaking. The white-clad landscape contrasted with a deep blue sky and the red-hued shale rock of this portion of the North Wall. Standing in the open meadow near our camp, I marveled at the scenery.

A stillness settled over the landscape as the elk along with the songbirds all but disappeared. I stood in an open meadow and heard nothing more than my heartbeat and breathing. The quiet seemed to cloak the land for the next three days until the weather moderated with the rising temperatures. During the day an occasional raven would fly by giving its guttural call, while at night we heard the great horned owl hooting a rhythmic hoo hoodoo hoooo hoo in the darkness. The seasonal change had taken place in the high country. Mother Nature had spoken and the cycles of life had listened.

On the fifteenth day, we left the high country of the North Wall, dropping in elevation down Red Shale Creek, past the Gates Park Guard Station, and onward to the North Fork of the Sun River where we dropped out of the snowy winter weather into a much more pleasant autumn scenario. I reveled in the warm sunshine as we spent the afternoon fly-fishing for trout in the deep holes along the stream. I even took a quick swim in the river to wash away the trail grime. The extremely cold water took my breath away as it was shocking to my senses. After thrashing and stumbling back on shore, my breathing slowly returned to normal, and the numbness faded. Afterward, I felt invigorated.

We still had three days of hiking left with a high mountain pass to cross to get to the trailhead. As we moved up the trail the next day along Headquarters Creek, we spotted a black bear with two cubs in a meadow above us. The mother bear was over 400 feet away yet made it known in no uncertain terms that she would not tolerate us coming any closer. She made short, aggressive charges in our direction challenging our presence. We slowly moved away before continuing to our next campsite.

Headquarters Creek was so named because the area was once the headquarters for the many tie hackers who lived in cabins in this area. From 1886 to 1899, the woodworkers provided over 200,000 railroad ties and 25,000 cords of fuelwood for markets outside of this area. Although Charles Biggs and others built a wagon road into this area, most of the wood was floated down the river. The venture ultimately proved uneconomical because of the long distance to the market and the unreliable water levels in the Sun River.

Our last campsite was in a high alpine basin to the west and below the mountain pass. Again, we entered the winter zone as a new storm moved in on us. The clouds were swirling in and out of the surrounding peaks creating a mystifying mood as the changing light patterns played havoc upon the landscape. I stood spellbound by the constantly changing scene. At one moment the sun sliced through the charging clouds sending golden shafts of light and color to the area, and almost in a blink of an eye, the scene rapidly changed to a dark and sinister countenance upon the landscape. This display was often followed by a curtain of clouds that blocked out everything before repeating the whole sequence in a dizzying fashion.

The storm system intensified, shaking and battering our tents throughout the night. Even though we had set our tents in a wind-protected area with thick, stunted trees, it was hard to sleep as the roaring wind strained at the tents. There were times when I thought the powerful blasting winds would rip the tents to shreds. Sometime before dawn the winds died down and I fell into a deep sleep.

I was surprised the next morning to find that it had not snowed all that much, but that a white rime frost had coated everything, providing a sensational scene of surreal beauty. It truly looked like a winter wonderland with rime crystals plastered to every rock, tree, and shrub while the vivid blue sky provided a backdrop. Golden rays of sunshine streamed through the mountain pass in the east lighting up the shoulder and summit of the unnamed peak immediately to the west of our camp.

Making our way over Headquarters Pass at 7743 feet was challenging as the trail was deeply drifted with hard wind-packed snow in many places. Parts of this trail on the west side of the pass had been blasted out of sheer cliffs so there was a degree of exposure to contend with while breaking trail over the pass.

Although cold and windy, the view at the top was breathtaking with beautiful scenery in every direction. Rocky Mountain, the tallest peak in the Bob Marshall Wilderness Area at 9392 feet, stood sentinel to the south, while to the north stood an unnamed peak at approximately 8560 feet. To the west, we saw the North Wall where we had spent so much of our time during the eighteen-day trip. To the east lay the South Fork Teton trailhead and beyond that, the plains of Montana.

Steve Lamar on a prior trip near Headquarters Pass in the Bob Marshall Wilderness.

The last few miles down to the trailhead offered some respite from the harsh weather above. To the east of the pass was a large natural spring where clear, cold water flowed from a pool in a scenic, amphitheater-like basin. We saw a large mule deer traversing a snowy talus slope below a shoulder of the steep cliffs.

The North Wall trip ranked as one of my favorite excursions. It seemed as if we experienced the full gamut of beauty, serenity, adventure, wildlife, weather, nature's mood swings, and physical challenges during the eighteen days in this untamed area of the Bob Marshall Wilderness.

CONNECTIONS
2002

◆

In 2002, I spent the first nine days of September in the rugged Swan Range of northwest Montana working as an instructor for the Northwest Connections' Landscape and Livelihood Field Study for college students.

A conservation and education nonprofit based in the Swan Valley, Northwest Connections (NwC) involved local people in the conservation of habitat linkages across rural landscapes. NwC operated for 19 years before merging with the Swan Ecosystem Center to form Swan Valley Connections.

The Landscape and Livelihood field course was an intensive two-month college course focusing on ecology and community-based conservation. Students could earn 15 college credits from the University of Montana as they studied the relationship between forest ecosystems and human communities.

Immersed in the high-paced regimen of learning, the small group of motivated college students enrolled in the 2002 Landscape and Livelihood course exuded energy and enthusiasm. Even more enthusiastic were NwC's Education Program Director, Andrea Stephens, and the founders of NwC, Melanie and Tom Parker, who were the other instructors on the trip.

The first morning of the backcountry trip found us at the Smith Creek Trailhead. Tom Parker gave everyone a quick overview of horse packing. Tom, along with a few friends, planned to pack some of the group's food and heavy gear into Condon Basin where we would spend several nights before moving camp. Along the five-plus miles of uphill trail to our destination, we would be free to study various interesting facets of natural history without being burdened with heavy backpacks. Before departing we answered student's questions about our route and discussed trail techniques such as foot care, pace, energy conservation, and hydration.

Donning our lightweight backpacks, we headed up the trail. The first mile of the trail roughly paralleled Smith Creek. This creek was named for E.F. Smith, an early-day Swan Valley trapper who in 1908 built a cabin near the confluence of Smith and Condon Creeks.

As we worked our way up the trail, we discussed plant identification, animal tracks found in the mud, birds singing in the trees, and other items of interest. We watched as a Northern Three-Toed Woodpecker searched for insects while perched on the side of a lodgepole pine tree that had been killed by mountain pine beetles. We flushed a ruffed grouse from the trail near a cluster of ripened Oregon grapes. Fresh deer tracks were visible in a wet boggy area along the trail. Bright red rose hips, one of the most concentrated forms of vitamin C found in

Tom Parker

the natural world, hung from the wild rose plant. Travel was slow and enjoyable as questions and answers flowed back and forth between the staff and the students. The students, with notebooks in hand, jotted notes and made quick sketches of the flora and fauna.

As we gained elevation, the instructors pointed out the changing vegetation. We left the mature stand of primarily ponderosa pine, Douglas fir, and larch, and entered a more even-aged lodgepole pine and Douglas fir stand that was borne from the aftermath of a forest fire in 1939.

After lunch, we conducted a mock first-aid scenario. The students put into practice what they had learned the day before in their Wilderness First Aid training. The second day of first aid training was planned for tomorrow in Condon Basin.

When we reached the three-mile mark we broke out into an open rocky area with a great view of the southern end of Swan Valley as well as portions of the Swan Front. Here we took a much-deserved rest break.

Continuing our trek toward Condon Basin where our first camp would be located, we saw a spruce grouse along with four juvenile chicks in an area laden with grouse whortleberries. I was sure that the grouse were feeding heavily on the delicious ripe berries. We stopped and ate some of the fruit ourselves. The tasty tart berries had a flavor of huckleberry and cranberry combined.

The views of the mountains were getting better as we gained elevation and came into the high subalpine meadows. Cooney Mountain and Smith Peak came

> I recalled my backcountry ranger days with the US Forest Service. Once, I found an old gray metal trail sign tacked to a tree opposite this open area. Upon examining the trail sign closely, I noticed that several people had signed their names and the date in the margins of the sign. One signature grabbed my interest. I read the name of my neighbor, Reuben Kauffman. Next to his name was the date 1940. Later, when I ran into Reuben at the local store, I told him about finding the old trail sign with his signature on it. He laughed and slapped his leg and told me how he and his brother had been some of the first people to use the trail after the US Forest Service built it in 1939. They were riding their horses from the old Condon Ranger Station over Smith Creek Pass and into the Bob Marshall Wilderness to hunt elk during the early fall. He went on to tell me in detail how the hunt had gone and the good times they had. I was amazed at the details he could recall some fifty-five years later.

into view. Many of the wildflowers had already bloomed and gone to seed. The smell of seasoned, cured vegetation permeated our senses.

As we topped the pass separating the Smith and Condon basins, we were rewarded with a sensational view of the rugged Swan Range to the north. Taking a quick breather for photos, I pointed out our campsite down below in a flat area of Condon Basin. There Tom and his friends had unloaded our heavier gear and supplies and were now in the process of riding back out to the trailhead. It had been a rewarding day on the trail, but with the weather threatening, we were ready to shed our backpacks, set up camp, and begin cooking the evening meal. With that goal in mind, we proceeded down into the basin.

The first evening at camp was a flurry of activity as we gave instructions on campsite selection, tent setup, water sources, operation of camp stoves, hygiene, cooking instructions, food handling, and proper disposal of body waste.

Ever cognizant of bear safety we went over the procedures for keeping a clean camp and putting up bear ropes for hanging our food, toothpaste, and garbage for the night.

With the camp chores completed and the weather threatening everyone retired to their tents to work on field journaling and homework assignments. Shortly after getting into the tent that first night, the thunder, lightning, and rain moved in for quite a long period.

Our first morning in Condon Basin was wet and cold as the clouds swirled in and out of the nearby mountain peaks. Despite the damp weather, the students participated in the Wilderness First Aid class taught by Dave McEvoy of the Aerie School for Backcountry Medicine. Previously, the students spent a day of instruction in first aid at the Northwest Connections facility. Building on what they

Condon Basin.

had previously been taught, the students practiced their newly gained knowledge in a backcountry situation. Dave conducted short sessions on a specific first-aid topic followed by a hands-on practice session.

Although the day started cloudy and wet, the skies cleared off by evening. At dusk, as we sat in camp discussing the land ownership patterns in Swan Valley and the surrounding areas, a Boreal Owl landed in a tree limb above us. It was approximately 10 inches tall. It occasionally flew from tree to tree but stayed close to us. We commented on how friendly the owl seemed. At first, we were not sure what kind of owl it was until we got out our bird book and identified it. One of the characteristics of a Boreal Owl is that it often appears tame and friendly. We were excited as Boreal Owls are rarely seen in this area. It was only the second Boreal Owl that I had witnessed here in Montana. Approximately a dozen years ago I heard one up in the higher reaches of Fatty Creek in the Mission Range while conducting owl surveys for the US Forest Service.

On the third day of the trip, we packed our gear and moved camp. It was a beautiful day with spectacular scenery as we trekked through Condon Basin climbing toward Smith Creek Pass along the Swan Divide. Just short of the pass, we took a short detour as Tom, who had returned to join us, showed us a section of an old Indian trail that crossed the pass just south and uphill of the present trail. Tom explained that early-day Swan Valley residents Joe Wilhelm and Harold Haasch told him about this old Indian trail. They said that years ago the two of them had followed the Indian trail for many miles from the pass down into the lower reaches of Little Salmon Creek. At that time, narrow travois drag marks could still be seen in places. Tom tried to duplicate the feat years later, finding the upper portions of the trail still visible, but the lower trail had blown shut.

As I topped the Swan Divide along this old trail, I was struck by how challenging this terrain must have been for the Pend d'Oreille Indians to bring their families and stock over the pass in their annual quest for food. Danger could have presented itself in many forms from steep cliffs to mountain storms to possible Blackfeet enemy lurking in ambush anywhere along the circuitous route. I had a newfound appreciation for the many native travelers who had come before me.

As we crossed Smith Creek Pass, we entered the Bob Marshall Wilderness. This area got its name from Bob Marshall, an explorer, and forester, who in the

NwC students and staff near Smith Creek Pass on the old Indian Trail.

1930s, was a leader in the conservation movement to preserve some of the last remaining wild areas left in the United States. Although this area has a rich human history, it is still relatively wild by today's standards.

The view from the Smith Creek Pass was incredibly beautiful and inspiring. Across the U-shaped valley to the east stood Steamboat Mountain with its fresh dusting of snow along its summit ridge. Below us were the small, emerald-colored lakes that we referred to as Little Salmon Lakes. These lakes were part of the headwaters of the Little Salmon Creek drainage that flowed off to the north for several miles before sharply bending to the east on its journey to the South Fork of the Flathead River.

With such an impressive view of the landscape for miles around, we stopped and conducted a geology and glaciology class. Andrea Stephens spent the next hour explaining the forces and processes that shaped the land that we observed in front of us. This class was followed by a period of field journaling and sketching.

> The Bob Marshall Wilderness Complex is a large area comprising over 1.5 million acres of congressionally designated Wilderness. The complex includes the contiguous Great Bear, Bob Marshall, and Scapegoat Wildernesses. Along with Glacier National Park, this area forms the backbone of the Northern Divide Ecosystem.

Steve Lamar standing on the Indian trail looking down at Little Salmon Lakes. —NwC Photo

While near Smith Creek Pass, I counted about four dozen Clark's nutcrackers flying through the notch in the Swan Divide as they traveled back and forth gathering whitebark pine nuts and caching the seeds. They were flying incredible distances as I watched them through my binoculars.

Clark's nutcrackers have a specially adapted storage area under their tongue that can store up to 80 whitebark pine seeds. The birds were collecting the seed far to the east of where we sat, storing the seed in their sublingual pouch, then flying toward the Mission Mountains far to the west across Swan Valley.

We could see their extended pouches loaded with seeds as they traveled west to cache the food. The birds prefer to seek out reasonably open subalpine areas, such as areas burned by forest fires, to store the seeds one inch deep in the soil for later use. They have remarkable memory capacity and through the use of triangulation can remember the location of their cache of seeds. They may bury 1 to 15 seeds per site while depositing seeds in as many as 30,000 sites during a season. Forgotten or unused seeds often germinate forming the next generation of Whitebark pine trees.

Also, of interest was the number of raptors seen as the fall migration was underway. I spotted a goshawk and a sharp-shinned hawk, as well as several golden eagles, merlins, and other raptors, cruising near the spine of the Swan Range as they flew south. Ground squirrels, pikas, and marmots often sounded their shrill alarm cries as the raptors flew overhead.

As we donned our backpacks and headed down to the Little Salmon Lakes to our next camp, we found recent grizzly bear diggings alongside the trail. The churned vegetation and soil had a rototilled look to it. Melanie dug up a few Glacier Lilies and Spring Beauties to show the group what the bear had been searching for. An amazing amount of nutritious energy was packed into the corm or bulb of each plant. Also edible for humans, the bulb of the Glacier Lily had a somewhat sweet and nutty flavor.

Later, we made camp near the smaller Little Salmon Lake. We spent the rest of the afternoon working on field journal entries and sketches. In the evening as the sky grew menacing with dark clouds spilling over the Swan Divide, we conducted a map reading exercise followed by a group reading from our biogeography booklets.

After a nighttime snowfall, we woke the next morning to a winter wonderland. Visibility was reduced to the immediate area around camp as the snow continued to fall. For many of the students, this was their first experience of camping in winter-like conditions. Finally, as we completed breakfast the snowstorm let up with an occasional patch of blue showing through the mostly cloudy sky.

After getting our gear ready for a day hike, we hung our food and garbage high from a tree, out of reach. We left camp and proceeded up the south end of the drainage toward the Albino Basin. We first observed part of the old Indian trail and campsite near the larger lake. We found remnants of an old hunting camp in the same area. It seemed probable that the campsite had been used throughout human history as it provided the needs of both humans and horses with a level, grassy area close to water and wood.

We followed the Indian trail for a short distance before cutting over to a series of potholes and mudflats. In that remarkable area, we found a variety of animal tracks along the shorelines and in the mud. There were both large and small grizzly bear tracks in the area. Tom and Melanie gave a quick lesson in track

NwC students examining animal tracks in the mud.

identification while the students took notes and made sketches. Other tracks included deer, elk, coyote, squirrel, mouse, vole, and the most interesting of all, wolverine.

As we hiked farther up the drainage we broke out of the protection of the forest into the open alpine meadows and boulder fields. The wind and snow buffeted us as we continued onward. Shortly, we came upon blood, bits of fur, and coyote tracks in the fresh snow. We stopped and investigated. By both forward and backward tracking of the coyote tracks, we were able to read the story of the hunt. The coyote had been gridding the area when he spotted a ground squirrel. The coyote stalked the ground squirrel until it was close enough to put forth a burst of speed and catch the ground squirrel before it could escape back to its hole. The coyote carried the ground squirrel a short distance before consuming it. A few bits of blood, hair, and the tail were all that remained. No doubt, we had disturbed the coyote, as all of the evidence was fresh. We could read the story in the snow where the coyote stopped, must have looked our way, and then left the area at a fast pace.

As we gained elevation, the weather conditions deteriorated. Visibility was reduced and the footing became slick and unstable. At that point, with the safety of our group in mind, we turned back toward camp. We continued to look at plants, new tracks, and other interesting items. We jumped a mule deer and watched as it moved away from us. As we dropped in elevation, the weather warmed and

> In his book, *They Left Their Tracks*, Howard Copenhaver, an outfitter from Ovando, told an interesting story about a 1950s snowstorm in the Bob Marshall Wilderness. He and one of his hunters found a small cave up in the basin above the Little Salmon Lakes. Inside the cave was a rocked-up fireplace with old cut tree branches stacked up on the floor. He surmised that natives or perhaps early-day mountain men had used the cave as a shelter. Howard and the hunter spent the night and part of the next day in the refuge as they patiently waited out the storm.

improved as the storm began to break up. By the time we reached camp, the snow at the smaller lake had melted. The students spent time that evening working in their field journals.

The next morning dawned crisp and clear, a beautiful fall day. After breakfast, we took the group along the old Indian trail to the precipitous cliff section that the natives had to negotiate when they traveled down the trail along Little Salmon Creek. This abrupt drop from the higher valley to the lower valley has often been referred to as a *step valley*, while others have called it a *hanging valley*. Regardless, it is an amazing geologic feature to observe, as well as a daunting obstacle while traveling along the old Indian trail. Getting horses, travois, and people safely down this section must have been a dangerous undertaking. The Forest Service relocated this part of the trail to the west and higher up to avoid this cliff section. Trail crews were able to blast rocky sections with dynamite and re-route the trail away from this obstacle.

On the way back to camp we found evidence of culturally modified whitebark pine trees. Indians peeled the bark to get to the sweet inner cambium layer of the tree. This food source was used both as a sweetener in their meals, as well as a survival food during times of scarcity. The tool marks at the top and bottom of the elongated scars were still evident. Unfortunately, the mountain pine beetles and the white pine blister rust had killed most of the other trees. Later, after talking to renowned whitebark pine authorities, Kate Kendall and Steve Arno, we found that our discovery might be the only known example of culturally modified whitebark pine trees in North America. It was much more common for Indians to use ponderosa pine and cottonwood trees as a food source.

Later in the day, we packed up camp and hiked to the Little Salmon Overlook where we stopped to enjoy the panoramic view. From this point, we saw the lay of the land before us and the immensity of the Little Salmon Creek drainage and surrounding terrain. Of special interest was the distant Stadium Peak with its distinctive round coliseum summit. We spotted a mountain goat up on the rocky face of a peak along the Swan Divide.

From the overlook area, the trail descended downward via several switchbacks through an expansive rocky boulder field. As we moved through this section of the trail, we did some trail work as a lot of rocks had rolled onto the trail. We kicked, shoved, and shoveled rocks off the trail as we hiked along this scenic area. We continued to lose elevation for the next six miles as we traveled to our next campsite at Little Salmon Creek.

As we hiked, we continued to study the natural history of the area. We traveled through a series of meadows at the toe of expansive avalanche paths coming down the leeward side of the Swan Range. The evidence of former snow slides lay scattered about the terrain. Snapped-off tree trunks and mangled tree parts were stacked ten feet deep in some places, demonstrating the tremendous power these avalanches wielded. Interspersed among the avalanche debris were Mountain Ash shrubs laden with bright orange berries, as well as quite a few bear scats near the trail.

Along the way, we saw a mule deer, several western toads, a couple of spruce grouse, and numerous songbirds including several beautifully colored Townsend warblers.

Tom knew this area intimately from earlier years when he and his brother hunted elk in this large drainage. He regaled us with a few of his past hunting experiences as we walked along. He pointed out the multitude of blowdown, thick vegetation, and the physically rugged terrain that made this area particularly tough to hunt.

Our destination that day was an old abandoned outfitter camp. Don Merritt once had a hunting camp there. Set back from Little Salmon Creek, the camp was nestled next to a spring in a dark grove of old-growth spruce trees surrounded by thick vegetation. Even on a sunny day, it seemed dark. As Tom put it, "It's so dark in here a guy needs to pump daylight into this place to see." It was quite a contrast to our earlier camps. Although I enjoyed the change, I was glad that we would only spend one night there.

Close to our intended camp, we discovered a pile of bear scat laced with candy bar wrappers on the trail. The bear had somehow eaten a human treat and that concerned us. Coming into our campsite we found that the campers before us had buried their garbage and unwanted food. A bear had smelled it, dug it up, and feasted on it. Once a bear is rewarded it often comes back hoping for more. We did not want a bear visiting us in our camp or along the trail.

With that possibility fresh in our minds, Tom gave a talk about wildlife encounters concentrating in particular on bears, but also mountain lions. Whereas earlier in the trip he gave general information to the students, he now gave detailed instructions and information on what to do in certain situations with particular animals. Afterward, we built a hot campfire over the area where the food and garbage had been buried, hoping to incinerate the leftovers and smells. Our group was even more vigilant in keeping a clean camp that evening.

In the waning light of evening, we heard a Pygmy Owl calling to the northwest. Later in the night as I lay in my tent I heard a bull elk bugling up in the high country to the west.

The next morning, we broke camp and continued down the trail until we came to the Palisade Creek junction. We crossed the creek and took a faint trail uphill to the site of Bud Moore's old trapper camp. Even though Bud had located his trapper camp close to the main trail, it remained hidden from plain view. At his campsite, we saw some of the surplus firewood and tent poles that were slowly decaying back into the landscape. Several young subalpine fir trees were growing where his tent once stood as nature slowly, yet tenaciously reclaimed the site.

Bud Moore, who began trapping at the age of fourteen, spent several winters in the 1930s running trap lines in the Lochsa backcountry. He worked for over 40 years with the US Forest Service before retiring in 1974. Wanting to get back to his roots and the land, he and his wife Janet moved to the Swan Valley. Beginning in 1983 at the age of 66, he spent a couple of winters living in a tent camp on Palisade Creek while he worked his trap line. That first winter Bud took 63 marten, 40 ermine, four mink, and two squirrels. Marten pelts were worth $40 while long-tail and short-tail ermine pelts were worth $5 and $3 each respectively. Interestingly, he observed very few snowshoe hares and pine squirrels in the area the first winter. He let the area rest the following winter before he returned the third winter to resume running his trap lines. By reducing the predator numbers, the third winter the pine squirrels, and to a lesser degree snowshoe hares were numerous, so much so that he inadvertently caught more than 60 squirrels in his traps. He was able to sell the squirrel pelts for $3 each. The third winter, in addition to the squirrel pelts that he jokingly referred to as *Swan Valley Sable*, he trapped 44 pine marten and 20 ermine.

During his first winter trapping in the area, Bud brought along several heavy traps for trapping Lynx but he did not see any sign that winter. The third winter he did not bring in the heavier traps and, as fate would have it, he discovered that a family of four Lynx often hunted that area.

After he saw wolverine sign for the first time in January that winter, Bud wrote in his journal, "Since a wolverine had robbed and destroyed a set about a mile above camp, I'm beginning to feel that, creature-wise, this is a whole wilderness after all." Bud saw wolverine sign during both of the winters he trapped the area but thought that the Mission Range to the west held higher numbers, especially family units.

The only set of fisher tracks he saw in the Palisade Creek drainage was during that first winter, with none seen the third winter.

From his tent camp at Palisade Creek, his trap line the first winter consisted of four spur lines. One spur went up the Little Salmon Creek drainage toward Smith Creek Pass, stopping short of the dangerous large avalanche path just north of the Little Salmon Lakes. The other spurs led down the Little Salmon Creek drainage, the Gill Creek drainage, and the Palisade Creek drainage.

Bud Moore at his home in Swan Valley. —John Fraley photo

In a journal he kept that winter, Bud commented, "The Little Salmon is dark country." He observed that even though he could look up on sunny days and see the sunshine on the high peaks, the sun never shone down in the Little Salmon Creek drainage. In another journal entry, he noted that three coyotes intersected with his snowshoe tracks in the powder snow one day. One coyote reacted by backing off, while the second bounded over his tracks careful not to touch his tracks. The third boldly walked upon Bud's trail before later jumping off and continuing through the forest. Bud commented, "Obviously, coyotes, like people, react in various ways to the same set of circumstances."

There were periods of bitter cold that winter. In a small way, I could relate to the conditions that Bud had experienced. On the very night that he was camped on Palisade Creek, I was camped on the west side of Swan Valley near Lindy Peak in the Mission Range. That night the temperatures in Swan Valley and Seeley Lake hit -45 and -52 degrees below zero, respectively. Winter camping took on a different character in that type of cold. There was no room for error, no room for getting sloppy or careless. I got a touch of frostnip on my nose while Bud got a bit of frostbite on the tip of his thumb.

Bud had a passion for the wildness of the mountain landscape. He took photos of the scenery but realized that although pleasing to the eye a photo could never quite capture the essence of wildness. In his journal, he wrote, "Photography falls short of recording the spell of wildness exhaled by the high country of the Swan Range in winter. Its bounty can only be seized by those who go there, who take time to reflect in its grandeur then let its wildness soak in to their personalities."

Leaving Bud's trapper camp, our group continued up the old, semi-abandoned trail toward Palisade Lake and Lion Creek Pass. The steep, high cliffs to the east of the Palisade drainage lived up to its name. The Palisade Cliffs rose like fortress walls to guard much of the drainage and surrounding terrain.

The huckleberries and grouse whortleberries were ripe and plentiful along the upper portion of the old trail as we hiked toward Palisade Lake and up to the Swan Divide where we would make camp. We took advantage of nature's bounty, collecting enough berries for a huckleberry-whortleberry cheesecake that would be our dinner dessert that evening. Black Bear tracks in the mud reminded us that we were not the only ones who enjoyed the delicious berries.

Our campsite south of Lion Creek Pass along the Swan Divide was very scenic with incredible views of Swan Peak, Tierra North, and the Lion Creek drainage. Swan Peak, at 9280 feet, is the second tallest mountain in the Swan Range.

We enjoyed a beautiful sunset that evening as we sat on a high rock bench overlooking the Lion Creek drainage to the west. The colors were striking with various shades of red, pink, and orange splashed against the western horizon of the distant Mission Mountains. While nearer to us were the darkening greens, blues, and blacks of the silhouetted canyons of Lion Creek.

As the light faded and the first stars appeared, Melanie gave a class on constellations. It was a crystal-clear night and at 7000 feet in elevation, the stars seemed to jump out at us. Of particular interest to me was the star Antares, located to the southwest in the constellation Scorpius. While I looked at the star through my binoculars, it appeared to constantly change back and forth from a red to a green color. It is a large star with a diameter 630 times that of our sun and is considered a red supergiant. It captivated my attention, as it seemed more beautiful than any of the other stars. We stayed up late that night watching numerous shooting stars as the group learned the various constellations and the stories behind their names. From time to time, we heard a distant Great Horned Owl calling in the darkness.

The next morning seemed to come quickly. After breakfast, we discussed the plight of the whitebark pine in this part of the country. Whitebark pine is considered a keystone species because it is a major component in the upper subalpine ecosystem of the mountains. Several wildlife species have historically depended upon the highly nutritious seed from the whitebark pine cone as a major food source including the Clark's nutcracker, pine squirrel, and grizzly bear. Each whitebark pine seed contains 50 to 60 percent fat. A variety of factors have caused the whitebark pine's demise. Fire exclusion and the resulting competition from shade-tolerant subalpine firs and spruce are crowding out the whitebark pine. Fire exclusion on the lower slopes has also resulted in overmature lodgepole pine becoming infested with mountain pine beetles that spread into the stands of whitebark pine.

White pine blister rust, a non-native fungus inadvertently introduced into this country in 1910, has ravaged the susceptible whitebark pine. It is speculated that global warming with its associated warmer temperatures, drought conditions, and the resultant stress may play an important role in the plight of the survival of whitebark pine. Because these factors are human-caused, the solutions could also come from humans. Restoration could come in many forms from putting fire back on the landscape, thinning out the competition, using pheromones to discourage insect attacks, planting genetically disease-resistant seedlings and seeds, and reducing greenhouse gas effects on a global scale. A couple of the biggest hurdles would be educating people on the seriousness of this problem and getting the support to accomplish the needed restoration. I remain optimistic that nature can overcome these obstacles with active help on our part.

After the discussion, we went on a day hike to Owl Peak. Located along the Swan Divide, this mountain at 8250 feet is the site of a former fire lookout. In the mid-1920s the US Forest Service stationed an employee at the site for the summer to look for smoke and forest fires. There was no structure, just a map stand on top of the peak with the fire lookout's campsite down the north ridge on a flat spot. This type of fire lookout was referred to as a rag camp. John Hulett, a lifelong resident of Swan Valley, was the Owl Peak lookout in 1934. As John told it, he had just been dropped off at his campsite by the packer when a thunderstorm swept through the area. He was in his tent when lightning struck nearby, paralyzing him. He was still conscious, but could not move. He later commented, "That was my first experience. I hadn't been there over half an hour when that happened to me." He recovered, spent the rest of the summer in the Owl Peak area, and lived to be 90 years old.

I could see why Owl Peak was chosen as an observation point to look for forest fires. The view from the top was not only spectacular and inspirational but also situated in a location that afforded unobstructed views of large expanses of forest in several directions.

Interestingly, John Hulett mentioned seeing blue grouse on the peak in 1934. Almost 70 years later, our group also saw blue grouse on the summit. While mountain goats were commonly seen on the peak in those days, we saw no sign of them the day we were there. From personal observations based on almost 30 years of exploring the mountains in both the Swan and Mission Ranges, it seems that the mountain goat populations are in serious decline. I have seen fewer and fewer goats as time has passed.

As we hiked through the country leading to the top of Owl Peak, we checked the condition of the whitebark pine trees in that area. It was not encouraging. The white pine blister rust and mountain pine beetles were delivering a one-two punch that was proving lethal to most trees. Still, there were occasional trees that had been spared, giving hope for the future. Because we saw Clark's nutcrackers in the area, we surmised that enough food sources were still available.

The summit of Owl Peak was tailor-made for a map-and-compass class dealing with triangulation. We demonstrated and practiced the skill of finding your location by taking a compass bearing of three nearby landmarks and transferring those bearings to the map. The point where the three lines intersected on the map was your location. The students practiced that skill as well as figuring out the names of distant peaks by using a map and compass. Later, drawing on the inspirational setting, the students spent several hours sketching and writing in their journals.

NwC students and staff on Owl Peak. —NwC Photo

Later on our way back to camp, we saw a mule deer as well as a flock of mountain bluebirds.

On the eighth day, we held an early morning map and GPS class before hiking into the upper Lion Creek drainage to conduct a couple of whitebark pine monitoring surveys. Northwest Connections has been monitoring whitebark pine stands in the Swan and Mission Ranges since 1998. Each site was surveyed for stand health conditions. The monitoring surveys were set up so that each site would be revisited every five years to record changes over time. The students seemed to enjoy the practical, hands-on experience and commented positively about being engaged in useful work. We measured all of the whitebark pine trees within our survey perimeter, recorded the diameters, heights, and foliage crowns, and noted any insect or disease damage. We recorded ground vegetation, aspect, and slope angles. We made notes of fire history evidence, avalanche damage, and wildlife sign. We noted whether the trees were producing cones and if Clark's nutcrackers were present. Careful notes were taken so that the site could be revisited in the future as we jotted down our position taken from our GPS units and marked our location on the map.

What we found at those sites was not encouraging. Signs of blister rust and mountain pine beetles were evident and wreaking havoc in both areas. But as in a lot of other areas, there seemed to be a few survivors that gave hope for the future.

On the final morning of the trip, we were up early preparing for a long day on the trail. We would descend over 3300 feet in elevation as we traveled over ten miles to the trailhead. We'd leave the upper subalpine terrain of whitebark pine, alpine larch, and subalpine fir and end up in the forested terrain of cedar, ponderosa pine, lodgepole pine, and western larch.

Hiking down the steep series of switchbacks near the scenic Lion Creek Pass was visually sensational in the early morning light. Swan Peak with its scattered bright patches of snow stood sharply outlined against the deep blue sky. The fall colors of the changing vegetation of the high country were bright and dazzling. The reds, oranges, and yellows of the various fireweed plants were especially appealing that morning.

A mile below the pass, situated on a reasonably flat spot close to Lion Creek and the trail, was the upper camp of the Lion Creek Outfitters. Owners Cecil and Isabelle Noble had used this Forest Service-permitted camp in the summer and fall guiding clients on fishing, hunting, and sightseeing trips by horseback for over thirty years.

We continued to quiz the students on plant identification. After nine days in the backcountry, they were getting better at recognizing the flora and fauna of this region. The Lion Creek drainage was more moist than the rest of the country that we had seen up to that point. We occasionally came across new plants that the students had not seen. We slowly worked our way down the trail, stopping often to look at something of interest.

Six miles from the trailhead, we came to the Lion Creek Falls. At that late time of the season, the waterfalls were a series of ribbons of water cascading over the rocky cliffs. Here we took a quick rest break, ate lunch, and took a few photos.

After hiking farther down the trail we came to an area of large, old cedar trees. It was hard to believe that we were in Montana. The area seemed more like what you would expect along the coast of Oregon or Washington. The maritime weather influence in western Montana was very evident in this area.

We crossed a barren, rocky, dry side streambed along the trail. Tom told a story about a tremendous thunderstorm that hit this area of Lion Creek with an incredible amount of rain in late July 1998. The upper portion of this northern side drainage blew out, sending a tremendous sediment load of soil and rock down into the main Lion Creek drainage and beyond. Sediment was deposited several feet deep through the area for quite some distance. So much sediment flowed downstream that the Swan River flowed a dark oatmeal color for several days. Evidence of this natural disturbance was still visible four years later below the trail with tell-tale mudflats that encased many of the trees in the riparian zone.

With three miles left to go, we came to the area known as the Pool of Eden. On a faint trail leading down to Lion Creek were two rounds of old remnant logs of a small cabin. I had come across this relic years ago and had asked several longtime Swan Valley residents if they knew the story behind it. None were sure although I heard several possible explanations. The most interesting explanation came from longtime resident Edna Kesterson who thought that it might have belonged to a turn-of-the-century outlaw and trapper who went by the name Soup Creek Harry.

As the story goes, Soup Creek Harry had come to Swan Valley in the early 1900s to evade the law. He settled and built a log cabin near the present-day Soup Creek Campground. It was said he had a few cabins scattered about that he used when he was trapping. When the law was closing in on him, he fled to Canada where he met his end in a gun battle with law enforcement officials.

The path leading to Lion Creek, with its interesting mix of geology and hydraulic action combined to produce an intriguing mosaic of slots, grooves, holes, and pools, was fascinating to explore. The actual Pool of Eden was a hundred yards downstream where the water funneled over a slot in the rock falling fifteen feet into a deep, beautiful, blue-green pool of cold mountain water. It occurred to me that natural features do not have to be large on a grand scale to be considered a gem of precious beauty.

We could see evidence of bygone days along the south side of Lion Creek from the number nine telephone wire lying on the ground. The wire once connected the Owl Peak fire lookout with the outside world.

We continued along the remainder of the trail until at last, we reached the Lion Creek Trailhead. It had been an extremely rewarding and worthwhile experience for the staff as well as the students. Our group spent the past nine days connecting with the landscape on a deeper level, cementing our relationship with the land and with each other.

Portable electric bear fence used in later years at NWC.

BEAR DNA PROJECT
2003

◆

I watched in fascination as a massive grizzly bear ambled down the trail in Glacier National Park, purposely veering off the trail toward a tree with polished bark. Standing up with its back against the tree, the bear rubbed its back up and down the tree with apparent enthusiasm. After some time, the bear dropped to the ground and ambled down the trail. Later, another bear came down the trail and repeated the rubbing behavior on the same tree. Sure enough, a short time later a third bear repeated the activity.

Along with dozens of other crew members at the 2003 Bear DNA Training Session, I was transfixed as I watched the video clip of the bears' behavior. We learned that bears naturally rub up against certain trees, posts, and other objects often leaving some of their hair behind. Some researchers think they do this to mark their home range or as a form of communication with other bears. Others think that bears rub up against these objects just to scratch an itch. Regardless of the reason, these trees, posts, and poles are rubbed repeatedly, often giving them a polished look. During the training session, we learned how to collect bear hair for eventual DNA analysis in the lab.

Of historic proportions, the Northern Divide Grizzly Bear Project was the largest non-invasive research study of bears to date. Led by Kate Kendall of the U.S. Geological Survey, this cooperative effort included federal, state, tribal, and non-profit agencies. Several hundred employees and volunteers were involved in this effort. The total area of the study encompassed over 8 million acres including Glacier National Park, the Bob Marshall Wilderness Complex, Swan Valley, Mission Mountains Wilderness, Rattlesnake Wilderness, South Fork Jocko Primitive Area, areas of the Flathead Indian Reservation, Blackfoot-Clearwater Valley, and portions of the Rocky Mountain Front. This large interconnected area was chosen for the study because it was considered occupied grizzly bear range.

The research study's primary objectives were to get a reliable estimate of the number of grizzly bears in the Northern Continental Divide Ecosystem and to build a genetic library to assess diversity and the degree of relatedness of the bear population.

Northwest Connections, a conservation and education non-profit organization based in the Swan Valley, contracted with USGS to collect bear DNA data in a vast area that included the Swan Valley, Mission Mountains, Swan Range, part of the Flathead Indian Reservation, and a portion of the Bob Marshall Wilderness Complex and adjacent lands.

In July 2003, one of the Northwest Connections teams including co-workers Randy Leventhal, Kieran Balazs, and I left on a three-day backpack trip into the Mission Mountains Wilderness to identify, record, and attach barbed wire to the bear rub objects along a designated route.

Randy and Kieran worked as a two-person team in the Swan Valley looking for bear rub objects along the various trails, roads, and power line corridors. When a bear rub object was found, they recorded and marked the location using a GPS unit. If the rub object was far enough away from the trail so as not to interfere with any stock use, they attached barbed wire in a zigzag fashion on the face of the rubbed area. If a bear rubbed up against the wire, some of the hair would be snagged in the barbs and would be collected for DNA analysis.

My job was to rotate among the crews checking for quality control as well as gathering information for the massive 2004 undertaking that would follow next season. All the field crew members needed to use the same protocols and procedures to ensure the accuracy needed in this type of research. This year was prep work for the next summer when we would collect the bear hair from the bear rub objects as well as from passive hair snag stations scattered throughout the study area.

Bear rub post.
—Luke Lamar photo

Tufts of bear hair left on barbed wire on a bear rub tree.

Our route took us through some of the most spectacular and rugged backcountry of the Mission Mountains Wilderness. Most of the route followed a series of trails to form a large arcing loop. A few miles on each end of the loop were trails that were maintained, but the majority of the route was on trails that in some cases had not been maintained for the past forty years or so.

We started our trip at the Hemlock Trailhead near Red Butte Creek on the eastern side of Mission Mountains Wilderness. The early morning was warm and pleasant, but the weather forecast called for continuing hot temperatures with highs in the 90s, possibly low 100s. Not only had the summer been very dry with little moisture in the previous several months, but the area had also experienced several years of drought. A few weeks earlier, several thunderstorms moved through Montana torching several forest fires. Many of those lightning starts were burning in the nearby Bob Marshall Wilderness where some of the other field crews were working.

We hiked the first mile or so up the trail mostly through an open, exposed area that had been logged several years earlier. We found our first bear rub objects upon entering the forest at the wilderness boundary. Three trees, complete with bear hair, showed some moderate rub history where some of the bark had been rubbed off the tree trunk. The trees were far enough away from the trail that we could attach three pieces of 14-inch barbed wire in a zigzag fashion along the rubbed section of the trees. We gathered and recorded the needed data in our field books before shouldering our backpacks to continue up the trail.

It felt good to be inside the designated wilderness with its shaded forest cover offering some relief from the heat. We moved steadily along the trail inspecting each tree for bear rub sign.

Approximately two miles into our hike we crossed Frenchy Creek. This stream was named after an early day trapper and miner, Frenchy Taylor who once lived in the Swan Valley. He was purported to have a mine in the area and claimed that he had found gold. His disappearance shortly after making that claim in 1914 led some of the local residents to wonder if he had met with foul play or had simply moved on.

A short distance past Frenchy Creek I pointed out several mountain hemlock trees that grew along the trail. The mountain hemlock tree derives its name from the smell of its crushed needles, which is similar to that of the hemlock plant. Its needles are arranged in a spiral or similar to a bottlebrush. A notable characteristic of this tree is its droopy-topped profile. Although this species of tree is not exactly rare in this part of the country, it is not common either.

The temperature was hot by the time we hiked the three-and-a-half miles to Hemlock Lake. Near the lake was an old trapper's cabin that was built in 1940 by sixteen-year-old Warner Lundberg and his homesteader grandfather Fred Roll. Unfortunately, this cabin would burn to the ground in the Crazy Horse forest fire less than a month later.

It felt good to splash the cool lake water on our heads before we took a quick lunch break at the scenic boulder-strewn outlet of the lake. From Hemlock Lake we left the relative ease of the maintained trail system with its unhindered and

Hemlock Lake trapper cabin. —USVHS Archives

easily traveled trail and exchanged it for the wilder, less traveled trails. We traversed around the lake, stopping at the inlet to fill up our water bottles before continuing up the brushy overgrown trail to Conko Lake.

A small lake with floating yellow pond lilies, Conko Lake was named for Eneas Conko, a Mission Valley resident of Pend d' Oreille and Iroquois descent. The path around the lake was overgrown with brush and numerous downed trees that blocked and hid the trail. It was difficult to find the trail in places as we left the lake and headed toward Spider Lake. I enjoyed this more remote and wild leg of our journey. I relished exploring the new country that I had only seen from afar.

A half-mile past Conko Lake we began a steep climb to a mountain pass that separated the Hemlock Creek drainage from the Elk Creek drainage. Bud Cheff Sr., a Mission Valley resident and former outfitter who had been coming into this area since the 1930s, referred to this pass as Hemlock Pass. We gained a thousand feet in elevation in the next half mile leading to the pass. The old trail traversed an open beargrass and rocky slope. The beargrass was in full bloom with large, white, showy flowers accenting the rich green ground cover and the browns and tans of the scattered boulders and rocky outcrops.

As we slowly worked our way up to the gap in the rocky band of cliffs that formed the headwall of the cirque basin, the afternoon heat was wearing on us. Once on top, we dropped our packs to rest and quench our thirst. The views were inspirational from where we stood. The rugged ridgelines curved outward from the cirque headwall in an easterly direction, forming a long horseshoe-shaped rim of rugged rock and steep forest that enclosed the Hemlock drainage. Beyond the broad valley lay the steep, formidable Swan Range. In the opposite direction from where we stood, roughly one mile to the west was Weisner Peak at 8367 feet. The late afternoon light with its accompanying play of shadows enhanced the beauty of the rugged landscape. We stood for some time soaking up the scenery that surrounded us.

After a long rest break, we hiked the last mile of the day dropping 700 feet in elevation down to Spider Lake. At 6778 feet, Spider Lake, a beautiful sub-alpine lake, was very picturesque in the late afternoon light. The shallow emerald-colored water near the shoreline quickly gave way to darker, blue-hued water of the deeper areas. The trout were rising as we searched for a campsite flat enough to pitch our tents.

I took a quick dip in the cold, clear lake water to wash off the trail grime. I was amazed that the water could be so cold in such a prolonged heatwave. It shocked my system, practically taking my breath away. As goosebumps formed on my skin, I staggered out of the water into the fading, warm sunshine. Several minutes after drying off, my breathing was back to normal, and I felt refreshed and invigorated.

Spider Lake.

After we shared the evening meal, I went for a short hike exploring the area around the lake. As I worked my way to the northwest side of the lake, I spotted a couple of mule deer feeding along the edge of a small meadow. From a tall rocky vantage point overlooking the lake, I could see directly down into the clear water observing several fish cruising around. Occasionally one of the trout would dash to the surface to feed on an insect.

The evening light cast a golden glow on the rocky limestone cliffs above the lake as I explored the route we would take in the morning. The old trail was faint, sometimes disappearing for short stretches only to reappear farther along the route. High cliff walls bordered the trail with steeply angled scree slopes. Several pikas and a marmot could be heard among the rocks. I found a tuft of mountain goat hair snagged on a low tree branch. I admired the white, showy Sitka valerian flowers mingled with yellow arnica, red Indian paintbrush, and purple explorer gentian. This was an incredible country with its carpet of colors splashed across the rugged terrain. I lingered until dusk before returning to camp.

Shortly after dawn the next morning, Spider Lake was tranquil with a slight mist hanging off its northern shore. Occasional outward radiating rings rippled as feeding trout broke the glassy surface of the lake. The coolness of the early morning was invigorating. As we ate breakfast, we studied the map. Overall, we would gain approximately 2000 feet of elevation and then descend 2000 feet as we crossed three mountain passes on our route to Mollman Lakes.

We hiked our way up and down the steeply rolling terrain past several small pothole lakes. I enjoyed this rugged wild country noting little sign of human use.

When the trail fizzled out, we had to scout around to pick it up again. We saw a couple of cow elk in a small meadow near the trail. Climbing up to what Bud Cheff Sr. termed Goat Foot Pass, we crossed over the Mission Divide into the Flathead Indian Reservation. Cheff claimed his horses needed goat's feet to clamor up and over this rugged pass.

As we crossed over into the Mission Mountains Tribal Wilderness, we were rewarded with outstanding views to the south of the imposing McDonald Peak and surrounding jagged country. McDonald Peak is the tallest mountain in the Mission Range at 9820 feet. Its sheer size and girth dominate the area. The peak was named after Angus McDonald, an early-day fur trader and settler in the Mission Valley. From 1846 – 47 he helped construct and establish a trading post at Fort Connah approximately six miles north of St. Ignatius. The first documented successful climb of McDonald Peak was in 1894 when Father Louis Taleman, a Jesuit priest at the Mission, and two students reached the summit. They built a cross from stones to *crown the Mission Range*.

To the northwest, we could see the impressive Mount Calowahcan which rises to 9061 feet. Earlier maps show this peak as Mount Harding. It was given that name in October of 1923 when a local climbing party led by Stanley Scearce and Mose Delaware summited the mountain and placed a flag on the top. In 1995, tribal elder Lucille Otter successfully led the campaign to change the name back to Mount Calowahcan, its former Salish name.

We soon realized that the trail location printed on the map did not match the true location of the trail. The actual trail led down and away from our intended route. We spent some time scouting around for the old trail but never found anything other than faint game trails. Finally, we decided to angle roughly northward to intercept the trail going over Elk Pass. We occasionally found bits and pieces of old trails to follow.

After a mile or so we intersected the trail from Summit Lake to Elk Pass. We continued up a short distance to the pass. We noticed more bear sign including scat piles along the trail and bear hair found on the boundary signpost. We recorded the required data and location, set the post with barbwire, and studied the country around us. We enjoyed the incredible panoramic views of rugged mountains and subalpine lakes as we gazed down into the Elk Lake area and beyond. We left the tribal side and crossed back into the Mission Mountains Wilderness.

At 6525 feet, Elk Lake is a good-sized lake, surrounded by a huge cirque headwall arcing around the northwest half of the lake. A few small remnant snow patches still hung in the more shaded recesses of the towering cliffs. Judging from the number of beat-up hitch areas and patches of old horse manure, the area appeared to get a fair amount of fall hunting and camping use from the tribal side. There were several well-used camping areas located in the vicinity of the

Elk Lake

lake's outlet. We stopped briefly at Elk Lake for a water break before continuing on our next leg of the journey.

Just north of Elk Lake was a smaller lake named Spook Lake. Bud Cheff Sr. was credited with naming this lake over 60 years ago when one of his hunting guides related a strange story to him. Ed Sias and Leo David were camping at this small lake when in the gathering dark of the evening a voice came across the water from the foot of the cliffs on the far side. The voice said, "Hey Ed! Hey Ed! Hey Ed!" A ball of fire came out of the cliff, rolling across the lake toward them. It spooked the two hunting guides so much, they immediately packed up camp and left.

After hiking past Spook Lake, we worked our way up toward Shangri-La Pass. We came across an area just below the pass decorated with a profusion of purple fireweed in full bloom. With the stunning backdrop of mountains, we decided to stop for a photo. That decision was nearly disastrous when Kieran stepped off the trail to the upside to take the photo. Kieran had a bundle of the barbwire strands wrapped in a protective sheath tied to his backpack. A few ends of the wire protruded out of the bundle. As Randy walked by Kieran, one of the wires struck her.

At first, I thought that she had taken a direct hit to her eye. As I rushed over to her aid, I realized we were in a tough spot for a rescue even if we could reach anyone with our radio. Luckily, the wire hit just below her eye. Nevertheless, the wound was swollen and painful to her. We administered first aid and took a long break until she felt better before continuing along the trail.

I could see why this saddle was named Shangri-La Pass. Rugged, wild mountain terrain rose stunningly. Shangri-La Peak was directly east of us. The fortress-like cliff walls to the west were so impressive that Kieran said "Castle Guard" would be an appropriate name as these walls of rock stood guard over the east entrance to Mollman Lakes. To the south and north lay ridge upon ridge of wild country. The beauty of this country excited my spirit while at the same time garnering peace and serenity.

Getting to Mollman Lakes from Shangri-La Pass proved to be tough in places as the old trail was brushy and overgrown. We were glad when we eventually intersected the trail that connects the Elk Creek Trailhead to Mollman Lakes. Even though the majority of the trail had not been maintained for at least a decade possibly two, it was still reasonably easy to travel. From the intersection, we climbed the last mile to our campsite along the eastern edge of the first large lake that makes up the Mollman Lakes.

These lakes are named after Charlie and Louie Mollman, who lived most of their lives along the creek in Mission Valley that now bears their name. According to Bud Cheff Sr. these two men, along with the help from other tribal members, built this trail as well as several other trails in the early years of the reservation as a means of both escape and attack if war erupted between the Indians and the whites.

Mollman Lakes

After a long day on the trail, it felt good to take off my backpack at our scenic campsite with its open vistas of steep, rugged mountain country. Again, I jumped into the lake to wash off the trail grime. Refreshed, we sat around our small camp stove and cooked supper. I brought out my binoculars to scan the cliffs for mountain goats but could not locate any that evening. A couple of mule deer fed close to our campsite. They did not seem to mind our nearby presence. We enjoyed a beautiful alpenglow with shades of yellow, orange, and red upon the high cliffs above us as the sun set to the west.

Leaving the scenic eastern gateway of the Mollman Lakes in the morning, we dropped down into the forested sidehill along the north fork of the Elk Creek drainage. We occasionally glimpsed the mountain scenery, but for the most part, we were surrounded by trees. After several miles, we began to see more bear sign and bear rub objects. Up to that point, I was surprised that we had not seen more bear sign in the more remote parts of our trip.

Although we had noted huckleberries in various places along our route, the amount of berries this season seemed sparse regardless of terrain or remoteness. It seemed to me that the bears were going to have to work hard to get a meal. We later wondered if many of the bears had moved down into the valleys to try to find food, as the human-bear conflicts seemed to be rising. Perhaps the green grass of residential lawns, dog food, and garbage provided the meals instead of the sparse natural foods.

It was another hot day with temperatures in the high nineties. As we broke out into an opening, we could see that off to the east one of the forest fires in the Bob Marshall Wilderness was making quite a run. We saw a huge mushroom cloud building above the forest fire. It had that exploding atom bomb appearance. We

Steve Lamar burning off barbed wire after collecting bear hair.

wondered about some of the other crew members who were working in that area. Did they have to backtrack and leave their work areas? We wondered if our previous work might be for naught as the fire raged that afternoon.

We had already been warned that if the fire season got much worse we would have to shut down the project for the season. The smoke from the forest fire was starting to pour over the Swan Range and settle into the valley below us.

We later learned that a couple of our field crews had indeed been forced to back out of the area that they had been working in. Several trails that had previously been surveyed for bear rub objects had burned, some extensively.

By late evening the visibility was low from the thickening smoke as we worked our way down the last miles to our vehicle. Although I expected to find more than the 17 bear rub objects we recorded along our route, we gathered important information needed for the next field season. As a bonus to the work we accomplished, we shared a rewarding experience in the incredibly wild, rugged Mission Mountains high country.

LAMAR MOUNTAIN
2003

◆

Back when I was 19 years old and very much afraid of heights, I climbed my first mountain as a student on a NOLS Course in the Wind River Range in Wyoming. To help overcome my fear of heights, I set a goal to climb at least 100 peaks during my lifetime. I never did overcome my fear of heights but at the age of 50, with my family at my side, I finally climbed my 100th peak on August 9, 2003.

On the eastern edge of Yellowstone National Park, Lamar Mountain, topping out at 10,585 feet above sea level, was named after one of my ancestors. From 1885 to 1888, Lucius Quintus Cincinnatus Lamar served as the Secretary of the Interior under President Cleveland. Lamar never visited the area but sent Arnold Hague, a friend and geologist with the U.S. Army to survey Yellowstone National Park. Though Lamar had never stepped foot in Yellowstone Park, Hague named several of the Park's features in Lamar's honor including Lamar Mountain and Lamar River.

Our trip to Lamar Mountain began early in the day when we drove from our home in Swan Valley to our campsite in Sunlight Valley, Wyoming, just east of Yellowstone National Park. Luke and I drove the most reliable vehicle among us, Luke's newly purchased Nissan pickup truck while Sharon and Annie followed in our vintage Subaru. Along the route, we were dazzled by the outstanding scenery. It's hard to beat the Rocky Mountain West for outstanding scenery. While reading about the local and natural history along the way, the landscape seemed to come alive in ways that excited my soul and imagination.

We arrived at the campground in the impressive Sunlight Valley after a short stop at the Sunlight Creek Gorge Overlook. Certain areas strike a chord with me and this was one of those places. A stunningly beautiful valley with its broad vistas of green ranch lands and rugged mountains in the background, Sunlight Valley immediately became one of my favorite places. It got its name from fur trappers in the 1940s who thought the area was so remote that the only thing that could get there throughout the year was sunlight.

John Kilgour, Annie's fiancé, and our future son-in-law, soon joined us at the campsite. We set up tents and cooked supper on our camp stove. In the evening, the weather was a bit unsettled with a few drops of rain, but overall, not too bad.

The next morning dawned gray and threatening. My heart was heavy as I had been so excited about this adventure and now the weather was threatening to thwart our plans. After a quick breakfast, we loaded the vehicles and headed to the trailhead located several miles up the drainage. Just getting to the trailhead would be a challenge. The jeep road was narrow and rough, with several stream crossings of Sunlight Creek on the way. A four-wheel-drive, high-clearance vehicle was definitely needed. Luke was already having misgivings about driving his truck over the rough terrain.

When we came to the first creek crossing, we parked the Subaru alongside the road. Sharon climbed in the cab, while Annie and John rode in the bed of the pickup.

When we reached the Sunlight Creek crossing, we discussed the best strategy for driving the rock-strewn bed of the creek. The water was deeper and moving faster than we anticipated.

As Luke put the truck in low gear, we shouted to Annie and John, "Hold on!" The water was up to the axle when we got to the middle of the stream. I had visions of the truck floating down Sunlight Creek. Sharon and I instantly became backseat drivers, giving Luke advice.

In unison, Sharon yelped, "Faster, faster," while I urged, "Slow down!" Cool-head Luke calmly drove at a steady speed through the swirling water. We all breathed a sigh of relief as the tires gripped solid ground.

When we arrived at the second creek crossing, we all readily agreed to park the truck and walk the extra mile to the trailhead.

At the trailhead stood the Painter Cabin, a remnant shell of an old log cabin that was slowly melting back into the earth. In 1890, John Painter filed the first mining claim in the Sunlight mining region. An early mining camp, Lee City was founded on Sunlight Creek about two miles upstream of its confluence with Sulphur Creek. Eventually, over a thousand claims were filed there.

My spirits were down as it began to rain. We decided to start hiking up the trail anyway and hoped the weather would improve. We began our hike in the Shoshone National Forest in a mature lodgepole pine forest. A short while later we crossed into the North Absaroka Wilderness and the forest became more open. Luckily, after an hour of hiking, the weather improved with clearing skies.

Approximately 3.5 miles up the trail we veered off and hiked cross-country for 1.5 miles toward Lamar Mountain. The scenery was outstanding as we worked our way up a sparsely forested ridge. We stopped often to take photos and gaze at the grandeur before us.

We continued on our way and crossed a beautiful basin below Lamar Mountain. The area contained pockets of healthy whitebark and limber pine trees loaded with cones, while the open meadows had a colorful array of wildflowers still in bloom. We saw several Clark's nutcrackers as well as some grizzly bear and elk sign.

The weather was starting to deteriorate, as distant thunderstorm clouds moved in from the southwest. We still had blue skies above us so we kept climbing toward the summit.

Upon cresting the pass along the eastern ridge leading to the summit, we stood on the boundary of Yellowstone National Park. We looked down into the headwaters of the Lamar River and saw the upper Lamar River patrol cabin where park employees stayed when working in this area.

The approaching thunderstorm clouds were looking more serious and we could hear distant rumblings. Still, we thought we might be able to get to the summit before the storm hit. We continued onward but were run off the ridge as the storm moved in quickly.

Annie, Luke, Sharon, and Steve Lamar with Lamar Mountain in the background.

Steve Lamar with Lamar Mountain in the background.

Luke, who was well ahead of the rest of us, made a mad dash to the top, reaching the summit just as the lightning started popping around the area. We all motioned to him to get off the mountaintop and join us down below.

All of us, including Luke, hurriedly baled off the ridge to a relatively safe area while the storm spent its fury. At this point, I thought we wouldn't make it to the top as a family. I was feeling pretty dejected as I wanted so badly for this peak climb to be successful. I was not sure we would get this opportunity again when all of us could participate.

My prayers were answered when the storm passed and another hole of blue sky opened up around us. We hurriedly set out again for the top. This time we were blessed and made it to the top. It was one of the most poignant times of my life. I had climbed my 100th peak with my family at my side. It was pure joy for me!

We celebrated with photos of the beautiful views in all directions as well as family photos. Our time on top was limited as the next round of thunderstorms bore down on us. We hustled off the summit, down the eastern ridge, and back into the pristine basin to the southeast. We continued to drop in elevation as we worked our way back to the trail and ultimately to our vehicles. It was an outstanding day that I will forever hold dear in my heart as one of my favorite experiences.

Sharon, Steve, Luke, and Annie Lamar on the summit of Lamar Mountain.

View from the summit of Lamar Mountain.

Sharon, John, and Annie saw a large grizzly bear later that day while driving back to camp. Luke and I were in the front vehicle, talking and not paying attention, and we missed seeing it.

Again, we camped at the Sunlight Creek campground, enjoyed a shrimp fondue dinner, and settled in for the evening. A beautiful full moon shone down on us that night.

We witnessed some very beautiful and impressive scenery while camping, hiking, and climbing in the Sunlight Basin of Wyoming. The trip was an incredibly rich time in my life. I felt fortunate that our family was able to experience the adventure together.

A BEAR FIGHT
2003

◆

In the late fall hunting season of 2003, I worked as a hunting guide for Buck Creek Guide Service. One day, I guided a client near South Barber Creek in Swan Valley. My client, a young man from New Jersey, was hoping for a nice-sized whitetail buck. We planned a long circuitous route that would take us through various habitats and terrain in our quest to find a big buck.

Because the fall rut was in full swing, it was a lively day with the deer on the move. We saw deer, off and on all day but my client never saw the size of the buck that he was hoping for.

As evening approached, with an hour and a half of legal light left in the day, we set up at the edge of an opening. After getting situated, I rattled a couple of deer antlers together and gave a few grunt calls from my grunt tube to lure in a buck deer. We waited in anticipation, but nothing materialized. After a busy day of sighting active deer, we were disappointed that the evening seemed so quiet.

Eventually, daylight faded, and darkness came. No deer would be harvested that day. We shrugged and stood up as my client unloaded his rifle. We packed up our gear and started back to the truck. We had taken but a dozen steps when all hell broke loose not more than 50 yards behind the spot where we had been sitting. It sounded like a couple of bears fighting!

In the dense alder brush, we could hear loud roaring, wrestling, and fighting with the sounds of tree limbs being broken and snapped off as the big bodies thrashed about. I had never experienced anything like this before. I pulled out my bear spray as my client started reloading his rifle. As we slowly backed away, we could hear what sounded like one bear being pinned to the ground by the other bear. It was making a submissive moan in defeat. We continued to back out of the area.

Later at the vehicle, we excitedly talked about the experience. My client had not harvested his deer that day but he certainly had an experience that he would never forget. Neither would I.

The next day, Tom Parker, the owner and outfitter of Buck Creek Guide Service, went back to check out the scene. In the shallow snowpack with the bear tracks all around, he could read the story of the events that had taken place the night before. Four bears had been within 50 yards of where we had set up for the evening hunt. After examining the tracks in the snow, Tom said it had been a sow grizzly and her 3 two-year-old cubs. Tom speculated that one of the cubs must have gotten out of line, and the mother bear had cuffed it around.

We later joked that the bears had gotten into a fight over which bear would get to eat us. One wanted the young guy, but the mother told him no, that he had to eat the old skinny guy.

It was a bit humbling to realize that we were within 50 yards of four grizzlies for over one and a half hours, not knowing the bears were so close until the fight broke out.

Grizzlies in Yellowstone National Park.

ALL MILES ARE NOT CREATED EQUAL
2006

◆

The aroma of ripe huckleberries filled the air as we hiked up the trail. It felt good to be in the mountains breathing the invigorating early-morning cool air.

Weeks of planning, preparation, and dreaming had morphed into reality when the alarm clock rang at 3:45 am that fine July morning. Excitedly, I splashed the sleep from my eyes, threw my loaded but light backpack into the truck, and drove two and half hours to meet my friend Rod Haynes at St. Mary's Lake in the Mission Valley. I followed him as he drove his truck to the trailhead of our final destination. We then drove my truck to the North Fork Jocko Trailhead where, after a few quick adjustments to our gear, we hit the trail.

As we walked across the footbridge spanning the North Fork of the Jocko River, we were amazed by the beauty around us. The stream was flowing briskly over the rock shelves and boulders, creating small waterfalls and cascades interspersed with deep emerald-colored pools of water.

As we ascended the trail, we noticed the terrain in the thick forest seemed to be one huge huckleberry patch with lots of purple ripe berries. We carried on an upbeat conversation as we hiked, stopping several times to eat handfuls of huckleberries. Our pace was slow, pleasant, and enjoyable.

Soon we reached Lost Sheep Lake where several people were camped. We took a short rest break to eat a snack before donning our packs and heading along a faint trail around the lake. We would soon leave the trail and head off in a westerly direction exploring seldom-visited terrain.

The landscape took on a wilder character as we left the lake. We quickly confirmed what we already knew, that the geology of the Mission Mountains is a series of tilted slab rock formations hindering easy travel. It reminded me of the blade of a handsaw that has been turned upside down, with each tooth gently sloping upwards to the apex and a steep undercut angle going down the other side.

After going up the gentle slab rock, we were often blocked from easily going down the other side. We had to work our way along the ridge until we found a break or opening that would allow us to climb down. This process of travel was repeated time after time along our route. In the distance, we could see our destination, but the circuitous, zigzag route soon made us believers in the phrase, *All miles are not created equal,* and soon became our motto on this trip.

After a series of angled slab rock formations, we crossed a prominent ridge to a rugged high valley that held a couple of small pothole lakes. The temperature had warmed by midday and Rod could not resist jumping in for a quick dip to cool off while I sat on the bank and soaked my feet. It was a refreshing rest break.

Afterward, we hiked to a pass along the Mission Divide that separates North Jocko Peak to the east from Vista Pinnacle to the west. From there we looked down into the Gray Wolf Lake area. What a grand view! The scenery was getting better all the time. A sea of rugged terrain and high mountains could be seen to the north and the east with the Swan Range being somewhat obscured by a smoky haze from nearby forest fires.

North Jocko Peak, at approximately 7760 feet, was named after Jacques (Jocko) Raphael Finlay, an assistant of David Thompson, Northwest Company explorer and fur trader. Jocko Finlay stayed in the area after Thompson left in 1812. The Montana Mountaineers aptly named Vista Pinnacle, at 8106 feet, in 1932 or possibly 1933.

After a short break, we worked our way in a southwesterly direction to another pass with a steep descent to the upper basin of the Deep Creek drainage. Things were about to get exciting fast.

The steep cliffs looked terrifying with no easy way down this sharply serrated ridgeline. After scouting around, Rod found a route that he thought might work. He suggested we lower our packs and then ourselves with a 9mm climbing rope that Rod brought along on the trip.

I've always had a fear of heights and this route was about to test me. My heart racing, my palms sweaty, my stomach queasy, I fought to concentrate on my immediate surroundings and the task at hand. I tried not to look far below.

Rod, cool as a glacial lake, led the way, picking the best route from ledge to ledge. I lowered our packs to him then lowered myself. We repeated the process several times, hoping each time that the route would not end abruptly with us being cliffed out.

I had often heard the phrase from wartime veterans, "There are no atheists in the foxholes." Well, I can tell you there were none on the steep, rocky cliffs that day either. Eventually, after several hours, we thankfully reached the scree slope at the bottom of the cliffs.

The high basin of upper Deep Creek was amazingly beautiful. It was enjoyable to walk along its wild, chaotic jumble of boulder fields interspersed with smooth, glaciated slab rock. We headed to the broad pass between Blacktail Peak and Vista Pinnacle where we set up our first campsite along the Mission Divide.

We each put up our small one-person shelters, cooked our meals, and enjoyed the spectacular scenery. Below us in a basin to the northwest was a series of small lakes. Farther below was the large Gray Wolf Lake. It was a stunning scenic view. The small lakes were labeled as Scenic Lakes on a 1933 US Indian Irrigation

Near our first campsite looking down on Gray Wolf Lake.

Service Map but the name did not stick. Instead, the name was shifted about one and a half miles to the southwest to a couple of lakes south of Gray Wolf Peak.

Vista Pinnacle was splendid with its sheer dark rock faces and interspersed chutes. A sliver of a quarter moon hung above the summit of Blacktail Peak. High peaks dotted the rugged landscape. We scanned the area for mountain goats but saw none. An occasional pika could be heard calling from the rocky scree slopes. The day faded and Weather Peak was silhouetted by a beautiful pink and orange sunset.

We woke early to a beautiful red sunrise over the eastern horizon from the smoke of the forest fires. A large red orb slowly rose through the haze before bursting above the smoke layer. A few scattered clouds quickly burned off with the coming of the day. The wind was blowing during the night but calmed down with the warm sunshine of the new day. Even at this elevation in August, there was a slight frost in the pockets of meadow grass around our camp.

An old, beat-up alpine larch tree stood near my tent. It was roughly a foot in diameter, growing on an exposed, windy ridge in thin, rocky soil. Its bark was a bit polished on one side, no doubt from being exposed to the blowing, stinging snow crystals during the long winters in this location, a veteran of many challenging campaigns. I wondered how old it was and marveled that it survived under the harsh conditions at this altitude. Its lime-green foliage radiated brightly in the early morning sunshine.

I admired the rugged landscape with the high towering peaks, the distant alpine lakes, and the white ghosts of long-dead whitebark pine trees, all bathed in the early morning alpenglow. The only sound was the dying wind whispering through the scattered trees. With the warm sunshine on my shoulder and the delicious crisp air to breathe, I soaked up the sensational experience that fine morning. I thanked my lucky stars that I could still negotiate this kind of terrain.

Later, we packed up, hoisted our backpacks, and traversed south, west, and then north around the base of Blacktail Peak hiking along the tilted slab rock, boulder fields, and scattered pockets of green vegetation. Rocks and boulders of numerous sizes were scattered on the slab rock, some as large as small houses. It was a bit of a balancing act teetering our way through the boulder fields and the rough terrain. We reached the pass to the west of Blacktail Peak. From this saddle, we looked directly down into the high basin of small lakes that had once been labeled Scenic Lakes. The blues and greens of the water and vegetation contrasted nicely with the browns and grays of the rocky terrain. From this angle, these lakes seemed on the same plane as the large Gray Wolf Lake far below, an optical illusion of sorts.

After a quick break at the pass, we angled southwest to the ridge to the west. We climbed north to the top of an unnamed peak at approximately 7880 feet. Again, we stopped for photos and gazed around at the awe-inspiring country. The Swan Range to the northeast stood out in sharp relief, as the smoky haze from the forest

Gray Wolf Lake in the background.

fires had cleared out. We angled down to a broad high bench between a sheer cliff that dropped off dramatically to the west and the rocky slopes of Weather Peak to the east. This section of the rocky shelf was interspersed with small meadows of vivid green vegetation with scattered wildflowers. Mountain goat hair hung in the branches along the faint game trails. We saw a blue grouse and heard a marmot and several pikas as we hiked along.

We eventually came to another pass just northwest of Weather Peak. From here we explored a safe passage down to the west into the Falls Creek drainage and the Scenic Lakes southeast of Grey Wolf Peak. The cliff band that we needed to descend was tall, steep, and formidable. It looked impossible to me as we poked along the cliff edge looking for a suitable route. Rod took the lead and explored several possible routes finally deciding on one that he thought might be safe. We saw four mountain goats while exploring.

While Rod was route-finding, I found the site of an old grizzly bear den located in an outcropping of rock and earth that formed a small opening. It led into a larger room in the small cave-like den. There were several inches of old, dried beargrass clippings matted down inside the den. It looked as though the den had been vacant for quite some time.

The trip down the steep cliff band was frightening. The unwieldiness of my backpack added to my apprehension, as my balance was less than stable. Rod seemed to easily negotiate the steep chutes. Once again, he brought out his climbing rope and draped the middle point around a tree, tossing the two ends down below. We now had a secure rope to hold onto as we slowly worked from one point of security to the next.

Sometimes, we had to lower our packs and then ourselves down a steep chute. It wasn't exactly rappelling, but close. Though my palms were sweaty, my heart rate up, and my breathing rapid, I forced myself to concentrate as we descended one section of the chute after another. It seemed like we spent several hours slowly down-climbing, never knowing if we would be stopped and truly cliffed out. Fortune smiled on us as the route Rod had chosen eventually popped out onto a steep boulder field.

Again, I said a little prayer of thanks as I unsteadily worked my way down to tamer terrain. As we hiked toward Scenic Lakes, we kept looking back at the route that we took. It looked impossible! Not only that, but it also appeared to be one of the few places to successfully descend.

As we were walking along the stream that flowed out of Scenic Lakes, we came to a short section where the water flowed down the smooth, tilted slab rock, forming a natural slide. We were tempted to take off our packs and try nature's playground. It looked safe enough, but we continued walking toward the lakes.

Lower Scenic Lake with Gray Wolf Peak in the background.

The wildflowers were plentiful and varied as we approached the lower lake. Vivid red Indian paintbrush, showy white Sitka valerian, bright yellow groundsel, and purple shooting stars created beautiful splashes of color in the foreground of the setting. The blue, crystal clear alpine waters of Scenic Lake formed the middle of the scene. In the background stood majestic Gray Wolf Peak. It loomed as a sentinel with its tall, sheer cliff faces and profile thrust upward like a sharp jagged tooth. Patches of snow lay in the shaded fissures and chutes of the mountain. We stood spellbound as we gazed at the incredible beauty of this area. Scenic Lakes were aptly named.

After setting up camp, we jumped in the lake to wash off some of the trail grime. The water was cold but refreshing. As we sat around camp resting, we marveled at the beauty of this area. It was rugged and wild, and we were grateful for the experience.

Later, we took an evening walk and headed toward the low ridge to the west and gazed into the next drainage that harbored Upper and Lower Riddell Lakes. The lakes were named in honor of Professor Riddell from the University of Montana.

As we sat on the ridge, the evening light cast yellow rays across the landscape. Below, we could see an evening hatch was in progress as the fish fed on the insects. The feeding frenzy produced a sight that looked as if rain was striking the surface of the water. Unfortunately, we left our fishing gear at home so that we could travel light.

With our binoculars, we glassed the surrounding terrain for wildlife, hoping to see a grizzly bear. None were seen, but we spotted a couple of mountain goats, marmots, and pikas. With a fresh, slight breeze blowing against our faces, we enjoyed our evening on the ridge.

We woke on the third morning to another light frost. Surrounded by the high-walled cirque at the head of this drainage, sunshine did not reach this beautiful spot in the early morning. As we ate our breakfast, we gazed at the cliff band to the northeast and discussed possible routes that would lead us to the pass east of Gray Wolf Peak. A long upward-curving rock ledge looked most promising. Donning our backpacks, we headed in that direction. The morning air was again crisp and a joy to breathe. We were in no hurry and often stopped to marvel at the wild country.

Our route wound upward until the rock ledge came to an end. From where we stood, there were several steep chutes leading upward. Again, Rod picked the most likely route. It was steep but not too sketchy. In several spots where things were a bit tight and steep, I lifted the backpacks to Rod. As we popped onto the top of the rock face, we found a small rock cairn that someone had left to mark the way down. Although we breached the rock cliff band, it was still some distance to the pass. The rest of this route was mostly a pleasant stroll through high alpine meadows of wildflowers, patchy snow, and plenty of high mountain scenery.

Upon reaching the pass, we were greeted with phenomenal mountain scenery, high-angled rock, splashes of snow, deep blue skies, and jagged mountains. We were experiencing what few others had ever seen. In the distance, we could see Gray Wolf Lake below us to the east, Sunset Crags, and Sunset Peak to the northeast, and Three Summit Peak to the northwest.

The east route to the top of Gray Wolf Peak looked tough from our vantage point. We decided to drop down into the high basin and skirt the northeast side of Gray Wolf Peak. Unfortunately, we could not find a break in the cliff band to drop into the high basin. As we hiked down the angled slab rock, we edged closer to Gray Wolf Lake. We were repeatedly cliffed out as we explored various routes. Eventually, we found a break in the tilted slab rock. We had to backtrack and regain all the elevation. The temperature was quite warm as we angled our way back toward Gray Wolf Glacier.

Walking along the strewn rubble below the remnants of the glacier was like visiting a patch of newly exposed rocky earth. The landscape had a stark, freshly-

View from the pass east of Gray Wolf Peak, Daughter of the Sun on the left and Sunset Peak on the right.

churned look to it. It had not been too many years ago when much of this terrain was still locked in glacial ice and snow. Because melting has accelerated in recent years, little is left of the Gray Wolf Glacier.

We hiked to the ridge that runs between Grey Wolf Peak and Three Summit Peak. Due to the extreme steepness and exposure, we quickly dispelled any notion of taking a shortcut through the Wind Notch down to No Fish Lake to the west.

Again, we had a breathtaking view of panoramic vistas of the East St. Marys Peak area to the northwest, Pass of the Winds to the north, and Gray Wolf Lake to the east. From this angle, it was easy to see why in 1923 Theodore Shoemaker and the Montana Mountaineers had originally named the lake *Dumbbell Lake*. The outline of the lake looked similar to a set of old-fashioned dumbbells (barbells).

The Montana Mountaineers named Gray Wolf Peak in 1923. Later, Thad Lowary wrote in a Forest Service memorandum, "There is a legend that the peak was named Gray Wolf because the silhouette of a running wolf can be seen from the north side of Gray Wolf Lake." Imagining the now melted-out areas, we tried to discern the shape of a running wolf in the remnant snowfield just below the southeast summit.

We descended from the Wind Notch area to the small alpine lake near Pass of the Winds. Cal Tassinari, the first wilderness ranger in the Mission Mountains Wilderness, referred to this body of water as Three Summit Lake. Earlier, in 1927, Theodore Shoemaker labeled this lake as Summit Lake on his sketch map of this area. Neither name appears on today's maps.

View from the Wind Notch area looking down to Dumbell Lake, renamed Gray Wolf Lake.

Gray Wolf Peak, 2006.

When we reached the Pass of the Winds, we contemplated making camp early but decided to keep exploring. As we moved along, I could only imagine the ferocious winds tearing across this open area during a wintertime storm.

Along the route, we saw a family of three white-tailed ptarmigan. These birds are somewhat rare and a species of concern. We heard them before we saw them. Ptarmigan have the adaptive ability to change colors with the seasons, a defense mechanism to help them elude predators. In the winter, the ptarmigan's feathers turn white to blend with the surrounding snow. At this time of the summer, they were a mottled gray, brown, and white mixture that blended into the rocky landscape in perfect camouflage. Another adaptation that ptarmigan use for coping with their harsh environment is their feathered legs and feet which allows them to better regulate their energy and remain warm during brutally cold weather conditions. In addition to the ptarmigan, we saw four marmots and several pikas.

As we worked our way through a high pass, we stopped to gaze at the stunning view of the Grizzly Lake and Freeman Pass area. Ringing this area were awe-inspiring mountains, snowfields, and small glaciers. We dropped our backpacks and brought out the cameras. As was often the case, our photographs didn't quite capture the immensity and flavor of this wild country. We were surrounded by alpine tundra with low grasses and vegetation that were suited to this exposed, gravelly, windblown terrain. Wildflowers dotted the moister, less exposed areas.

View of the Grizzly Lake Basin and Fissure Glacier, Lowary Peak on the left.

Below us was a varied landscape with stringers of trees, slab rock benches, open meadows, potholes, and a jumble of rocky glacial deposits. In the background, Fissure Glacier ringed Grizzly Lake while Lowary Peak, the Freeman Needles, and Black Buck Peaks formed an amphitheater encasing the scene in front of us. It didn't seem possible, but the wild character of the landscape intensified with each passing hour of this amazing journey.

As we worked our way down and around Freeman Pass, we could barely perceive that we had crossed the Mission Divide. Freeman Pass was named for Dr. Freeman Daughters, a member of the 1923 Montana Mountaineers exploratory trip into this area.

View from Freeman Pass with Gray Wolf Peak in distance.

In the waning hours of daylight, we made our last camp near a small lake west of High Park Peak. The scenery, much like the bulk of this trip, was simply stunning. We soaked up the tranquility while scanning the landscape looking for grizzly bears, mountain goats, and other wildlife. A mule deer walked past. We spotted six mountain goats. Again, no bears were sighted. A muted pink sunset capped off a wonderful day.

On the last day of our trip, we woke early and went for a day hike to Grizzly Lake and Fissure Glacier. It was a clear, cool beautiful morning. The mountains stood sharply against the deep Montana blue sky. Grizzly Lake at nearly 8000 feet was ringed on its west and north sides with snowfields and the remnants of the Fissure Glacier where a large bergshrund crevasse sliced across its top. The still waters of Grizzly Lake reflected the surrounding scenery. Large icebergs floated in its deep blue-green waters. Alpine wildflowers grew in the thin gravelly soils on the exposed rocky benches - cushion phlox, Indian paintbrush, buttercups, glacier lilies, shooting stars, and moss campion.

In 1956, USFS employees Herb Styler, Bob Van Gieson, Thad Lowary, and Dick Peltier were camped at this unnamed lake when they were awakened by a commotion outside their tent. They were surprised to see a grizzly bear swimming around and playing in the lake. They watched as the bear climbed the snowfields of Fissure Glacier and then slid down to the bottom, climbed to the top, and slid down repeatedly. Thad Lowary, who had a large camera with a tripod, tried to get close enough to the bear to take a photograph. The bear turned from playful to aggressive and bluff-charged Lowary. After witnessing the amazing performance, the four men decided that the lake should forever be known as Grizzly Lake. Thad Lowary who worked in the regional office in Missoula saw to it that Grizzly Lake was labeled in the next printing of new maps several years later. Lowary, a strong advocate for the Missions Mountains becoming designated wilderness, died in 1969. In 1970, Lowary Peak was named in his honor.

Grizzly Lake

Aptly named by the Montana Mountaineers in 1923, the Fissure Glacier meltwaters flowed out of this basin down a deep rocky fissure forming Fissure Creek. This stream continued the long cascade down the rocky fissure and eventually flowed into High Park Lake.

After spending a few hours exploring the area, we went back to camp and packed up. Heading in a southerly direction, the terrain became rugged and challenging. A series of sharply angled slab rock benches interspersed with small streams made for a lot of up and down, meandering here and there, as we slowly traveled in this scenic wonderland. The small meadows were filled with wildflowers. Lewis's monkeyflower grew in grand profusion. Previously, I had seen this flower primarily along flowing streams in small stringers and patches, but here it grew as the primary plant from one side of the meadow to the other.

We stood on a high rocky knob looking down at Dry Lake with its emerald green waters contrasting with the dark colors of the surrounding rocky terrain.

As we hiked the rocky terrain, we contoured our way toward the area above No Fish Lake. Getting there was more challenging as the land became more rugged and broken. It was a puzzle locating a passable route. We cliffed out on a few occasions and had to backtrack and explore other options. I was thankful that the weather was excellent. Most of the country that we had traversed these past four days would be extremely challenging in stormy weather.

As we moved through the rough terrain, we began to see more wildlife, sometimes startling them at close range. I doubt whether the wildlife in this area has seen many humans. We had observed eight mountain goats and five mule deer so far that day. Later, we would sight a group of 16 mountain goats on the cliffs above us.

From above No Fish Lake, we headed in a southwesterly direction up the slab rock toward the long south ridge flowing from East St Mary's Peak. From below, accessing this ridge looked difficult. The problem of finding a passable route through the slab rock was a constant challenge. Looking for a route on the topographical map with contour intervals of forty feet was sometimes deceiving as a seemingly straightforward route might, in reality, contain several cliffs of thirty-nine feet or less.

Again, we found ourselves negotiating a route where the exposure and steepness were a bit daunting. We tried not to look down. We climbed systematically, moving carefully so we didn't dislodge loose rock upon each other. Eventually, we topped out above the last remaining rock band and walked up to the broad graveled ridge. Here we took a long, well-deserved rest break.

It felt good to gaze at the astounding beauty. Especially impressive was the sheer west-facing wall of Gray Wolf Peak that dominated the view to the east.

Earlier, while meandering our way from No Fish Lake, we stumbled upon a large rock cairn that was built as a memorial to three sisters who along with their

Rod Haynes standing in a meadow of Lewis's monkeyflowers.

No Fish Lake

uncle had died in an airplane crash. Their airplane had crashed into the sheer walls of Gray Wolf Peak in 1992. The event evoked sadness within me and I found the memorial touching.

We hesitated to leave this spot along the long sweeping ridge, as we knew that the rest of the trip would be anticlimactic. We reluctantly left the heart of the wilderness and hiked the final two miles that dropped approximately 4600 feet in elevation back into the summer heat and civilization. In a lifetime of exploring, living, working, and playing in the outdoors, I rated this trip as one of my most memorable.

West face of Gray Wolf Peak

DECADES OF APRILS
2007

◆

In our nook of Swan Valley, we are lucky that our house is situated near many wet meadows, marshes, and ponds that are part of a larger wetland complex that extends over much of the Swan Valley. This labyrinth of water systems makes the Swan Valley very diverse with a multitude of plant and wildlife species. While living near a variety of habitats, I have observed plenty of wildlife through four decades of Aprils.

As the April temperatures increase, so does the corresponding wildlife activity. When the wet meadows, pothole ponds, and lower-elevation lakes begin to melt, the return of the migratory species gains momentum. As the Canada geese return around our place, the resulting goose music becomes common. Who needs an alarm clock when the Canada geese begin their music at the crack of dawn each morning? Add to the ensemble several sandhill cranes, various ducks, and songbirds, and it gets too noisy to sleep. It makes a good excuse to get up and go for an early morning walk.

On nearby waters, the courtship and mating activities of the various duck species are in full swing in April. The male mallards always seem to outnumber the females around our neighboring wetlands. This causes a lot of fighting and chasing about the area. Several pairs of buffleheads, hooded mergansers, and ring-neck ducks nest on the nearby waters.

Wood ducks occasionally use the nest box that I put up more than twenty years ago. Wood ducks will sometimes engage in a practice called egg dumping when one female enters the nest and lays eggs on top of the resident female's eggs while the resident female is away feeding. I witnessed the results of this practice in the 1990s when I saw a male and female wood duck with a line of 24 small ducklings swimming along behind. The predators wasted little time in noticing the abundance of prey. The number of ducklings decreased with each new sighting. The total was down to six the last time I saw them as a family unit.

While standing on our front porch one day, I watched as two mallards in the wet meadow to the east became very agitated. Their quacking became very loud and vocal. I could not figure out what was bothering them when out of the sky a bald eagle dive-bombed toward them. The mallards easily avoided the attack, quickly flushing and maneuvering away from the eagle.

Thirty years ago, sandhill cranes were rare around our area, but have since increased in numbers to the point where they are now common. They are a watchdog type of bird. They are always alert and give a loud guttural call when there are intrusions in their territory.

During the first ten years that we lived in this location, the American bitterns and great blue herons were a common sight. One day, five great blue herons and two American bitterns were feeding in the wet meadow at dusk. I observed bittern parents with two young ones feeding in the wet meadow. The American bittern has a distinctive primordial call. The bittern throws its head back while making a sound similar to a booming, *glunk-glunk*. It is a large bird that can hide amazingly well in the cattails. They seem to have disappeared for the past ten years with only a rare sighting now and then.

Frequently, northern harriers (marsh hawks) visit the wetlands. Their white rump patch is a common identifying characteristic. Although they usually glide around the openings low to the surface and dive down to nab their prey, I once watched as a northern harrier tried to get into a large nest of sticks perched high on top of an old-growth ponderosa pine tree. A raven was in the nest fighting off the northern harrier. I wondered whose nest it was and which was the actual predator that day. Had the hawk left its nest only to be robbed by the raven or was it a raven nest with the hawk trying to run the raven off? A quick look in a field guide straightened me out, as northern harriers are ground nesters.

Owls are usually present around our area in April. We often see and hear great horned, great gray, northern saw-whet, and northern pygmy owls.

Signs of grizzly bear activity are common in April. We occasionally see prints in the mud or snow, but rarely see the actual animal this time of the year. We usually don't see signs of black bear around our place until May.

As the snows melt exposing the elk sedge on the dryer slopes near the wetlands, the elk move into the area and feed heavily on it. Later, when things have greened up, elk can be seen standing knee-deep in the pothole pond feeding on the emerging vegetation. They put their head underwater to nip at the vegetation, reminding me of moose behavior.

Surprisingly, I have not seen many moose in what appears to be good moose habitat in the area. In the past thirty years, I have seen moose only once or twice a year at best. Last year in mid-summer, a cow moose and a newborn calf walked through our wet meadow.

An unwanted wildlife species that usually starts to become noticeable around our place in April is the mosquito. Although mosquitoes are considered a pest to humans, they are nevertheless important to many birds and fish. In particular, the tree swallows key in on this abundant food source in our area as they dart around the wet meadow at amazing speeds gorging on mosquitoes. As we seem to have more than our share of mosquitoes, I cheer the tree swallows on with words of encouragement.

April would not be April in our area without the return of the common snipe (recently renamed Wilson's snipe). The snipe, during courtship, will fly in a loop-like fashion, then dive, swooping in an exaggerated arc back to close the loop. On the descent, the sound emanating from the wind through its tail feathers sounds like winnowing *huhuhuhuhuhu*. It's a unique sound that I never tire of hearing.

As yet another April comes to a close, the spring renewal of life in Swan Valley is once again upon us. Look, listen, and enjoy.

Great Gray Owl. —Sara Lamar photo

MCDONALD PEAK
2008

◆

It is curious how life sometimes plays out with its twists and turns. Opportunities come and go and seemingly arise again out of the blue. And so it was with me regarding my first ascent of McDonald Peak.

In 1981, a friend and I planned to climb McDonald Peak. We had talked about it for weeks. We were packed up and ready to go when we heard the news that the Confederated Salish & Kootenai Tribe had closed the peak and surrounding area for most of the summer. This area was to be part of the large Grizzly Bear Conservation Zone that would be closed annually from July 15th to October 1st so that bears could take advantage of the seasonal food source that this area offered. The high rocky alpine terrain dominated by McDonald Peak had long been a magnet to certain insects in such great numbers that grizzly bears had annually made the pilgrimage to this area to feed on this important food source.

In many early accounts, people observed the phenomenon of grizzly bears feeding on insects high on the slopes of McDonald Peak. Theodore Shoemaker noticed several grizzlies feeding on ladybird beetles (ladybugs) in 1923 while scaling the peak. In 1932, Jack Romer recorded up to twelve grizzly bears turning over scree rock in a high basin just below the summit of McDonald Peak. He noticed that the bears were feeding on something that was not readily apparent until the bears moved on. When he investigated, he found hundreds of ladybird beetles among the scree rock. That same summer, John Stark, a Swan Valley resident, witnessed essentially the same thing on the rockslide areas of McDonald Peak. More recently, Stacy Courville, CSKT biologist, sighted as many as 13 grizzly bears during the annual flyovers to monitor the feeding activities on McDonald Peak.

In 1952, researcher John Chapman teamed up with both Romer and Stark to determine if the bears were still utilizing the ladybird beetles as a food source. They collected bear scat for analysis and were surprised when the samples were found to consist almost entirely of army cutworm moth remains. No ladybird beetle remains were present in those samples. Finding the army cutworm moths (ACM) in such huge numbers was surprising because these insects originate in the Great Plains and Intermountain West. At that time, it was thought that the ACM (Euxoa auxiliaries) was strictly a plains insect. It was later discovered that these insects migrate in mid-summer to high-elevation areas such as McDonald Peak.

Army cutworm moths have been found to congregate in certain locations in the mountains of Montana and Wyoming. The ACM feeds at night on the nectar of alpine flowers and finds shelter during the heat of the day under the scree rock found on the mountain slopes. The bodies of the moths grow to the size of a jellybean and contain over 70% fat. One study found that in 30 days, a grizzly bear feeding extensively on ACM could consume 47% of its annual energy needs. By late September and early October, the moths migrate back to the plains to lay their eggs.

Because of increased recreational use in the McDonald Peak area during the 1970s and 1980s, grizzly bears abandoned these preferred feeding sites. After learning of this important food source, the Confederated Salish and Kootenai Tribes decided to close the McDonald Peak area to human use to prevent conflict between bears and humans. Keeping the bears in the high country as long as possible would be advantageous to both bears and humans.

Busy with other pursuits, I did not seriously consider climbing McDonald Peak until 27 years later in 2008. My interest in climbing the peak was rekindled as I researched place name information about the various mountains, lakes, and streams in this region of Montana. I kept finding interesting stories and documents about McDonald Peak.

In addition, my son Luke had climbed to the top of the peak several times. He whetted my appetite by showing me his outstanding photographs of that incredible alpine area. Realizing that I was not getting any younger, I decided it was time to give the peak another try. Several days before the annual closure took effect, I packed my gear.

I hoped that a friend could accompany me on this trip, but his work schedule was too busy during this particular time. Rather than cancel the trip, I decided to go alone. Although there is a certain amount of risk when outdoors, I have always felt comfortable being in the forests and mountains by myself. Being careful, deliberate, and focused, I planned to pace myself and not take any unacceptable risks.

As my base camp, I planned to hike to Island Lake or if I was feeling very energetic, I would go farther to Cliff Lake. I was confident that either location would be close enough to attempt the peak climb. After several hours of hiking, I reached a gap in a cliff band and popped out into open sub-alpine terrain high above Island Lake. I was just a short distance from the Post Creek Saddle, a mountain pass along the Mission Divide. A path through this gap led down to Cliff Lake. Although most of this area was still snowbound, I found a dry bench with a flat spot for my tent with a nice view. I decided not to push any further that day.

After setting up my tent, I rested on a rock outcrop in the sunshine. From this vantage point, I looked down at Island Lake far below me. In 1922, while leading a joint USFS and Northern Pacific exploratory trip into this area, Theodore Shoemaker noted the prominent island in the middle of the lake and named this alpine treasure Island Lake.

After resting a bit, I decided to hike up to the pass to have a look at the terrain that I would travel tomorrow. Because of the deep snow at this elevation, I donned

A view from Heart Lake of Post Creek Saddle, the low pass to the right.

my crampons and grabbed my ice axe for the steep walk to the pass. As I crossed Post Creek Saddle, the beauty and wildness of the landscape jolted my senses. Looking down into Grizzly Basin at the head of Post Creek and up at the dominating, majestic McDonald Peak was simply stunning. Silently, I stood in awe and gazed at the scene before me. The terrain both excited me and at the same time sent shivers of anxiety through me.

Was I serious about getting to the top? Maybe I was tackling too much. I fought down the doubts and tried to stay philosophical. I'd give it a good effort tomorrow. If I made it to the top, that would be great. If not, maybe next time. Maybe never.

I have always been somewhat fearful of heights, and don't consider myself much of a mountaineer. Still, I love alpine landscapes and I am a sucker for a good view. Through the years I had managed to climb over a hundred peaks, mostly in northwest Montana. The bond to Swan Valley and the adjacent landscape was in my blood, and I wanted to explore and learn about it as much as possible.

Later back in camp, I rested and enjoyed the evening. The only sounds were the whispering wind and an occasional bird song. The cool breeze felt good on my face and even better to breathe. As the sun dipped to the west, the slanting light worked its magic on the landscape and the beauty of the high alpine country intensified. To the south in a deep blue sky, a silvery quarter moon hung behind Lindy Peak.

I was awake by 4 am, refreshed, and ready to go. After a quick breakfast, I hung my extra food and utensils from a rope high from a tree limb out of reach from any wandering bears or other wildlife. I grabbed my pack and headed toward McDonald Peak.

McDonald Peak, at 9820 feet, is the tallest mountain in the Mission Mountains. This mountain was named for Angus McDonald, a fur trader for the Hudson's Bay Company, who established a trading post north of St. Ignatius at Fort Connah in 1846 - 1847. The first documented successful climb to the summit was made by Jesuit priest Father Louis Taleman and two of his students in 1894.

As the sunlight broke over the eastern sky, the view of the peak was spectacular with its early morning pinkish-orange alpenglow radiating from the ample snow that still draped most of the mountain. Bracketed by a clear, deep blue sky, the scene was sensational.

While I worked my way down the steep trail to Cliff Lake, I was glad that I had my crampons and ice axe. Because the snow at this early hour was hard as a rock, any travel would have been very slow and treacherous without this gear.

Cliff Lake was still half frozen and the landscape was deep in the past winter's snow. Only an occasional patch of bare ground hinted that it was indeed summer. Pine marten tracks were visible in the snow near the outlet of the lake.

Cliff Lake with McDonald Peak in the background.

Because of the tall cliffs jutting out into Cliff Lake along its south side, it appeared that I would need to wade across Post Creek somewhere below the lake's outlet and hike around the north and west sides of Cliff Lake to access the route I wanted to take. The stream was moving fast and looked deep. I explored downstream to Disappointment Lake but could find no safe way to cross the creek. If I could not get on the other side of the stream, there would be no attempt to climb the peak. Dejected, I walked back to Cliff Lake and sat down to mull over my options.

I looked at my map and studied the terrain. From where I sat, the only option that looked remotely feasible would involve climbing up a steep snowfield to the south of the cliffs along the southern side of the lake. This route might skirt the cliff section. I decided to give it a try. Luckily, fortune smiled on me that morning as the route proved easier than it looked. Once down on the other side of the cliffs, I saw a massive snow bridge that covered the inlet stream making for easy access to the other side.

After another half-mile of hiking over mostly hard-packed snow, I stood below the incredible 600-foot waterfall that flowed down the cliffs from Lake of the Clouds. It was an amazing sight. The roar of the falling water splashing against

Waterfall pouring out of Lake of the Clouds into Grizzly Basin.

the cliffs and rocks below bombarded my senses. The mist from the churned-up water floated through the air for quite some distance and sprayed my face. I stood in awe and enjoyed the beautiful spectacle before me.

Another half mile brought me to Icefloe Lake. The Montana Mountaineers, led by Theodore Shoemaker, named Icefloe Lake on the exploratory trip into this area in 1923. The lake was named for the floating ice that came from the remnants of an old glacier that had calved ice chunks into the lake.

Icefloe Lake was mostly frozen over with some ice floating in its open waters. This area was a mix of snow and open ground with a scattering of wildflowers. Pasque flowers, buttercups, and moss campion dotted the patches of thin soil in the open rocky terrain.

Ice Floe Lake

I continued to work my way up toward the Ashley Creek Pass. As I gained elevation I left behind the last few trees and entered a world of rock and snow. Fresh marmot tracks led from a rocky bench across the snow to a pile of boulders. I kept alert for grizzly bear sign but saw none. I was enjoying the wild, rugged, beautiful landscape as I moved along.

As I neared the pass and curved northward, I was startled out of my reverie to see nine climbers coming from the Mission Valley and over the ridge ahead of me. After spending the past two days alone, I suddenly felt like I was in Grand Central Station with people everywhere. Things did not seem so wild and remote anymore. I stood and watched them traverse a steep section of snow to gain access to a rocky south face of McDonald Peak. Once they gained the face, they spread out and climbed to the summit. A lot of rock was dislodged in that phase of their

View from near the summit of McDonald Peak looking south toward Glacier Peaks in the center and Daughter-of-the-Sun Mountain on the left.

Glacier Peak on the right with Daughter-of-the-Sun Mountain on the left.

climb and I lingered back on the snowfield to stay out of harm's way. Fortunately, they moved through the rocky section quickly and did not stay long on the summit.

Once I felt it safe to move on, I continued to the top. After the rocky section, I hit snow again for the final push to the summit. I topped out on the broad summit ridge. Because this summit ridge had several protruding snow cornices overhanging the precipitous north face, I was careful not to get too close to the edge as I walked the final distance. I had finally made it to the top of McDonald Peak!

From the incredible view from the summit, I saw a jagged mountain landscape dominating the immediate view and a mix of forest, mountains, lakes, and flat agricultural lands down in the Mission Valley. The sizable McDonald Glacier filled the north basin below the summit. To the northwest lay McDonald Lake at an elevation of 6224 feet. To the west was West McDonald Peak. Sonielem Ridge stood slightly above the jumble of mountainous landscape to the south. I enjoyed the view of the southeast with the impressive Glacier Peaks jutting up like sharp teeth into the deep blue sky.

Far off to the northeast stood Holland Peak, the tallest peak in the Swan Range. My son and a friend were attempting to climb to its summit that very day. I looked through my binoculars to see if I could spot them but saw nothing. I waved anyway.

With a slow methodical pace, it had taken me seven hours to climb the peak. After a short time on the summit, I headed down and back to camp. It was a beautiful evening as I worked my way back. The evening light again worked its magic as it made the beautiful scene even more supreme. Although tired, the return trip to camp was enjoyable, capping an unforgettable day in the mountains.

FIVE BEARS TIMES TWO
2009

Within the past few years, I have been fortunate to see five bears together on two different occasions. The first sighting in the spring of 2008 involved five grizzly bears in the large meadow east of our house here in Swan Valley. I was outside loading firewood in my truck when I heard a loud commotion coming from the forested island in the large wet meadow east of our house. I heard a lot of crashing about with a rapid huffing sound that was unfamiliar to me. We had several elk hanging around in the vicinity that spring, but the sounds coming from the island did not sound like an elk.

I rushed to the house to ask my son Luke to come outside and identify the sounds I was hearing. He grabbed his binoculars, scanned the island, and blurted, "They're grizzlies! And they're heading to the meadow."

Just then, a female grizzly bear and two of her two-year-old cubs ran out into the opening. The mother grizzly stopped, spun around, and stood up on her hind legs peering back at the island. In a matter of seconds, the family of bears was quickly followed by another large bear that was being chased by a huge male grizzly bear. Five bears were now in front of us about 200 yards away. "Wow, this is unbelievable!" I said.

In all my years in the mountains I had never seen so many bears together and now, standing next to my house, were five grizzlies together! Realizing this was a once-in-a-lifetime event, I tapped Luke's shoulder and whispered, "Get the camera, get the camera!"

He screeched back, "No, I don't want to miss this"!

Again, I urged him to get his camera. Finally, he ran into the house and grabbed the camera. Just then, all the bears returned to the island, and fighting broke out. The loud snapping of branches, thrashing about, bawling, growling, and general mayhem followed.

Luke followed some of this action with his binoculars. He whispered, "Here they come again!"

Once more, the mother grizzly and her two cubs ran into the meadow quickly followed by the adult bear being chased by the huge male grizzly. The mother grizzly kept between her cubs and the adult bears to protect them.

Luke excitedly snapped off several photographs while the bears ran around in the meadow before finally exiting to the south. I looked at Luke and excitedly announced, "We've just experienced a once-in-a-lifetime event!"

Five Grizzly Bears, 2008

We stood around gazing at the meadow to see if the spectacle was truly over. After a few minutes, the huge male grizzly bear came back into the meadow and loped around the far edge of the meadow disappearing behind the island. We soaked up the moment. What an experience! I chalked it up as something I would probably never see again, one of life's phenomenal moments.

———•———

During the following summer of 2009, I was working along the foothills of the Swan Range conducting bear DNA hair collections for the Northern Divide Grizzly Bear Project. I was kneeling at one of the natural bear rub sites collecting bear hair from some barbed wire that I had attached to the tree several weeks earlier when I heard something in the thick brush a couple of hundred feet away. I stood up and moved a few feet down the trail to get a better look. Through the brush, I could see the coal-black back of a black bear. It was angling away from me. I thought, "Cool, a black bear." I watched as it disappeared and reappeared a few times in the thick brush.

I noticed that it was heading toward a small opening between a couple of larch trees on a sidehill. I thought of digging my camera out of my pack but didn't want to miss watching the bear. The adult bear walked quickly through the opening. Right behind the bear came a small bear cub that was the same color as its mother. I thought, "Wow! A sow with a cub."

This thought had barely registered when a second cub came scampering after the first cub. Then in rapid succession, a third and fourth cub sprinted through the opening. Four cubs! All were small, coal-black miniature versions of the adult bear.

Excitedly, I dug through my pack for my camera, but the bears had quickly disappeared into a thick brushy area. I berated myself for not having my camera more accessible. I could have used the video function if only I had realized there were five bears together. I waited around hoping to see them again but to no avail. I couldn't get the silly grin off of my face, realizing that I had just witnessed five bears together again!

Autumn splendor

THE REAL PANORAMIC PEAK
2013

◆

The bold scenery of the original Panoramic Peak bombarded my senses while I stood on the summit and slowly turned 360 degrees to grasp it all. Incredible beauty splashed across a wild, rugged landscape and completely held my attention in rapture. Sheer mountains with significant vertical relief, deeply crevassed glaciers, many lakes of all descriptions, and tumbled and tortured rock were interspersed with alpine meadows exploding with a rainbow of alpine wildflowers.

The original Panoramic Peak at 8650 feet was aptly named. In 1922, Theodore Shoemaker led a joint Northern Pacific Railway Company and U.S. Forest Service exploratory trip into this area of the Mission Range. Many features were mapped and named during this trip. According to Shoemaker, this peak was named "because of its superlative view."

Although Shoemaker named this peak in 1922, somehow in the subsequent years, the map makers nudged the name to the peak west of the original, a shorter mountain that Shoemaker had descriptively named 'Round Top'. This broad round-topped peak seems out of place in the throne room of seemingly upside-down geology with its sheer-walled jagged landscape.

My friend Rod Haynes and I made a couple of trips to this peak in recent years. In 2013, we went on a five-day backpack trip exploring this area before heading through Crazy Horse drainage to Hemlock Lake. It was a journey of 27 tough miles and over 10,000 feet in elevation gain before it was over. It was a trip that covered a mixed route of maintained trails, old Native American trails, and plenty of off-trail travel that included some challenging bushwhacking.

A small, almost perfectly round alpine lake northeast of Panoramic Peak aptly named Mirage Lake by Shoemaker, has a manicured appearance with open space of sedges and grasses, wildflowers, and rock. Only a thin line of stunted alpine larch trees are downslope and to the east of the lake. I saw three blue grouse in this stand of trees. The view from this exposed area is limited but outstanding, particularly to the east toward the Swan Range.

Rod and I made camp on a flat spot to the east of Mirage Lake. After taking a rest break, we spent the afternoon climbing to the top of Panoramic Peak and Round Top. We enjoyed exploring the area and taking in the fantastic views from different angles and perspectives.

Climbing Panoramic Peak involved some scrambling along the jumbled rocky ridge leading to the summit. The descent to Round Top was steep but on more moderate terrain. Round Top is an open broad rounded peak that has a weather-beaten

Mirage Lake with McDonald Peak to the left.

View of McDonald Peak from along the ridge to the original Panoramic Peak.

View of Lake of the Clouds and Glacier Peaks from Round Top.

look to it. Most of the vegetation is short, and mostly free of trees. A few bands of short, snow-blasted trees clung tenaciously to life in this environment of thin soils, short growing seasons, and brutal winter conditions. When the prevailing wind reached gale force, the blowing snow sandblasted the exposed portions of the trees. The exposed side of the trees had few if any branches and needles.

I watched an incredibly colorful sunrise the last morning we were camped near this lake. I awoke when there was only a hint of predawn light forming over the Swan Range. With a camera and notebook in hand, I found a rock ledge to perch and watch the show. It didn't disappoint. The sky changed from a thin orange line behind the darkly silhouetted Swan Mountains and, over the next half hour, gradually built in intensity and color.

The sky had a scattered thin cloud layer that reflected the yet-to-be-seen sun's rays as it slowly rose behind the distant range. The colors morphed from a faint orange to a vivid display of pinks, reds, oranges, yellows, and blues gaining color and brilliance until the sky was brightly lit. What a feast for the senses! I attempted to capture the grandeur of the scene unfolding in front of me but my camera could not do it justice.

Exploring wild areas like the real Panoramic Peak and Round Top excites the human spirit. It reminds me of our past human history when our forebears were hunters, gatherers, and wanderers. Born to explore and wander, I was thankful to be surrounded by wilderness.

Sunrise

View of Turquoise Lake with Daughter-of-the-Sun Mountain on the left.

A CLIMB UP MOUNT SHOEMAKER
2014

◆

I sat on our front porch enjoying a cup of caffeine waiting for the predawn darkness to fade when the wolves started howling nearby. When I heard that primal sound, something in my DNA stirred and responded.

I get a similar feeling when I hear an elk bugle, a loon crying its mournful call, or a vee of geese making goose music. It dredges up something down deep that modern life has glossed over and tamped down. But it's there and only needs a prompt and it comes rushing to the surface.

I take this early morning wolf music as a sign that today's adventure will be just what I'm looking for, a quest for the unique. I'm looking for grand scenery, challenging terrain, and a sense of adventure balanced with serenity and peacefulness.

I know that where I'm going, I probably won't see other people or very few at the most. I'll use the main trail to access part of the route but the rest will be off-trail. That's the best part, where I will enjoy a feeling of true wilderness.

In August 2014, a few months shy of 62 years old, I decided to climb Mount Shoemaker in the Mission Mountains Wilderness. This goal had been on my list of things to do for a long time. My friend Rod Haynes who usually teamed up

Turquoise Lake with Mount Shoemaker upper left and Sunrise Glacier in upper center. —USFS photo, Lowary collection

with me for our yearly Missions Mountains adventure couldn't make it this year. A few years earlier we had spent the better part of a week exploring in this rugged, stunning alpine area of the Mission Range. At that time, we had traveled near the base of Mount Shoemaker but hadn't taken the time to scale it. Itching to get back up in that country, I decided to go solo rather than wait another year.

At 8644 feet, Mount Shoemaker was named in honor of Theodore Shoemaker, a U.S. Forest Service employee who led a joint USFS and Northern Pacific Railway Company exploratory trip in this area in 1922. He was also instrumental in forming the Montana Mountaineers, an outdoor club based out of Missoula, Montana. On the 1922 trip, as well as trips in subsequent years, many of the features in this rugged area were mapped and named, culminating in one of the first maps produced of this area of the Mission Mountains. The Montana Mountaineers fondly referred to this peak as Mount Theodore as early as 1923 to honor their enthusiastic leader. Unfortunately, somewhere in the mapping process, the location of Mount Shoemaker was mislabeled on subsequent maps. The U.S. Board for Geographic Names corrected the mistake in 2014 but has yet to be corrected on later maps.

I yearned to stand on top of the peak so that I would have boots-on-the-ground first-hand knowledge of the peak and its surroundings. I set a date and went about packing my gear and food. As I have aged, I exchanged some of my heavy-duty backpacking gear for newer, lighter gear, some of which I'm still a bit leery of.

It sure feels great to carry what seems like a comfortably heavy daypack versus a large cumbersome backpack where I feel more like a pack mule than a hiker. Now, I have a bit more spring in my step which is a bit like turning back the clock somewhat.

When I grabbed my backpack and stepped outside, I was greeted by a beautiful, supermoon. The full moon was closer to the Earth than it had been in many years. It certainly looked impressively larger than usual.

While driving to the Glacier Lake Trailhead, a stunning smoky sunrise spread across the eastern horizon. It was the time of year when the air was likely to be filled with smoke from forest fires scattered across the west. Although unhealthy to breathe, the smoke particulates produced some colorful sunrises and sunsets. The sunrise this morning was a vivid display of reds and oranges silhouetted by the dark outline of the Swan Range.

Once at the trailhead, I made a few adjustments to my backpack and headed up the trail. It felt good hiking in the early morning coolness. I wanted to hike several miles and gain the bulk of the elevation before the day heated up. But the ripe huckleberries lining the trail were a distraction, often inducing me to slow down, and even stop to snack on the tasty morsels. The huckleberry crop was good, a

Sunrise through the smoke

boon to both bears and humans, as well as other wildlife species that feed on the bountiful purple fruit.

As the day heated up, the forest took on the familiar late-summer scent of dried and curing vegetation that was slowly baking under the hot sunshine. It is a smell that I will always associate with the Rocky Mountains.

By midmorning, I arrived at Lagoon Lake where my pace slowed considerably as I waded across a narrow section of the water and bushwhacked to Jewell Lake. In 1922, Asahel Curtis, the professional photographer for the joint USFS/NPRC exploratory trip, took a photograph of a lightning-scarred whitebark pine tree near Jewell Lake. Disease and time have taken their toll on this ancient tree. The tree is still standing but in bad shape and may not be standing much longer.

From Jewell Lake, I picked up a faint trail that would eventually lead me to Lone Tree Pass. I hiked by Surprise Lake and Prospector Lakes, named in 1922 and 1923 respectively. Unfortunately, the names of these bodies of water were not printed on subsequent maps. Both look like small ponds rather than lakes but are interesting nonetheless.

Mount Shoemaker upper left, Sunrise Glacier upper center, Turquoise Lake below.

As I topped out on a rocky ridge above Jewell Lake I was greeted with a stunningly picturesque view of Sunrise Glacier and its surrounding rugged alpine landscape all reflected in the small pond of Surprise Lake. Farther along the faint trail was Prospector Lake, named by the Montana Mountaineers when they found old mining tools nearby. The tools were so old that the handles were weathered and rotten.

After scrambling through a series of cliff bands and lengthy scree fields for several miles, I finally reached Lone Tree Pass. Apparently, the lone tree is long gone. From there, I hiked about a quarter mile southeast of the Lake of the Clouds staying just inside the border of the Flathead National Forest of the Mission Mountains Wilderness where I made my camp. Although it would have been nice to camp at the scenic Lake of the Clouds, that area is closed to humans between July 15th and October 1st each year. It is part of the Confederated Salish Kootenai Tribe's Bear Management Area where bears can feed and roam without human interference. The nearby McDonald Peak attracts many bears each summer that come to feed on the proliferation of army cutworm moths that inhabit the scree fields near the upper reaches of the peak. These moths that feed at night on alpine flower nectar and hide under rock scree in the daytime can grow to the size of jelly beans that contain up to 70% fat. Needless to say, the bears key into this nutritious source of food to help gain weight for the upcoming winter hibernation. The view from my campsite was spectacular with broad panoramic views to the north and east. To the south and west were several bands of alternating snowfields and rock benches. The heat generated from the sun was melting the snow producing small rivulets and pools of water from which I filtered my drinking water. At 8000 feet, I was now camped in the land of rock and snow with some small scattered meadows full of alpine wildflowers.

I woke the second morning before daylight, had a quick breakfast, packed a few items for the climb, and secured my camp. In the faint predawn light, I began scrambling my way to the base of Mount Shoemaker which was over a mile away.

Mount Shoemaker. McKay Collection. —UM Archives

A good portion of my intended route to the base of the peak would require traveling on snow that was frozen firmly after the cool night. I strapped my crampons to the bottom of my boots to make my footing more secure and safer. I used my hiking poles to further help balance myself. I carried an ice ax on my pack that I would use if the terrain became too steep.

As the morning sky lightened, the sun burst over the Swan Range to the east. I was rewarded with the sight of a beautiful pinkish-orange alpenglow splashed against the high country of the Mission Mountains. The dazzling bright colors reflecting off the snow and rock contrasted the dark terrain still in shadows. The smoky haze of yesterday was gone. As a slight breeze swept down the slopes, I stood inhaling the deliciously cool, crisp air and soaked in the beauty of the high alpine landscape.

As I worked my way along the edge of the northeastern toe of Sunrise Glacier, I encountered wolverine tracks in the snow. I surmised that the tracks were no more than one day old, probably made yesterday evening. Older tracks would have quickly melted in the hot sunshine.

My son, Luke, who worked as a wilderness ranger in the Missions, saw a wolverine at Turquoise Lake a few weeks before. Could these tracks be made by the same animal? Carrying binoculars, I scanned the glacier and surrounding terrain hoping against hope to see the wolverine, but no such luck. Still, I shared the same environment that the wolverine seemed to prefer. Its presence here brought a smile to my face.

During the 1922 exploratory trip led by Theodore Shoemaker, well-known photographer Asahel Curtis named the Sunrise Glacier. Shoemaker wrote in his report, "Every morning the sun glints from the big glacier which hangs under Glacier Peaks long before it shines on its lower points, and so we called it Sunrise Glacier."

Because I have hiked here in the past, I knew the route to take. Route finding in the Mission Mountains can be challenging at times. The numerous cliff bands can be difficult to negotiate and time-consuming. You can sometimes literally zigzag as if in a maze. If the route were drawn on a map it would look like a ball of loosely scrunched-up yarn. Or as the old mountaineering saying goes, "Sometimes you have to go north to get south."

From the base of the mountain, the climb to the summit of Mount Shoemaker was mostly straightforward up the southeast ridge. It was a mix of snow and rock with a bit of route finding around some protruding rocky gendarmes and cliffs. The view from the top, as with most peaks, was sensational. The 360-degree view was inspiring and beautiful. There was so much to see for miles and miles.

The nearby jagged landscape captured and held my attention. The Salish used a word to describe the Mission Mountains, *Coul-Hi-Cat*, which means, "to turn upside down" in describing the sheer upheaval of the mountainous terrain found here. I couldn't agree more as I stood gazing at the scene around me.

Daughter-of-the-Sun Mountain.

AN UNSETTLING EXPERIENCE
2014

The early morning hike into the high country started at o-dark-thirty with my headlamp blinking off as soon as I turned it on. "No problem," I thought, as I pulled out a small flashlight that I kept in my hunting pack. The snow was falling steadily with a skiff of new snow on the ground.

As my son, Luke and I hiked up the trail I became overheated, sweating more than I usually do. I was wearing wool clothing with a base layer next to my skin. My new synthetic shirt didn't seem to be wicking the moisture away as well as my old one.

As we gained elevation, the wind picked up and the snowfall became more intense. While traveling through the steep terrain, I kept slipping causing me to exert more energy. My new boots did not seem to grip as well as my beat-up pack boots. Because I often braced myself to keep from falling, my fleece gloves became saturated with moisture.

Hiking in adverse weather was nothing new to me. Over the years I have skied, hiked, and camped in sub-zero temps, blinding snowstorms, and pummeling wind. In my younger days, I camped in the winter not too far from here in temperatures that dipped to -45 degrees below zero.

I have always relished hunting the high country for elk. I like the feeling of wildness that the high country offers and the solitude that I often find in these places. I enjoy landscapes that offer views of beautiful scenery along the way. I'm partial to hunting with fresh snow on the ground as I can readily see what other animals are traveling around whether it is elk or voles. I savor the crisp, cool air hitting my face as I hunt into the wind. I like the challenge that the high country offers.

But on this day, the tables were turned. It was one of those days that did not work out as usual. I'm lucky my son was there to help me. Although I was slow to admit it, the situation was turning from bad to worse. The combination of wind, snow, and wet clothing was taking its toll on me. My energy level was dropping fast. My fingers were getting cold and stiff from the wet gloves. I had disposable hand warmers in the gloves, but they did not seem to be providing heat any longer. Usually, I carry a spare pair of gloves but had inadvertently left them at home that morning. I stopped to get new hand warmers out of my pack. I felt like I was all thumbs, fumbling to open the packets.

"Are you okay?" asked Luke when he saw me floundering. Luke sensed that something was wrong and that I was not doing too well.

I replied, "My gloves are soaked and I can't seem to keep warm."

"Do you need my spare gloves?" he wanted to know. I gladly accepted his offer.

Even though my judgment was getting foggy, I realized I needed to get out of my wet clothes and warm up. "I'm going to head back to the truck," I announced. I sensed Luke's disappointment about turning back, especially after spending hours getting to this point.

Knowing that Luke would want to continue hunting, I advised, "You keep hunting." I pointed downhill and added, "I'll head back to the truck." Bewildered, Luke said, "That's the wrong way." He told me I needed to go down a different ridge.

In my mind, I was sure I was right. After all, I had hiked and hunted this area many times in the past. I've been hiking in the high country for over 40 years.

At that point, Luke insisted, "I'll hike with you to make sure you get back okay." We stopped, ate some food, and drank some hot tea. The food, warm liquid, and dry gloves with new hand warmers in them, seemed to bring me back from the edge. As we worked our way down, I was feeling more like myself.

After we reached the forest, the trail was easy to follow. "I'll be fine now that I've got a trail to follow," I assured Luke.

As I slowly hiked back to the truck, I mulled over the whole experience. It was unsettling, to say the least. I had been on the edge of hypothermia. If Luke hadn't been with me, the outcome might have been much different.

Winter snow scene

ALONG THE SWAN RANGE
2015

♦

The cool rain felt good after days of hot, smoky weather. The misty rainfall kept my friend, Rod Haynes and me comfortable as we hiked the 25 switchbacks and 4000 vertical feet in elevation in less than four miles. We were once again heading into the backcountry to explore the wild but this year there was a twist to our strategy.

Considering our advancing age, we hired a local outfitter to haul our backpacks up the first leg of our five-day journey. This allowed us to hike unencumbered to the high country with enough energy to move beyond the trail system into the more remote parts of the wilderness. At age 63, I was the old man while Rod was the youngster at 60.

With only light daypacks, we left the Holland Lake Trailhead shortly after the wrangler, Kyle O'Brien, and his two horses headed up the trail with our backpacks. A few hours later we joined him for a leisurely lunch at the old Holland Lookout site. Although still cloudy, the weather was beginning to clear.

With one foot in the Bob Marshall Wilderness and one foot outside, the 360-degree views from this vantage point were impressive, to say the least. At 8053 feet, this spot was well chosen in 1921 (or possibly 1918 by some accounts)

Kyle O'Brien, packer, getting ready to head down the trail.

for a Forest Service fire lookout. It was initially a tent camp, often referred to as a rag camp. In 1931, a fire lookout building and shelter cabin were built on this site. The lookout was burned by the Forest Service in 1957 but the shelter cabin still stands and was recently renovated in 2013.

With a slight breeze, the sky was showing signs of clearing. We shouldered our backpacks and headed along the ridge to the north. It felt good to be back in the high country. I turned briefly to see the packer leading his stock down the trail for the return trip to the trailhead.

With a spring in our steps, Rod and I felt fresh and ready to see what the backcountry had to offer. We were not disappointed. The scenery was outstanding.

Top right: *Holland Lookout, burned in 1957. Van Gieson Collection.* —USVHS Archives

Top left: *Henry Thomason, Holland Ridge Rag Camp, 1921.* —USFS photo

Bottom right: *Holland Lookout, 1949. Montana Mountaineers.* —UM Archives

Bottom left: *Holland Ridge Shelter Cabin, renovated in 2013*

We had planned to stay on the ridgeline and go up and over Woodward Peak, but steep cliffs prevented that from happening. Given enough time and effort we could probably have found a route but with our heavy backpacks, we decided not to chance it. We opted to backtrack a bit and headed east down an old packer trail that skirted around the peak. After a bushwhack up to Rubble Lake, we made camp just south of the lake on a small rise with a good view. At 7600 feet, Rubble Lake and the expansive scenery were beautiful.

Our first camp above Rubble Lake.

It was a colorful sky that evening with varying hues as the sun sank into the western horizon. The crisp, cool air felt good to breathe as we stood enjoying the scenery around us. We glassed the nearby slopes for wildlife but didn't spot anything. As the light faded, we crawled into our tents for a welcome night's rest.

I woke once during the night to heed nature's call. The sky was bright to the north, possibly a hint of northern lights.

At one point during the night, Rod saw a Boreal Owl fly around him before landing in a nearby tree. The Boreal Owl sighting was remarkable as very few folks ever get to see this species of owl.

We were up at dawn at the start of the second day of the trip. It was a beautiful morning with a half-moon overhead to accent the scattered bright pink clouds above the Swan Range. The air was crisp and cool with a hint that fall would soon arrive in the high country. We again glassed the slopes for wildlife without success. I thought we should have spotted more wildlife than we were seeing in this remote area.

We got busy around camp and made a quick breakfast and hot drinks. We packed what we would need for the day. Before setting out, we secured our camp and hung our extra food from a nearby tree. Although a bit tired from yesterday's exertion, we were eager to explore the country. We quickly found a game trail on the south side of Rubble Lake that led west to a low pass along the Swan Divide. Once on top, we hiked the ridge south to Woodward Peak. The scenery was fantastic with views of the expansive Bob Marshall Wilderness on one side and the Swan Valley with its western guardian Mission Range on the other side.

The slight breeze and cool air were invigorating and put some spring into our step. I felt young again with that boyhood wonder and excitement that thankfully has never quite left me as I have grown older. I was fortunate to be able to experience this incredible wild country.

Rod Haynes with Buck Peak just to his left and Holland Peak in the background.

We explored the ridge and eventually reached the twin summits of Woodward Peak. This mountain at 8450 feet, was named for Karl Woodward, who led a group of US Forest Service and Northern Pacific Railway Company employees in 1907 and 1908 on a joint mapping survey of the Swan Valley and the South Fork of the Flathead River country. Several natural features were named for the various crew members of these survey parties. For some reason, the name Woodward Peak didn't get printed on present-day maps. However, the large Woodward Lake to the northeast did retain his name. The Necklace Lakes chain of lakes to the east and southeast were appropriately named. The high basin was full of lakes sparkling like jewels as the sun glistened off their watery surfaces.

After we lingered on top taking in the immense countryside, we snapped a few photos and wandered back the way we had come. We decided to keep running the ridge to the north. We climbed an unnamed peak at 8485 feet before we peeled off on a side ridge to the east and headed down the slope to the north side of Rubble Lake. What a great hike and a fun experience.

The view from near Woodward Peak looking north to Rubble Lake.

Woodward Lake

The clouds continued to move out of the area as the day lengthened. By dusk, the sky was completely clear as a strong cold wind blew through the high country. Rod and I walked down to Rubble Lake to catch the last remaining light of the day and watch the wind play on the surface of the lake. Wild choppy whitecaps whipped the surface water this way, then the opposite way. A golden eagle flew by seemingly unfazed by the strong erratic winds.

The morning of day three broke clear and cool after a breezy night. I walked down to the lake to get some water for the morning's hot drinks and stood spellbound at the scene before me. As the sun rose, the alpenglow reflecting off the

Terrace Lakes to the left.

mountains and Rubble Lake was sensational. The deep crimson red gradually turned orange, and finally bright yellow. It was beautiful beyond words. As luck would have it, my camera was back in my tent.

After breakfast, we packed up and hiked over to Terrace Lakes. Its name is derived from a series of terraces, each with a small lake or two. It only took us an hour to get to our new camp which was situated east of the westernmost lake.

After setting up our tents and hanging our food in a nearby tree, we headed up the southeast ridge of Buck Peak. At 9003 feet, Buck Peak, at the head of Buck Creek drainage, is another local designation named for the seasonal gathering of deer along the ridges north of the stream.

The climb was a long steep trudge but the scenery was outstanding. The views got better and better as we ascended to the summit. The vista from the top was incredible. I slowly turned 360 degrees to take in the expansive views. Only nearby Holland Peak at 9356 feet was taller.

When seen from the west down in the Swan Valley, this mountain appears as the tall pyramid-shaped mountain south of Holland Peak. Compared to other people's Bucket List, mine is local in nature. I had just accomplished something that I had wanted to do for the past 40 years. Rod and I spent over an hour on the summit enjoying the scenery before we reluctantly headed back down to camp.

We relaxed around camp while taking in the beautiful scenery. It was peaceful and serene. It felt great to be experiencing this wilderness landscape.

Later in the evening, we explored the area. The lake near our campsite had quite a bathtub ring around it. We estimated that the water level had dropped eight to ten feet from its original high-water mark.

There were still many wildflowers blooming in the high country including Indian paintbrush, explorer gentian, arrowhead groundsel, alpine St. John's Wort,

Looking south from Buck Peak.

Lewis's monkeyflower, fireweed, and showy fleabane. The beargrass, elk thistle, and pasque flower, for the most part, had already gone to seed.

Our wildlife count that day included a couple of mule deer, two blue grouse, one sharp-shinned and one Cooper's hawk, a bald eagle, a pika, and four Clark's nutcrackers. Although there were plenty of whitebark pine trees that had died from the mountain pine beetles and blister rust, there were still enough live trees producing cones to attract Clark's nutcrackers.

We found a few tracks in the mud around the lakes, mostly deer and elk. We thought an old weathered set of tracks could be from a grizzly bear cub or possibly a wolverine. The tracks were too old to tell conclusively.

We woke on the third day to a frost that covered everything. It was only August 8th but it felt like an autumn morning. There was a bank of red clouds on the eastern horizon but otherwise clear blue skies were overhead.

After breakfast, we packed our gear and headed up the drainage toward Buck Pass just south of Buck Peak. It was an interesting walk to the pass as we ascended one small terraced basin up to the next. In one place we found the scattered bones and the broken antlers of an elk. We surmised that the bull elk had triggered an avalanche and died from the trauma in a rough and tumble descent into this small basin. It would have taken quite a force to bust up the antlers like it did. We figured a grizzly bear or wolverine came by after the winter's snow melted and had quite a meal. The bones were scattered here and there all over the basin.

The view from Buck Pass was grand from east to west. It is a rugged and beautiful place. We looked down to the west at the old forest fire that burned through this area several years ago. Although local outfitter, Frank Jette once used this pass to access the Bob Marshall Wilderness, it would be tough to access the pass from the

Swan Valley side after a forest fire burned through this area in 2006. The resulting toppled dead trees had fallen haphazardly across the landscape.

Instead of going down to Buck Basin, we traveled along a side hill toward Holland Peak to the north. We jumped four mule deer along the way. It was a tough route through the steep scree and outcrops. We were tired when we finally made it to the easier terrain of the pass on the north side of Buck Peak.

We took a break and enjoyed the view looking east into the Dart Creek drainage and beyond. The Bob Marshall Wilderness is such a treasure, one of this country's crown jewels. We could see a lot of wild country and we were only skimming the very edge of it. After years of grassroots effort, the Swan side of this area nearly became part of *The Bob* back in the 1980s but President Reagan vetoed the bill even though all of Montana's congressional representatives supported the proposal.

At this point, we were weary and had run out of energy. If the weather had been clear, we might have camped somewhere in the area but thunderheads were forming off in the distance. Being in such an exposed high area was not a good option.

If we were younger and had more energy, we would have climbed up to what I call Marmot Mountain, the small bump of a mountain at 8852 feet south of Holland Peak. The few times I had been there in the past, a hoary marmot had been on its broad summit. Instead, we decided to cut over to the goat trail that climbers use to access this country from Upper Rumble Lake.

When we reached the goat trail, we found ourselves among 10 mountain goats who were obviously used to being around humans. They seemed unconcerned

Mountain Goat with Holland Peak to the left.

Looking down on Upper Rumble Lake with Holland Peak on the right.

with our presence as they slowly worked their way up the ridge while we snapped a few photos and enjoyed the dramatic scenery of this rugged area. I was alarmed at how well-defined the trail had become from the impact of human use. It looked like it was regularly used rather than the occasional use it got in the past.

We worked our way down the trail to the lake and found a nice spot to camp. From our campsite, we saw two climbers on the summit of Holland Peak, two others along the lake, and three more hikers going up the goat trail - a busy place.

After having the backcountry to ourselves for several days, it suddenly felt too crowded and not very wild. Although we were in spectacular scenery, sharing it with so many others in this sudden fashion put a damper on our experience.

Upper Rumble Lake is such a beautiful place, one of the more scenic areas of the Swan Range. It is a high mountain lake at 7890 feet and offers good fishing if you hit it right. I have fished it when you would swear there wasn't a fish in the whole lake. Other times the fishing was outstanding. High mountain lakes seem very temperamental in that regard.

The terrain is open with very few trees in this area, and only a tree or two tall enough to hang the food bag from. There are several mini ridges of exposed rock that parallel the lake and offer tent sites and privacy in between them. Bordering the east side of the lake is the scree slope with the sheer headwall of Holland Peak dominating the landscape.

The large snowfield that once covered a large portion of the southern cirque and extended to the edge of the lake is disappearing as it melts away. At the current rate of melting, it will completely disappear in several more years. It's

Remnant snow field on the southern end of Upper Rumble Lake.

Looking down on Lower Rumble Lake.

hard to believe so much of the snowfield has melted since I was first here about 40 years ago.

The mountain goats that passed us on the ridge above the lake earlier in the day, returned by evening and were hanging close by. They were waiting for us to pee so that they could lick the salt and minerals. The goats were so habituated to humans that they could be a nuisance. We made a point to relieve ourselves far away from our campsite.

It was a beautiful evening as the soft alpenglow colors splashed across the face of Holland Peak lighting up the area for a brief time before the sun dipped behind the Mission Mountains to the west.

On the last morning, we woke early and headed down the well-worn hiker trail to Lower Rumble Lake with its beautiful waterfall and bright blue water. We worked our way down the steep trail to the trailhead. It had been a great trip with my good friend in a spectacular country. Who could ask for more?

LAKE OF THE CLOUDS
2019

◆

In the summer of 2019, my friend Rod Haynes, my son Luke, and I took a four-day trip to the Lake of the Clouds in the rugged Mission Mountains. We timed our trip a few days before the annual closure of the area from July 15th to October 1st as part of the CSKT Bear Management Zone.

The first six miles were all uphill on a maintained trail. It was obvious that this would be a good huckleberry season as the bushes were loaded with green soon-to-be-ripe berries. That was good news for humans, bears, and other wildlife.

Pockets of wildflowers were plentiful splashing vivid colors across the landscape. The next 4½ miles were a tough combination of bushwhacking through thick brush, climbing around rock cliffs, searching for the easier goat trails, and using crampons while crossing steep snow fields. We saw six mountain goats, a blue grouse, a bald eagle and heard a couple of pikas and Clark's nutcrackers as we worked our way to the lake.

At age 66, these kinds of trips are not getting any easier but are still my favorite type of adventure. When we leave the maintained trails behind, along with 99% of the people, trips in the backcountry take on a different flavor, more substance, and more refreshing to the spirit.

Bushwhacking on the way to Lake of the Clouds with Glacier Peaks in the background.

Route finding is a challenge, especially in the Mission Mountains Wilderness as its geology is full of steeply angled cliffs of all heights and difficulty. Some of the cliffs are relatively easy to negotiate while others are maddening difficult to find a safe route up or down. You can rarely hike a straight line from Point A to Point B. Instead, you sometimes meander all over the place finding a route that works. Sometimes you get cliffed out and have to back off. Sometimes a climbing rope is needed to negotiate a tricky, steep section of cliff rock. Other times the crampons are strapped to your boots with your ice axe ready to chop steps, or to self-arrest if you slip and fall on the steep snow. The bushwacking and route finding can swing from peaceful serenity to terrifying adrenaline rushes.

The first day's hike of 10½ miles and 4800 feet in elevation gain was tough for Rod and me. We were both tired when we finally made it beyond Lone Tree Pass to an area north of Lake of the Clouds. Luke, at 36 years old, seemed to take it all in stride and was as fresh as he was 10 miles earlier. Ah, the stamina and energy of the young and fit.

In 1922, Theodore Shoemaker and Jack Clack, Forest Service employees, led a group of photographers and writers into the Mission Mountains. The objective of the exploratory trip sponsored by Northern Pacific Railway was to scout the area for future tourism promotion. In addition, they named several lakes and mountains during this trip. After a subsequent trip in 1923, Shoemaker was able to produce the first map of this area of the Missions. Later, Shoemaker wrote this entry about the Lake of the Clouds: "Cloud ghosts seemed always moving down beneath its surface; so we called it Lake of the Clouds."

An incredibly beautiful area, Lake of the Clouds, at 7800 feet, was still mostly frozen over with a few open areas of water. The 360-degree views were sensational as this part of the Mission Mountains was rugged and jagged. The Indians referred to the Missions as *Houl-Hi-Cat*, a phrase that meant "to turn upside down" referring to the sheer upheaval of the terrain when viewed from the Mission Valley.

To the south and southwest are remnant glaciers with visible crevasses and a bergschrund arcing along the top cirque of snow and ice. Towering above the glaciers were the two jagged Glacier Peaks at 9060 and 9407 feet. Among other unnamed peaks to the west was the impressive McDonald Peak boldly dominating the scene to the northwest. At 9820 feet, McDonald is the tallest mountain in the Mission Mountains. Off to the north were more distant mountains of all shapes and sizes.

To our immediate east was Round Top at 8400 feet. It is shaped like a giant beach ball half buried in the ground. It appears as a geologic oddity in this world of jagged peaks and rugged terrain. Many of today's maps have labeled this mountain Panoramic Peak but the original Panoramic Peak (8650 feet) is located to the east of Round Top.

Frozen Lake of the Clouds and Glacier Peaks

McDonald Peak from our camp north of Lake of the Clouds.

The scenery was dramatic and awe-inspiring and I was thankful to once again experience it. What a feeling of exuberance, awe, happiness, serenity, and freedom all rolled into one. I felt alive in this landscape and was profoundly grateful that I was there to soak it all in.

We each set up our lightweight one-person tent and ate our supper. We settled in to enjoy the changing colors of the varied landscape as the sun set in the west. With our binoculars, we glassed the slopes and basins for wildlife. We spotted mule deer and a few elk off in a distant basin. Finally, tiredness overtook me and I headed to the tent for the night. I felt contented as I drifted off to sleep.

I crawled out of my tent in the middle of the night to relieve myself. The sky was a mixture of stars and clouds. The moon was especially beautiful as it began to set behind a peak to the west. The thin clouds behind the peak reflected that portion of the sky with a halo surrounding the peak. A dark shadow extended from the top of the peak across the basin to the east. I thought that an appropriate name for the peak would be Moon Shadow Peak (8963 feet). I stood in amazement and soaked up the scene before finally heading back to the sleeping bag.

I awoke at daybreak to the music of hermit thrushes announcing the coming of the new day. When I emerged from my tent, I found dark ominous clouds cloaking the summits of the taller peaks. I could see some blue sky to the south but things looked dark to the north. By the time we cooked our breakfast, dark stormy clouds quickly rolled in and it started to rain. We retired to our tents to wait it out, hoping that it would be short in duration.

After an hour or so the weather improved and we decided to go exploring. If the weather allowed, we planned to climb at least one of the Glacier Peaks and traverse the Garden Wall.

After loading our packs with gear, water, and food for the day, and hanging our food bags from a stout limb in a whitebark pine tree, we set out in a southeasterly direction to the Lone Tree Pass area and then south towards Sunrise Glacier. Due to the amount of snow in this area, we soon donned our crampons for better footing on the hard snow of early morning. The high alpine scenery was indescribably beautiful with views of jagged peaks and rocky outcrops protruding from a world of snow. We eventually made it to the Sunrise Glacier and took a westerly, northwesterly route to the northern end of the Garden Wall and the base of the lower Glacier Peak.

In 1922, Sunrise Glacier was aptly named by Shoemaker and crew. "Every morning the sun glints from the big glacier which hangs under Glacier Peaks long before it shines on the lower points, and so we called it Sunrise Glacier," Shoemaker wrote.

Several years ago, I found an old cowboy hat at the toe of Sunrise Glacier and wondered about the story behind the hat. Whose was it originally? How long had it been here? Was the owner perhaps still buried in the snow? Had it blown off the owner's head while he stood on a nearby peak and it ended up here?

Getting to the top of the Garden Wall involved the use of crampons and ice axes to negotiate the steep snow near the headwall. The adrenaline was flowing through my body as I'm sure it was with Luke and Rod also. I was relieved when we safely topped out along the northern end of the Garden Wall. The views were sensational, especially looking down and along the Garden Wall to the south.

Sunrise Glacier on the left.

Lake of the Clouds with Sunrise Glacier on the left and Glacier Peaks (and glaciers) on the right.

According to Miriam and Robert Underhill, early mountaineers who climbed in the area in 1946-47, the Garden Wall was named because of its likeness to the Garden Wall in Glacier National Park.

We decided to first climb the lowest of the two Glacier Peaks, then determine if it was possible to climb the taller peak from this route. We took off our crampons as the remaining route to the top was snow-free. The route zig-zagged through a series of cliff bands but was relatively easy. The views from the top of any mountain are spectacular and the view from here was no exception - breathtaking.

Rod Haynes on the northern terminus of the Garden Wall.

Luke Lamar on Sunrise Glacier with Daughter-of-the-Sun Mtn. in the background.

View looking south from the top of Garden Wall, Mountaineer Peak in the background.

Usually, mountaintop vantage points offered views for miles in all directions. In this case, the taller Glacier Peak stood looming off to the west, blocking a slice of the scenery. From this angle, it looked like a difficult ascent to its summit. We decided to save that challenge for a different day and settled in on the top of the lower Glacier Peak. We took quite a few photographs, gazed at the sensational view, and enjoyed the moment. It was a special time sharing this experience with my son and good friend.

Luke Lamar and Rod Haynes on the summit of the lower Glacier Peak.

After a pleasant time on the summit, we proceeded down to the northern edge of the Garden Wall. The traverse along the top of the Garden Wall to its southern terminus was enjoyable. The wall was approximately 1¼ miles in length and was broad in many places on top. It was an easy stroll. We enjoyed the scenery, stopped to take photos, glassed the various peaks and basins for wildlife, and breathed in the sharp, cool, fresh air of the high alpine country.

We found the rare Mission Mountain Kittentail flower growing along the top of the ridge. Luke said that there are only 30 known occurrences of this species of plant.

I felt fortunate to be experiencing all of this wild country. Ridge Running is my favorite form of exploring in the wild, with wide-open breathtaking views that allow me to see what is close up and also into the far distance. It is about as good as it gets.

Traversing the Garden Wall had been on Rod's *Mission Mountains Bucket List* for quite some time. Through the years we had hiked nearby but never climbed to the top. I was glad that we finally got to experience it.

Mission Mountain Kittentail flower.
—Luke Lamar photo

Luke Lamar glassing for wildlife on the Garden Wall.

After spending an hour or two on the Garden Wall, we backtracked to a point where we could safely glissade down the Sunrise Glacier as we worked our way back to camp. What an amazing day!

Back in camp, I was content to sit around, write in my journal, and soak in the scenery. Rod and Luke had other ideas. Rod found an opening large enough in the frozen lake to take a quick dip (too cold for me – Rod's thermometer registered 42 degrees!) while Luke decided to climb Round Top Mountain (ah, to be young again).

For company, a mountain goat came by and decided to hang out. He wanted to lick the minerals in the area where we had recently peed. No doubt, the goat spent

Round Top in the foreground with the original Panoramic Peak directly behind it.

more time down at Turquoise Lake where hoards of people visit. He didn't seem overly concerned with our presence.

Later in the evening, we enjoyed glassing the peaks and basins for wildlife. Near dusk we spotted two cow elk below us in Grizzly Basin to the north. The hermit thrushes serenaded us as the evening light faded into darkness.

I woke early in the morning to enjoy the alpenglow splashed across the mountains, always a special treat in the high country. Although the very top of McDonald Peak was covered by clouds, the nearby mountains lit up as the sun rose over the eastern horizon and cast its low-angle brightness on the mountains. As the sun rose, the alpenglow changed from a deep red color to a reddish-orange to a brilliant orange before transforming to the bright morning sunshine. Glacier Peaks were especially stunning with bright alpenglow. As the light show continued, the hermit thrushes sang a high country symphony.

It was a lazy morning and we lingered around camp eating breakfast while glassing the slopes and basins for wildlife. We saw a mule deer in the basin to the north. Luke spotted a large grizzly bear high on the slopes of McDonald Peak. It was on a ledge that looked more suitable for a mountain goat. The bear was probably foraging for numerous army cutworm moths that inhabit the peak and surrounding areas at this time of the season. High in fat content, the Army cutworm moths attract the bears that congregate here to feast on these moths from mid-July until the end of September. This dynamic is the reason the CSKT closes this area off to humans during this period.

Due to his work schedule, Luke had to pack up and head out. I was glad he was able to join us for this experience. Ever since he was around five years old, he was eager to explore the Swan Valley and surrounding mountains, to know it all very well and he has worked diligently toward his goal for the majority of his life.

Rod and I put a few necessities in our packs, hung the food bags, and headed up the westerly ridge on the north side of Lake of the Clouds. We crossed the outlet stream of the lake, a slit in the rock that forms a northerly channel. The channel was snow-clogged this season and we were able to find a safe place to cross. The water flowing under the snow didn't travel far before it poured over a dramatic waterfall plunging over 600 feet to the bottom into the Grizzly Basin area. Although we couldn't see the waterfall from the Lake of the Clouds area, we saw it from a previous campsite in Grizzly Basin several years ago. We were camped for several days and watched the various moods of the waterfall – from large amounts of water gushing down on a warm afternoon, to wildly spraying mist as breezy conditions pushed and pulled the water in different directions. On cold below-freezing mornings, there would be very little water flowing down the waterfall. This incredible waterfall has no name and because of its location in a seldom visited area, is rarely seen by humans.

Waterfall pouring out of Lake of the Clouds, 2010.

Rod and I hiked up the westerly ridge that hooked to the south as we continued to climb. We wanted to see if there was a route up to the taller Glacier Peak. As we climbed, the views from this ridge were becoming more fantastic and dramatic. This was a wild, rugged country and incredibly beautiful.

Unfortunately, my age was acting up. I felt a bit dizzy and didn't trust myself around the areas with some exposure. I had to swallow my pride and tell Rod that

I couldn't go farther on our intended route. We stopped and took a very long rest break, drank some water, and ate some snacks. I still didn't feel good about continuing so we headed back to camp.

Back at camp, we took it easy for a couple of hours, ate supper, and then went for a walk around the area scattered with lots of colorful buttercups, spring beauties, and pasqueflowers. We glassed for wildlife but saw nothing except for Uncle Billy, our nearby mountain goat. It was another pleasant evening in camp.

We woke early on our last morning. The weather looked menacing to the north as thunderstorm cells were floating by. With the rising sun, the combination of reddish-orange alpenglow on the nearby mountains and the same blaze of colors on the passing thunderheads was quite stunning.

Uncle Billy

Sunrise on the last day.

Beargrass in bloom

As we packed up and headed out, thunderheads drew nearer and moved closer in our direction. Several clouds rolled through just to the north of us. A few sprinkles fell, but we didn't need to don our rain gear. The day was interspersed with thunderheads, warm sunshine, and blue sky. Our route took us by several patches of beargrass in full bloom, a splash of creamy white upon the rugged landscape.

Again, we used our crampons to safely walk over several steep patches of snow. The early morning snow was set up like hard concrete and would have been challenging without the crampons.

By the time we dropped in elevation to Jewell Lake, the mosquitoes had emerged in force. Once we got back to the maintained trail, we met many people heading to the various lakes along the popular trail. We kept a steady pace with a few rest breaks here and there until we finally reached the trailhead in the afternoon.

It was a great trip for two old geezers and one young buck. I felt so grateful for the experience.

RED MOUNTAIN
2023

Years ago, as I sat at the kitchen table poring over a topo map of the Scapegoat Wilderness, Red Mountain caught my eye.

At 9411 feet, Red Mountain is the tallest mountain in the entire Bob Marshall Wilderness Complex that includes the Bob Marshall, Great Bear, and Scapegoat Wildernesses encompassing over 1.5 million acres.

Climbing Red Mountain looked easy enough as there was a trail to the summit where a USFS fire lookout once stood. I figured it would be a three-day trip approaching the peak from the Heart Lake area. However, time kept marching along year after year without the trip coming to fruition.

Upon turning 70 years old, I decided that if I was ever going to scale Red Mountain, I had better do it soon or I might never get the opportunity again. I checked with my son Luke, daughter Annie, and son-in-law John about my plans. They were all up for joining me on the adventure.

Instead of a three-day backpack trip, we figured that Red Mountain could be climbed in one day if approached from the network of roads to the south near the Scapegoat Wilderness Boundary. Our route would be a bushwhack with no maintained trails.

Our trip began early in the morning at 4:00 am. We drove miles and miles of gravel roads before arriving at our starting point. We were in an area of old mining operations, mostly copper but also other minerals of value. This part of Montana in the Lincoln area was dotted with both old and new mining claims and ventures.

The bushwhack through a combination of thick brush, fallen trees, and steep terrain was challenging. We eventually emerged from the arduous terrain to a long, open ridge system. Traveling became much easier and enjoyable for a couple of miles as we hiked toward the summit, traversing the edge of the southern boundary of the Scapegoat Wilderness.

Along the way, we saw nine mountain goats with five young kids of the year. We observed an interesting interaction between a golden eagle and the mountain goats. The golden eagle flew low over the mountain goats and landed on a snowfield close to the goats which caught the attention of the momma goats. The golden eagle then flew up and buzzed the mountain goats before flying off. The young goats looked too big for a golden eagle to prey on, but who knows?

We found lots of bear sign as we climbed along our route. Grizzly bears had dug up roots from the scattered vegetation, particularly feeding on biscuitroot.

Luke found a couple of day beds that the bears had used among some rocky outcrops. The bears also feed on Army Cutworm moths that inhabit the extensive scree fields found on this mountain. The Army cutworm moths migrate from eastern Montana to spend the summer nights feeding on the nectar of wildflowers but spending the warm daylight hours hidden under the scree rocks. Army cutworm moth bodies are roughly the size of small jelly beans and are 70% fat. The bears relish these tasty, nutritious morsels.

On Top of Red Mountain. L to R: John and Annie Kilgour, Steve and Luke Lamar.

The Red Mountain area is noted for having both whitebark pine and limber pine trees. Both trees are five-needled pines and produce pine nuts, an important food source for many species including Clark's nutcrackers and bears.

The views got better and better as we climbed higher in elevation. After four hours, 4.3 miles, and 3400 feet of elevation gain, we reached the summit of Red Mountain.

The views of miles of wild country were amazing, especially to the north and west of where we stood. The Scapegoat was designated Wilderness in 1972 with a total of 239,936 acres. We could see far beyond the boundary of the Scapegoat Wilderness.

Remnants of the former fire lookout - stacked rock work, anchor points, and other bits and pieces - were visible. According to the records, the fire lookout structure, a D-6 cupola cabin, was completed in 1929 and was used until the 1940s when it was abandoned. Anyone standing in the fire lookout commanded a view of the immense country, but the lookout was logistically challenged without a nearby water or firewood source. A new fire lookout was later built atop Stonewall Mountain to replace the Red Mountain Lookout.

Annie Kilgour on the Red Mountain Lookout stonework.

Wildflowers on Red Mountain.

The skies were mostly clear when we started the ascent but the clouds were increasing by the time we reached the summit. We ate a quick lunch, took photos, and enjoyed the scenery before starting back down. The clouds became more menacing and darker as we descended. We enjoyed the walk along the ridge but kept a wary eye on the cloud buildup. We left the long, open ridge and entered the forest just as thunder rumbled from the direction of the mountain.

We continued to descend through the thick timber and brush with some sprinkles of falling rain. At one point, we came across a mine tunnel in the side of the mountain.

We eventually bushwhacked our way back to our vehicles without getting too wet. Although it had quit raining down below, it continued to rumble and storm in the high country, a reminder of the raw power of storms in the mountains.

A day in the mountains rarely disappoints and today was no exception. It was an especially good day in the wild country sharing the experience with my family.

WINTER OBSERVATIONS
2010 - 2024

◆

Early in the New Year, Sharon and I went skiing in the Loon Flats area of Swan Valley. The landscape was picturesque, draped in a white blanket of fresh snow. We noticed some recent deer tracks along the trail as we skied along. Later, I noticed from reading the snow tracks that the deer had been startled and had bounded away. Only half paying attention, I figured that the deer had seen or heard us and that we were the cause of its alarm.

I quickly realized that the deer had not run away from us but had bounded toward us before jumping off the trail. Now our curiosity heightened! We skied a short distance and found that a young mountain lion had intersected the path traveling east to west. As it was snowing steadily and these tracks were very well defined with no fresh snow in them, we realized this interaction had just taken place possibly minutes before we arrived on the scene. What had been an enjoyable ski outing all of a sudden became a heightened and memorable experience.

While skiing in Swan Valley another day, I came across an interesting scene. A lone Townsend solitaire was sitting in a Rocky Mountain juniper tree loaded with pale-blue juniper berries (actually berry-like cones). With heavy snow clinging to everything, this bird was undoubtedly content in finding this bonanza food source and had it all to itself. That situation changed rapidly as a large flock of bohemian waxwings descended on the tree and began voraciously feeding on the juniper berries. The Townsend solitaire was **not** happy about this turn of events! It squawked and whined quite loudly as it protested having to share its bounty of food. The waxwings fed for a half-minute or so, then retired to a nearby western larch tree to perch. The Townsend solitaire flew to the top of a tree between the waxwings and the juniper tree as if to serve notice that it intended to guard its food source and would challenge the raiders of its food supply.

I got the impression that the waxwings could care less what the solitaire's intentions were as they once again descended on the juniper tree for another round of feeding. Again, the solitaire protested long and loud. Smiling at the interaction, I continued skiing down my planned route. An hour later, as I returned to this point on my way back home, the bohemian waxwings were again perched in the nearby tree, and the Townsend solitaire was still attempting to guard its food source.

Sometime during the night, a small herd of elk fed along the forested edge of our yard. They pawed through the ten inches of snow and fed on the elk sedge that grows in this area, mostly on slightly east and south aspects. By morning they were gone. Later in the day, I saw six of them as I drove to work.

We sometimes experience crazy weather patterns in the winter. The area received up to a foot of heavy, wet snow followed by frigid cold temperatures down to -19 degrees below zero. A few days later, the cold snap left our region, replaced by warm temperatures and rain. The rain and resulting melting action then froze into ice. This up-and-down pattern has redefined our winter weather patterns here in Swan Valley. I definitely preferred the good old days when winter was winter.

An interesting phenomenon took place when the temperatures dropped to -19 degrees below zero this past week. Outside in the forest, I heard what sounded like a gun battle going on. But it wasn't rifle shots that I heard. When the temperature dipped into this range, the water in the tree's sap expanded as it froze. The loud sounds were produced when the tree bark split as the wood contracted from the cold and the sap expanded from the freezing action. Interestingly, to the native cultures of the Dakota Sioux and the Cree, the first new moon of the new year is known as the *Moon of the Cold-Exploding Trees*.

While out skiing, I saw a bald eagle perched on top of a tall ponderosa pine tree. For several winters now, we often have an eagle that roosts for part of the day in this area. We are not sure if it is the same eagle but we call him, Baldwin. But what if it's a she? Maybe we should be calling it Baldwina.

We woke to 6 inches of fresh snow to go over the old 8-inch base of snow. Sharon and I took our dog, Smokey, and went for a ski on our loop trail of about 1½ miles. It was excellent, cold snow. While skiing, we saw a cow elk, a bald eagle, several ravens, and a flock of juncos. Due to thick cloud cover, we couldn't see the mountains but all the nearby trees were draped with a mantle of snow. I told Sharon, "Look, the Christmas trees are already decorated!"

We met friends and skied the thin snowpack along the Holland Lake shore before deciding that the ice on the lake was safe enough to ski. Several people were ice fishing on the lake. Even though it was mostly cloudy, the mountains looked amazing. We skied from one end of the lake to the other end then skied back to our vehicles near the boat launch area. We capped off the afternoon with a fun and delicious tailgate party. It was a good, enjoyable workout, with great friends in a beautiful setting.

Holland Lake was talking today! We couldn't believe how vocal it was. At first, we thought the group of people ice fishing out in the middle of the lake had a stereo playing some kind of music but we soon realized that wasn't the case. It was the continually expanding and contracting of the ice making sounds that reminded us of a whale talking. I was skiing on the ice about 10 feet from shore when I heard a loud sound coming toward me. I could see the ice splitting as the crack went right under my skis! I have heard ice on lakes talking before but not as vocal as today. What an experience!

When the big game hunting season ends, the world seems to take on a quieter and slower pace. With that in mind, we load our skis, packs, and dogs into the truck and head up a side road to a favored area to go skiing. Winter usually comes early here in the Swan Valley but so far, the snow isn't too deep to get to where we want to go. It is a sunny day with bright blue skies and snow-covered mountains, simply beautiful. The white mountains stand out sharply against the bright blue sky. The views along our chosen ski route are vast and stunning as we can see for miles to the north, east, and west. There is a subtle breeze from the north that makes the air crisp and delicious to breathe. It feels good to ski along our route for the first time this winter. The *swish, swish* of our skis gliding through the snow makes a rhythmic sound. The dogs are like school kids at recess after being cooped up inside for too long as they romp with reckless abandon, enjoying their new-found freedom. The feeling is infectious. We can't keep the silly grins off our faces as we marvel at our good fortune. Today, no one is richer than we are at this moment in time.

Sharon Lamar skiing Annoyance Ridge.

REFERENCES

Chapman, J.A., Romer J.I., Stark, J. "Ladybird Bettles and Army Cutworm Adults as Food for Grizzly Bears in Montana." *Ecology*. Vol. 36, No 2. (Jan. 1955). Pp. 156-158.

Copenhaver, Howard. *They Left Their Tracks*. Stevensville, MT. Stoneydale Press Publishing. 1990.

Graetz, Rick. *Montana's Bob Marshall Country*. Helena, MT. Montana Magazine. 1985.

Hall, Elihu N. *Ballads from the Bluffs*. Elizabethtown, IL. Elihu N. Hall. 1948.

Holterman, Jack. *Place Names of Glacier National Park*. Helena, MT. Riverbend Publishing. 2006.

Incashola, Tony, Director of the Selish-Qlipse Culture Committee. Personal communication with Steve Lamar. 2007.

Kendall, Katherine C., "Northern Divide Grizzly Bear Project." USGS. March 30, 2005. http://www.nrmsc.usgs.gov/research/NCDEbeardna.htm.

Kresek, Ray. *Fire Lookouts of the Northwest*. Spokane, WA. Historic Lookout Project. Third Edition. 1998.

Lamar, Steve. *Swan Valley Place Names: A Mosaic of History, Stories, and Local Lore*. Condon, MT. Rumble Peak GeoData. 2008.

McKay, Kathryn L. *Trails of the Past: Historical Overview of the Flathead National Forest, Montana 1800-1962*. U.S. Forest Service, Flathead National Forest. Kalispell, MT. 1994.

Moore, Bud. "Journals of the Little Salmon." Unpublished document. 1983.

National Outdoor Leadership School. NOLS. Jan. 29, 2025. https://www.nols.edu.

Shaw, Charlie. *The Flathead Story*. Kalispell, MT. U.S. Forest Service, Flathead National Forest. 1967.

Shoemaker, Theodore. "Trails End and Beyond." *American Forestry* 16 (April 1923): Volume 29 (352) 218-228.

_____. "Report of an Exploring Trip on the Flathead National Forest. The Northern Pacific Railroad and the Forest Service Cooperating." Flathead National Forest. October 20, 1922.

Stockstad, Dwight. "The Mysterious Missions." *Montana Sports Outdoors*. 1(2): 1959.

Stromnes, John. "Form of Survival." *Missoulian*. Feb. 2, 2003. https://missoulian.com/uncategorized/form-of-survival/article_fed42c8e-4867-5a0b-9d2c-db-66f7481ab8.html.

Styler, Herb. Interview with Suzanne Vernon and Steve Lamar. February 2007.

The Diggings. "Montana Mining Claims." Jan. 29, 2025. https://thediggings.com/usa/montana/claims.

Tomback, Diana F., Arno, Stephen F., Keane, Robert E. *Whitebark Pine Communities: Ecology and Restoration*. Washington DC. Island Press. 2001.

USDA Forest Service. "The 1988 Canyon Creek Fire" [folded brochure]. Missoula, MT. No. R1-89-3. 1989. https://www.frames.gov/catalog/29953.

Underhill, Robert and Miriam. "Climbs in the Montana Rockies: Mission Range." *Appalachia*. December 1950: 145-167.

Vernon, Suzanne. *Montana: Voices of the Swan*. Condon, MT. Upper Swan Valley Historical Society. 2011.

White, Don Jr., Kendall, Katherine C., Picton, Harold D. "Grizzly Bear Feeding Activity at alpine Army Cutworm Moth Aggregation Sites in Northwest Montana." *Canadian Journal of Zoology*. Vol. 76, No. 2. Feb. 1998.